*The Jazz Poetry
Anthology*

The Jazz Poetry Anthology

EDITED BY

Sascha Feinstein and Yusef Komunyakaa

Indiana University Press
BLOOMINGTON AND INDIANAPOLIS

The paper used in this publication meets the minimum requirements of American National Standard for Information Sciences—Permanence of Paper for Printed Library Materials, ANSI Z39.48-1984.

Manufactured in the United States of America

Library of Congress Cataloging-in-Publication Data

The Jazz poetry anthology / edited by Sascha Feinstein and Yusef Komunyakaa.
    p. cm.
   ISBN 0-253-32163-8 (cloth : alk. paper). — ISBN 0-253-20637-5 (pbk. : alk. paper)
    1. Jazz music—Poetry 2. American poetry—20th century.
3. American poetry—Afro-American authors. I. Feinstein, Sascha, date. II. Komunyakaa, Yusef.
PS595.J34J39 1991
808.81'9357—dc20

90-5237
CIP

2 3 4 5   95 94 93 92 91

For my father, who helped introduce me to the music, and in memory of my mother, who liked to listen to Louis Armstrong while she painted.

S.F.

In memory of Lorenzo Robinson, who first said to me the name Louis Armstrong.

Y.K.

Contents

Preface   xvii

Sam Abrams   *In the Capability*   1

James Baldwin   *Le sporting-club de Monte Carlo*   1

Amiri Baraka   *AM/TRAK*   2

George Barlow   *In My Father's House*   7

Gerald Barrax   *The Singer*   9

Marvin Bell   *The Fifties*   10

Carol Bergé   *Piaf and Holiday Go Out*   12
    The Recounting of Gods   13

Paul Blackburn   *Listening to Sonny Rollins at the Five-Spot*   15

Horace Julian Bond   *The Bishop of Atlanta: Ray Charles*   16

George Bowering   *Pharoah Sanders, in the Flesh*   16

Edward Kamau Brathwaite   *Trane*   17

Ray Bremser   *Blues for Harold*   18

Sterling A. Brown   *Cabaret*   22
    Ma Rainey   24
    New St. Louis Blues   26

Richard Burns	*The Song of the Yellow Star*	27
Hayden Carruth	*Paragraphs* [Sections 11, 26, 27, 28]	28
Cyrus Cassells	*Strange Fruit*	30
Maxine Cassin	*Three Love Poems by a Native*	31
Grace Cavalieri	*The Liberation of Music*	32
Fred Chappell	*The Highest Wind That Ever Blew: Homage to Louis*	33
Wanda Coleman	*At the Jazz Club He Comes on a Ghost*	36
Claire Collett	*Midsummer*	37
Leo Connellan	*Mommy's Hubby*	37
Gillian Conoley	*The One*	39
Clark Coolidge	*The Great*	40
Gregory Corso	*For Miles*	41
Jayne Cortez	*Into This Time*	42
	Rose Solitude	44
	Solo Finger Solo	46
	Tapping	47
Robert Creeley	*The Bird, the Bird, the Bird*	48
	Broken Back Blues	48
Tom Dent	*After Listening to Monk*	49
	For Lil Louis	50
Owen Dodson	*Yardbird's Skull*	52
George Economou	*33⅓ RPM*	53
Richard Elman	*Chet's Jazz*	53
	Driving Home	54

John Engels   *In the Palais Royale*
                            Ballroom in 1948   55

Clayton Eshleman   *Un Poco Loco*   56

Fatisha   *From Star to Sun*
                            We Are Going   57

Sascha Feinstein   *Buying Wine*   58
                            Monk's Mood   59

Lawrence Ferlinghetti   *Sometime During Eternity . . .* 61

Calvin Forbes   *Drum Crazy*   62

Alice Fulton   *You Can't Rhumboogie in a*
                            Ball and Chain   63

Christopher Gilbert   *Horizontal Cosmology* [Sections
                            1, 4]   64
                            Resonance   66

Dana Gioia   *Bix Beiderbecke (1903–1931)*   66

Elton Glaser   *Elegy for Professor Longhair*   67

Vince Gotera   Hot Club de France *Reprise*
                            on MTV   68

Lee Meitzen Grue   *Billie Pierce's Jazz Funeral*   69
                            Jazzmen   70

Marilyn Hacker   *Elegy*   72

Michael S. Harper   *"Bird Lives": Charles Parker*   74
                            Cannon Arrested   75
                            Dear John, Dear Coltrane   77
                            Elvin's Blues   78
                            Here Where Coltrane Is   79

Howard Hart   *Ben Webster and a Lady*   80
                            Sonny Greer   81

ix

Robert Hayden   *Homage to the Empress of*
                           the Blues   81
                       Soledad   82

David Hilton   *Blind Saxophonist Dies*   83

Everett Hoagland   *Jamming*   84
                       The Music   85

Andre Hodeir   *Outside the Capsule* [Excerpt]   87

Garrett Hongo   *Roots*   91

Langston Hughes   *Dream Boogie*   93
                       Jazzonia   94
                       Morning After   95
                       The Weary Blues   95

Lynda Hull   *Hollywood Jazz*   96

Lawson Fusao Inada   *Plucking Out a Rhythm*   98

Ken Irby   *Homage to Coleman Hawkins*   99

Rod Jellema   *Four Voices Ending on Some*
                           Lines from Old Jazz Records   101
                       Stop-time   103

Ted Joans   *Jazz Is My Religion*   104
                       Jazz Must Be a Woman   105
                       Lester Young   106

Joe Johnson   *Cecil Taylor* [Excerpt]   107

Steve Jonas   *One of Three Musicians*   108

Bob Kaufman   *Bagel Shop Jazz*   109
                       Battle Report   110
                       Walking Parker Home   110
                       War Memoir   111
                       War Memoir: Jazz, Don't Lis-
                           ten to It at Your Own Risk   112

x

Sybil Kein	*Jazz*	114
Jack Kerouac	*221st Chorus* [From *Mexico City Blues*]	115
	239th Chorus [From *Mexico City Blues*]	116
Etheridge Knight	*For Eric Dolphy*	116
	Jazz Drummer	117
Kenneth Koch	*The History of Jazz*	117
Yusef Komunyakaa	*Elegy for Thelonious*	120
	February in Sydney	120
Richard Kostelanetz	*STRINGFOUR*	121
	STRINGFIVE	122
Art Lange	*Blues Five Spot*	123
	Monk's Dream	123
	Monk's Point	124
Philip Larkin	*For Sidney Bechet*	124
Philip Levine	*On the Corner*	125
Larry Levis	*Whitman:*	126
Lyn Lifshin	*Alberta Hunter*	127
N. J. Loftis	*Black Anima* [Section 9]	128
John Logan	*Chicago Scene*	132
Mina Loy	*The Widow's Jazz*	133
Nathaniel Mackey	*Ohnedaruth's Day Begun*	135
Clarence Major	*Un Poco Loco*	138
Dionisio D. Martinez	*Three or Four Shades of Blues*	142
	Three or Four Shades of Blues (2)	143

xi

William Matthews   *Alice Zeno Talking, and Her*
    Son George Lewis the Jazz
    Clarinetist in Attendance   144
    Blues for John Coltrane, Dead
    at 41   146
    Bmp Bmp   146
    Bud Powell, Paris, 1959   147
    Coleman Hawkins (d. 1969),
    RIP   148
    Listening to Lester Young   148
    Unrelenting Flood   149

Victoria McCabe   *For Albert Ayler*   150

Kenneth McClane   *At the Bridge with Rufus*   151

Colleen J. McElroy   *The Singer*   152

Heather McHugh   *Sleep, after Ray Charles Show*
    and Hurricane Report   153

Jack Micheline   *Blues Poem*   153

Vassar Miller   *Dirge in Jazz Time*   154

Roger Mitchell   *For Stephane Grappelli*   155

John Montgomery   *Snowmelt from Yesteryears*   156

Jack Mueller   *Death Jazz: A Review*   157

Lisel Mueller   *January Afternoon, with*
    Billie Holiday   158

Harryette Mullen   *Playing the Invisible Saxophone*
    en el Combo de las Estrellas   159

James Nolan   *Jazz Poem for the Girl Who*
    Cried Wolf   160
    Presenting Eustacia Beau-
    chaud: Ward 3   160

Frank O'Hara	*The Day Lady Died*	162
Kenneth Patchen	*Latesummer Blues*	163
Robert Pinsky	*History of My Heart* [Section I]	165
Sterling D. Plumpp	*I Hear the Shuffle of the People's Feet*	167
Ishmael Reed	*Poetry Makes Rhythm in Philosophy*	173
Kenneth Rexroth	*Written to Music*	174
Kate Rushin	*The Black Back-Ups*	179
Ira Sadoff	*At the Half-Note Cafe*	182
Sonia Sanchez	*a/coltrane/poem*	183
Carl Sandburg	*Jazz Fantasia*	187
Robert Sargent	*Tin Roof Blues*	187
	Touching the Past	188
Mandy Sayer	*Choofa*	189
Asger Schnack	*Aqua* [Excerpt]	190
Jan Selving	*Dancing to Ellington*	191
Léopold Sédar Senghor	*Blues*	192
	New York	192
Kazuko Shiraishi	*Dedicated to the Late John Coltrane*	194
Aleda Shirley	*Ellington Indigos*	198
	The Last Dusk of August	199
	21 August 1984	200
John Sinclair	*humphf*	201
Gilbert Sorrentino	*Broadway! Broadway!*	202

Jack Spicer	*Song for Bird and Myself*	203
Wallace Stevens	*The Sick Man*	206
Michael Stillman	*In Memoriam John Coltrane*	207
John Taggart	*Coming Forth by Day*	207
Melvin B. Tolson	*Lambda* [From *Harlem Gallery*]	208
	Mu [From *Harlem Gallery*]	210
William Tremblay	*Song for Jeannie*	215
Jon C. Tribble	*Anaximander Lewis*	217
Quincy Troupe	*The Day Duke Raised; may 24, 1974*	219
	Four, and More; for Miles Davis	220
	Snake-Back Solo	223
Jean Valentine	*Coltrane, Syeeda's Song Flute*	224
Anne Waldman	*Bluehawk*	225
	Eric Dolphy	226
Joy Walsh	*Ferguson's Conquistadores 77*	226
Marilyn Nelson Waniek	*It's All in Your Head*	227
William Wantling	*A Plea for Workmen's Compensation*	229
Jerry W. Ward, Jr.	*Jazz to Jackson to John*	231
Paulette C. White	*Nina Simone*	234
Sherley Anne Williams	*Any Woman's Blues*	235
	1 Poem 2 Voices A Song	235
William Carlos Williams	*Ol' Bunk's Band*	237
David Wojahn	*Satin Doll*	238

Joel "Yehuda" Wolk   *Elegy for Kenny Dorham*   239

C. D. Wright   *Jazz Impressions in the Garden*   240
    The Substitute Bassist   240
    Treatment   241

Robert Wrigley   *Torch Songs*   242

Al Young   *A Dance for Ma Rainey*   243
    Jungle Strut   244

Bill Zavatsky   *Elegy*   245
    To the Pianist Bill Evans   245

Paul Zimmer   *The Duke Ellington Dream*   248
    Zimmer's Last Gig   248

Biographical Notes and Statements of Poetics   250
Music Appendix   279
Acknowledgments   285

Preface

I

The short-lived success of the poetry & jazz movement in the 50s unfortunately colored the opinions of many critics with regard to jazz-related poems. Even at the height of the poetry & jazz readings, there was significant criticism, much of it justified, that the cross-medium relationship seemed forced—that neither art form was allowed to breathe. As Kenneth Rexroth wrote in his introduction to Kazuko Shiraishi's *Seasons of Sacred Lust:* "Poetry read to jazz had only a brief popularity in America. It was ruined by people who knew nothing about either jazz or poetry." For the purposes of this anthology, that debate is not terribly relevant; aside from the controversial efforts of the Beat movement, many poets have tried to write about music and to keep the musical rhythms without relying on a live combo to set the pulse. In fact, since the turn of the century there have been hundreds of poems responding to jazz in all its musical and cultural overtones. In this anthology, the range of poetic and jazz aesthetics, not merely from writers across the United States but from countries around the world as well, strives to represent the many poetic voices and to explore the broad responses to jazz as poetic inspiration.

As with any anthology, of course, this section offers only a limited palette of the poems and writers available. Nevertheless, it is the most complete project of its kind. Some notable collections of jazz-related poems, such as Langston Hughes's *The Weary Blues* (1926) and Ted Joans's *Black Pow-Wow* (1969), refer only to one poet, usually the author; others, such as Rosey Pool's *Beyond the Blues: New Poems by American Negroes* (1962), are limited by the date of publication and therefore by the scope of music and writers. Jeremy Robson's *Poems from Poetry and Jazz in Concert* (1969) and other, similar collections concern themselves mainly with the performance element of reading poetry to jazz, and many of the poems have little or no direct relationship with the music. Jim Stephens's anthology of jazz-related poems, *Bright Moments: A Collection of Jazz Poetry* (1980), includes a number of valuable pieces but, finally, is not so extensive as such a project deserves; in keeping with the jazz tradition of sharing individual sounds, it seems important to compile a great variety of poetic voices.

As a result, this anthology includes a number of well-known poets, several foreign writers, a slightly expanded selection for those who have written extensively about jazz, and a large percentage of lesser-known poets, many of whom deserve more recognition than they have received.

Obviously, when attempting to place African-American poetry in its historical and social perspective—from Langston Hughes to Chris Gilbert—it is impossible not to address the synthesis of verse and music (specifically jazz and blues). Much has been written critically on this topic, most notably Stephen Henderson's introduction to his *Understanding the Black Poetry* (1973); and, of course, when considering the overall importance of black music in the American cultural psyche we cannot overlook W. E. B. Du Bois's classic statement in 1903 from his *The Souls of Black Folk,* where he refers to the music as "the singular spiritual heritage of the nation and the greatest gift of the Negro people." That's now a given. And, yes, undoubtedly much of black poetry has been associated with black music, and at times almost stereotypically so; what is surprising, however, is to realize how widely jazz has influenced poetry outside the black community—*internationally.* The music has broken social and cultural barriers, leapfrogging the guard gates of the black literary community, and has significantly influenced much of contemporary poetry.

II

Because the subject matter in this anthology pertains to both poetry and music, the academic uses are also not limited to one medium, though perhaps the most obvious application is in courses in poetry. Syncopated rhythm and varied meter, a sense of movement, lyricism and drama—all these qualities are certainly not unique to jazz-related poems, but they become immediate issues because of the nature of music. This lyricism and musicality would make the book useful for any classes concerned with contemporary poetics, whether they be creative-writing workshops or introductory courses in poetry. The poems can be studied and compared, not merely with regard to specific genres of music or particular figures addressed, but also in terms of standard poetic sensibilities.

From a more music-oriented and chronological standpoint, the works cover most of the periods in the history of jazz, from the early blues to free jazz, and when taken out of their alphabetical order the poems allow for a special reading of jazz history. (The Music Appendix lists an extremely general grouping for this purpose, but it at least offers a partial guideline for more precise categorizing.) True, the various approaches to jazz taken by the poets do not allow for any serious effort to cover a complete history of modern American music. But even those readers unfamiliar with the chronology of jazz can begin to see the different musical stages through their respective poetic treatments.

What becomes apparent, of course, is that certain modern figures and periods in jazz dominate as inspirational sources, partially as a result of the poetry and jazz movement from the Beat generation's taking flight during the bebop revolution. Consequently, some of the major figures in jazz are either absent or denied the weight they deserve. Where several poems in this anthology concern Duke Ellington, for example, only one focuses on Count Basie. And despite an imbalance of jazz-related poems with regard to particular eras or jazz periods, valuable comparisons can be made when several writers choose the same era or figure. Poets writing about Charlie Parker have approached their subject through personal experience, distant admiration, posthumous reflection, even through the voice of Walt Whitman. John Coltrane has probably been the focus of more poems than any other jazz musician, but the portraits of the man and his music vary as much as his own creative endeavors—from bebop and modal music, to hard bop and "sheets of sound," and eventually to free jazz.

Finally, some well-known poets have been left out, not because of the quality of their work, but because of astronomical permission-to-reprint costs. For the most part, however, those who deserve to be represented in this genre have been included.

III

This anthology thus offers several approaches to poetics and to jazz. An exciting collection of contemporary poets mixed with a host of other twentieth-century international writers, it presents variations on a number of integral themes, from personal portraits of famous jazz artists to meditations on the music itself.

None of the poets denies the rhythmic pulses shared by modern poetry and modern music. At the same time, few share the same influence of or passion for jazz: some admit that jazz has inspired their work more than any other creative source; others freely admit that they know little about the technical aspects of the music but feel drawn to the beat. Their Statements of Poetics briefly touch upon those differing relationships. Nevertheless, it is precisely that disparity in appreciation which makes the collection of writers playful and engaging.

Indeed, jazz has attracted such a diversity of voices and temperaments that one wonders at Anaïs Nin's surprise when she says in a letter to Julio Cortazar: "How long were you in America that you could write so marvelously about Charles Parker or jazz language and jazz life? Don't answer"—*don't answer* because the work itself is the answer; but this also points to how jazz has crossed cultural boundaries through the transference of emotional and imagistic energy. That is what Robert Hass touches on in his "A Poetry Craft Lecture" in *Poetry Flash:*

> One of the problems for me with listening to a lot of music is that it makes me despair of poetry. (laughs) I was listening to Charlie Mingus's *Blues and Roots* a couple of weeks ago. Especially the beginning of the fourth part—if

you divide the piece into five movements—is the most astonishing thing in it, to me. It's one of those places in music where—the only thing like it I can think of in literature that *almost* approaches it is the Caddy section of *The Sound and the Fury,* the Benjy section of *The Sound and the Fury,* when he's howling for his sister who's lost, only you can't hear him howl because he's the narrator of the book, and you only know he's howling because everybody's saying to him, hush up now, while this cascade of images is going through his head.

There is a similar energy surging throughout this anthology, cascading with images and verbal music, and it all cumulates in a more comprehensive definition of jazz poetry.

Ralph Ellison touches upon the contrasts in jazz that relate directly to poetics in *The Invisible Man:*

Sometimes now I listen to Louis while I have my favorite dessert of vanilla ice cream and sloe gin. I pour the red liquid over the white mound, watching it glisten and the vapor rising as Louis bends that military instrument into a beam of lyrical sound. Perhaps I like Louis Armstrong because he's made poetry out of being invisible. . . . And my own grasp of invisibility aids me to understand his music. . . . Invisibility, let me explain, gives one a slightly different sense of time, you're never quite on the beat. Sometimes you're ahead and sometimes behind. Instead of the swift and imperceptive flowing of time, you are aware of its nodes, those points where time stands still or from which it leaps behind. And you slip into the breaks and look around. That's what you hear vaguely in Louis' music.

In part, the act of *visualizing* jazz accounts for the range of poets engaged in the music's elusive accessibility: young black writers steeped in the tradition of black music, using poetry in part to achieve a political voice; older white poets attracted to the spirit of syncopated rhythms; some writers who feel bebop ruined the spirit of jazz; others who see modernism as surpassing all previous forms of the music; men pining over the women they wanted to love; women lamenting over the men who have done them wrong; people transported by the live drama on the bandstand; others, years later, transported still by memories and recordings; poets interested mainly in a detailed narrative; poets trying to break apart the language to imitate sound; friends of jazz musicians eager to keep their spirits alive on the page; jazz appreciators engaged in the spirit of an era; and all those who have tried to capture the swing, the sex, the dance, the violence, the laughter, the brutal rhythms and the tender sway of jazz.

The Jazz Poetry
Anthology

SAM ABRAMS

In the Capability

          of one man's breath
as marion as strings
shape vibrations in air
& memory

on purpose
a music which fights
environment rings phone rings
cash register clench yr teeth

close yr eyes you have
to hear the bass

                up tight for
this or that good sounds do
not good vibrations make

hard ass city

st marks place 19 67
ornette patted joshua on the belly
& said "hey man"

JAMES BALDWIN

Le sporting-club de Monte Carlo

(for Lena Horne)

The lady is a tramp
    a camp
    a lamp

The lady is a sight
    a might
    a light

1

the lady devastated
an alley or two
reverberated through the valley
which leads to me, and you

the lady is the apple
of God's eye:
He's cool enough about it
but He tends to strut a little
when she passes by

the lady is a wonder
daughter of the thunder
smashing cages
legislating rages
with the voice of ages
singing us through.

AMIRI BARAKA

AM/TRAK

1
Trane,
Trane,
History Love Scream Oh
Trane, Oh
Trane, Oh
Scream History Love
Trane

2
Begin on by a Philly night club
or the basement of a cullut chuhch
walk the bars my man for pay
honk the night lust of money
oh
blow-
scream history love

2

Rabbit, Cleanhead, Diz
Big Maybelle, Trees in the shining night forest

Oh
blow
love, history

Alcohol we submit to thee
3x's consume our lives
our livers quiver under yr poison hits
eyes roll back in stupidness
The navy, the lord, niggers,
the streets
all converge a shitty symphony
of screams
  to come
  dazzled invective
Honk Honk Honk, "I am here
to love
it." Let me be fire-mystery
air feeder beauty."

Honk
Oh
scream—Miles
comes.

3
Hip band alright
sum up life in the slick
street part of the
world, oh,
blow,
if you cd
nigger
man

Miles wd stand back and negative check
oh, he dug him—Trane
But Trane clawed at the limits of cool
slandered sanity
with his tryin to be born
raging
shit

3

Oh
blow,
            yeh go do it
            honk, scream
            uhuh yeh—history
                        love
                        blue clipped moments
                        of intense feeling.
"Trane you blows too long."
Screaming niggers drop out yr solos
Bohemian nights, the "heavyweight champ"
smacked him
in the face
his eyes sagged like a spent
dick, hot vowels escaped the metal clone of his soul
fucking saxophone
tell us shit tell us tell us!

4
There was nothing left to do but
be where monk cd find him
that crazy
mother fucker
            duh duh-duh duh-duh duh
            duh duh
            duh duh-duh duh-duh duh
            duh duh
            duh duh-duh duh-duh duh
            duh duh
            duh Duuuuuuuuuuhhhhhh
Can you play this shit? (Life asks
Come by and listen

& at the 5 Spot Bach, Mulatto ass Beethoven
& even Duke, who has given America its hip tongue
checked
checked
Trane stood and dug
Crazy monk's shit
Street gospel intellectual mystical survival codes
Intellectual street gospel funk modes
Tink a ling put downs of dumb shit
pink pink a cool bam groove note air breath
a why I'm here

a why I aint
& who is you-ha-you-ha-you-ha

Monk's shit
Blue Cooper 5 Spot
was the world busting
on piano bass drums & tenor

This was Coltrane's College. A Ph motherfuckin d
sitting at the feet, elbows
& funny grin
Of Master T Sphere
too cool to be a genius
he was instead
Thelonius
with Comrades Shadow
on tubs, lyric Wilbur
who hipped us to electric futures
& the monster with the horn.

5
From the endless sessions
money lord hovers oer us
capitalism beats our ass
dope & juice wont change it
Trane, blow, oh scream
yeh, anyway.

There then came down in the ugly streets of us
inside the head & tongue
of us
a man
black blower of the now
The vectors from all sources—slavery, renaissance
bop charlie parker,
nigger absolute super-sane screams against reality
course through him
AS SOUND!
"Yes, it says
this is now in your screaming
recognize the truth
recognize reality
& even check me (Trane)
who blows it

5

Yes it says
Yes &
Yes again   Convulsive multi orgasmic
                Art
                Protest

& finally, brother, you took you were
  (are we gathered to dig this?
  electric wind find us finally
  on red records of the history of ourselves)

The cadre came together
the inimitable 4 who blew the pulse of then, exact
The flame the confusion the love of
whatever the fuck there was
    to love
Yes it says
blow, oh honk-scream (bahhhhhhh - wheeeeeeee)

(If Don Lee thinks I am imitating him in this poem,
this is only payback for his imitating me—we
are brothers, even if he is a backward cultural nationalist
motherfucker—Hey man only socialism brought by revolution
can win)
                Trane was the spirit of the 60's
                He was Malcolm X in New Super Bop Fire
                Baaahhhhh
                Wheeeeeee . . . Black Art!!!
Love
History
   On The Bar Tops of Philly
in the Monkish College of *Express*
in the cool Grottoes of Miles Davis Funnytimery
Be
Be
Be reality
Be reality alive in motion in flame to change (You Knew It!)
                              to change!!
                (All you reactionaries listening
                Fuck you, Kill you
                get outta here!!!)

Jimmy Garrison, bass, McCoy Tyner, piano, Captain Marvel Elvin
on drums, the number itself—the precise saying
all of it in it afire aflame talking saying being doing meaning

6

Meditations
Expressions
A Love Supreme
(I lay in solitary confinement, July 67
Tanks rolling thru Newark
& whistled all I knew of Trane
my knowledge heartbeat
& he was *dead*
they
said.

And yet last night I played *Meditations*
& it told me what to do
Live, you crazy mother
fucker!
Live!
  & organize
  yr shit
  as rightly
  burning!

GEORGE BARLOW

In My Father's House

Always first to rise
he usually slipped into daybreak
like a phantom—heading
(in jacket jeans white socks & loafers)
for Alameda
the drowsy traffic
& buzzing electronics of Naval Air

But he plays a horn
& some mornings caught him
aching with jazz—reeling
in its chemistry & might:
Duke Bird Basie
riffs chords changes
softly grunted & mouthed

in his closet
in the hallway in
all the glory of the sunrise

Who knows what spirits
shimmer through the neurons
& acoustics of his sleep
before these mornings:
black Beethoven
shunning his own deafness
for the sake of symphony
a Haitian drummer—
eyes shut in the moonlight—
mounted by divine horsemen
who flash through his hands
pretty Billie
eating gardenias with a needle
singing the blues away

Maybe urges older than oceans
startle him in the shower
or in the livingroom
on his way out the door
compel him to swipe moments
from time he doesn't have
to inch notes across
pitiless lined sheets
that have waited on the piano all night
for beat & harmony to marry

On these mornings
he met the man with ease
didn't carry no heavy load
Car horns were trumpets
fog horns bassoons
train whistles blushing saxophones
On these mornings
he jammed with angels
popped his fingers
to music in his head
filled his great lungs
with cool air

GERALD BARRAX

The Singer

for Nina, Roberta, Aretha.
Sarah, Ella, Carmen.
Dinah, Billie, Bessie. And Ma.

Black Angel
Doing what she's gotta do
The sister sings

"Like a stone bird"
He said, intending to praise her.
But no bird has such a choice.

They speak, too,
Or whatever twittering means
But does that explain human song?

Maybe this more than natural impulse
Surprised even the creator
Who let the possibility

Slip his mind.
Not unintended.
Just not thought of.

   Suppose
There was a creature
not yet human
who cocked his head, dimly quizzical
at birdsong
and did something—
roared, screeched, howled—
something purely joyous in imitation
and those birds filled the prehistoric air
in flight from his obscenity.

Who was to tell him
he wasn't created for that? Or
   suppose Eve.
Giving a name

to something dull Adam
didn't know about:

What's that? What are you doing?

And she, holding the doomed child,
stopped and looked at him as if listening
and smiled, and said

Singing.

Not like birds
Who are doomed to sing
Her doom and ours is her silence.
    The sisters sing
        Doing what they've gotta do
    Black Angels

MARVIN BELL

The Fifties

Miles Davis on a night off
comes up the street
to Birdland, in the days
before his solos turned
to astronomy, he's in shades,
I'm on the sidewalk
waiting to hear J.J. and Kai
with Roger, who recently
soloed on "The Minnehaha Waltz"
with a stuck third valve.
There it is in a look—
the barrel-chested horn men
with calloused lips,
cushion-rim mouthpieces
for long nights and a rubber
embouchure drying out
and chipping away at *schmaltz,*
vibrato and the "shakes,"

10

until you might as well be Clyde
McCoy with a flutter tongue
and a plumber's helper
to *wah wah* the white blues.
We've come from Basin Street
where Cat Anderson, once the scourge
of the high registers,
has to play in the staff for Basie.
The second man covers.
Before that, Burke solos
with the Goldman Band in the park
and leaves out the high counterpoint
(optional) virtuosi stuff,
though he steps it up a notch
to where you can hear the holes
in the valves and pipes
lining up with tiny, rapid explosions
of spit and breath, and he bows quickly.
I've got a Bach cornet,
used to belong to Burke's second chair,
and later I'll belong to
a Mendez trumpet with two triggers,
but now I've got that sweet tone
and I'm fast, but it's not enough.
I see notes for solos—bad.
I'm hung on the chords—bad.
I can't stay up—bad. Clifford Brown,
Thad Jones, Miles, nobody knows
Nat Adderley yet—they don't have to
see the notes, take off
the glasses, or look outside.
It's already clear to me
that it's bad to be too clear
about some things—solo voice things,
pitch things, next phrase things.
At jazz-conscious WNEW,
the hippest jockey
has locked himself in the studio
to play one record all afternoon—
it's "Mr. Sandman," the McGuires.
Miles has started to use a mute
on all standards.

CAROL BERGÉ

Piaf and Holiday Go Out

Bracelet eat into the flesh/ the gangrene of
applause   Strange fluids aim up
                              the spirit
the Lights
              up Out, she is dead.
                            Dead in the skin
blue red lights/ brown white on black red gone
gone/ out. It was all those black dresses
did it, parade of buckling under, underlines
magnified by sound, those spotlights   music
the drug toward love.
                            How it is its own sadness
disease. With no name but its own.
                              Spotlight
on the lips how they move and the hands make hands
move. Eyes out.
                    It is a too smooth structure,
they silent, their cunts wired for sound
toward the fine misery put them down.
                                        It was
'a certain man in this here town' made a shape
but his shape changed and did not matter.
Thick or thin if he gave what was needed.
                                          Scat/
a word with two meanings, 'Lover where can you'
It was joy, joy, joy until then and turned fast
like the lights.
              Went
                    the quick hard way.
The dead women inhabit a room, fill it with their
perfume their songs.
                          Can we all burst with them
their memory their wide music of the sad flesh.
This room   like all the others   to contain them
in this shape.
                    'It was bad at home, so now we
stay up any way we can these long nights'
                                          Soon
it will be easier.   Sing it loud.

12

The Recounting of Gods

I.   My own history bores me, texture of my skin, of
the problems of my allies. A recounting
of ordinary travails 'How are you' not rhetorical.
Like spade skin, sound of Chinese waiters, ordering
the same food week after week
Construct of the days
the nights/ a sweater worn back to front/
obsessed
with forms the way a coin-collector wails with drums
or a drummer collect stamps.
In your oriental face
I see all the delicacy of evil. The cardsharp, as
story thrice-told (w. tarot) and never dull. Mark
of the line running off the page, ragged fingernails
or bone jutting through skin. Color of whiskey
color of bars/ or music of lights of all our years:
It is no longer romantic or will always continue.

II.   It is always so romantic to me: my own history.
Precious cardsharp whose texture is known although
untouched. You as yr own scuba-diver, motionless
through ice. My ally, my enemy whose ideas obsess
with old mythologies. Teeth like dice. Moving out
off the Florida Keys, a toast to the creative arts,
how boring we all are, with our cute malnutrition
and diets of strange solids formed in sea water.
Poems/ written on the backs of blank checks, as our
aging audience mutters, 'Get off your saddle,
Charlie Chan, the crap game is over.'
o your innocent
mask, it is all so dull by now/ the frail slow walks
down wooden streets where a foreign language is heard
The forms distant, the music (Ah! you know the music!)
The Detestable Pain/ our recognition of its shape
Our endless editing and the endless circumscribing.

III.   Good to know we will all be liquid and fit into
our individual ghastly history. My teeth are like
dice. I notice. All painters love music and dance.
Musick it is shaped like pain like magick. Boring.
Like stories of the endless Muses dressed as waiters,

the recounting of the gods
of agony of loud laughter
of discord monumental and distant. Counting them
like items in a collection. The pills, getting high,
who one's friends are, today yesterday: line-breaks.
That dreadful parade of faces of the ex-lovers
The charade of memories/ I ask you: what is shaped
like a grand piano, and screams? Sound of their voices.
A tenuous thread/ binding us to reality or each other.
He hates rain falling on his face, he collects his hates
in a bucket, in two months he has enough to drown in,
No scuba suit, o my friend he has no scuba suit, I've
learned not to tell him,
I've learned not to talk so much.

IV.   I have not learned to stop writing: that most desirable
of gods. I keep thinking of Virginia Woolf, a mad girl,
her fantasies, there is one Leonardo in this my odd life,
there have been few.
Head structuring gently on the neck,
a certain majesty to us, not the editorial, not the regal
but thee and me, how we move or take stance to face it.
Drum beat to the core.
You can become my intimate easily.
I will answer the bell or not, when you ring. You *know*
what I mean, that's what counts! So you can become my
intimate, so easily. I shine at the beginning, then glow
in the center of it all; that radiance; that light; and
then the screaming. The sleepless death.   Drum smell.

V.   Smell of drums. When it
happens, when the deep lessons
are learned, without abbreviations. Crow Jane taught me
many lessons. Let us sleep this night like cubs, like
children, curled glistening and simple. Away from all
fluids, all threatening liquids. Bones indent
at certain pressures. I can use/ the hour you give me
whenever I wish! Audacity to spend one's life
as one chooses. I choose: to be spoiled rotten, to get
whatever I wish, soon or late, to throw things away
before they are used up, opinion no longer moves me,
young love is an illusion, no illusion, I remain
despite the infinite losses.
You, in yr scuba outfit,
finding me atop your invented undersea mountains, o you

14

Genius! You are a poem, a god, you are Charlie Mingus
on a rainy day, the water almost up to his eyes,
6th Ave/8th St., trying to catch a cab/ and looking
like everybody else. Nobody recognizes us. He fails.
The cabs and buses pass. But with courage he stands.
Howls at the audience of wills,
                              in the face of beauty.

PAUL BLACKBURN

Listening to Sonny Rollins at the Five-Spot

THERE WILL be many other nights like
be standing here with someone, some
one
someone
some-one
some
some
some
some
some
some
one
there will be other songs
a-nother fall, another—spring, but
there will never be a-noth, noth
anoth
noth
anoth-er
noth-er
noth-er
              Other lips that I may kiss,
but they won't thrill me like
                    thrill me like
                              like yours
used to
        dream a million dreams
but how can they come
when there
              never be
a-noth—

15

HORACE JULIAN BOND

The Bishop of Atlanta: Ray Charles

The Bishop seduces the world with his voice
Sweat strangles mute eyes
As insinuations gush out through a hydrant of sorrow
Dreams, a world never seen
Moulded on Africa's anvil, tempered down home
Documented in cries and wails
Screaming to be ignored, crooning to be heard
Throbbing from the gutter
On Saturday night
Silver offering only
The Right Reverend's back in town
Don't it make you feel all right?

GEORGE BOWERING

Pharoah Sanders, in the Flesh

Walking east on 3rd street
to listen to Pharoah Sanders
I have to step around rotting junk,
wearing my sorcerer's gloves,
blue, orange, red & grey

to enter out of fear, short
of breath, into Slugs' bar, warm
as crowded bodies can make it,
warming the small mugs of ale,
warming already to the unfamiliar

setting to be welcomed as the new
familiar, as Japan played in Africa
on vinyl, in Quebec. This is my first
encounter east of avenue B,
having given up my money, my coat,

16

my Kanadian white face, knowing
they dont know I've heard that music
for years in my best friends' blood-
streams; I look for the face
on my typing room wall, he's there,

Pharoah, fey row, little boy lost
leaning on the wall of the little stage
banging two tambourines together,
legs bent & straightening, coming
northeast from Arkansas, east again

to Sun Ra's bar & his continent
laid open by the Nile. We arent far
from the East River, the slug
floating heavily to the sea. I've
got a seat, Pharoah Sanders

has pickt up his magnificent horn,
chasing these warmed up pictures
from my mind; I've come out of
literature, right into the roar
of that belly's horn, I wish I could

just run up & grab him &
stop saying that's Pharoah Sanders,
that's really Pharoah Sanders.

EDWARD KAMAU BRATHWAITE

Trane

Propped against the crowded bar
he pours into the curved and silver horn
his old unhappy longing for a home

the dancers twist and turn
he leans and wishes he could burn
his memories to ashes like some old notorious emperor

of rome. but no stars blazed across the sky when he
   was born
no wise men found his hovel. this crowded bar
where dancers twist and turn

holds all the fame and recognition he will ever earn
on earth or heaven. he leans against the bar
and pours his old unhappy longing in the saxophone

RAY BREMSER

Blues for Harold . . .

*for Harold Carrington, friend & poet, who died of
an overdose of New Jersey, 25 years young . . .
July, 1964 . . .*

you took
all the solos
& now yr/ax is in hock
somewhere in Trenton,
New Jersey State Prison
               , 2-wing, down
an abolished corridor . . .
                   some white-man blows yr/horn . . .

you were born enslaved
& died free—who's happy,
harold? you are not!

       (Harold was the most beautiful boy
       that ever came out of a reformatory
       unchanged)—no one cld ever put you down/or
       we who cld/wldnt!

Harold, i see yr proud wool-head held high
   now, (nobody realizing how symbolic
of *being* high this is) whosoever you defy to-
   day will need *not* reason to hurt you,
no returns—no demand for it anyway
   —you look about you now . . .

18

I remember the long nite talks
or shutting-ups we had,
you & Nick & Carl & Stewart & I;
Jimmy Smith, earlier, tearing up his organ
with the 'Champ'—or Miles blowing a Blue-Haze
all over us, first stirrings of Coltrane—1957, 56;
Ghandis in our gray department of institutions &
agencies sheets—(in Trenton & Rahway
                    they're the same 2,
                    every week! talk a-
                    bout funk . . .)

Harold, i own up no guilt:
having never been guilty of it!
   those who enslaved you
   stink of it—
   they wallow in it, yet
it betrays them not
                    for who knows the whch
                    of the 2 stinks more is almighty
                    indeed . . .

those who hate you have slain you
& your father before—presently,
your mother, who (as i cld) wld
call you nigger with a comparable love
the likes of which-with
you yrself loved your mother
in the adolescent resentment you contained
in no come-back; grown here to permit / now / this
thru all yr days long done & gone;
blown up like a fart,
& demolished . . .
for what, Harold?

for that fucking moon!
for that wretched bird you see flying
; the wall that's about you—(?)
for its eventual, ultimate fall
& failure to contain yr/hatred
whch was love they read,-nor-read-not, ever!
for that complacent bitch
whose bull-dyke heart is all meat
& whose theme-music is a violent

19

& perennial lewd assault—a degenerate
who'll piss & expectorate in yr/ear
& call that music . . . that hydraulic-metallic soprano! Vie/
for the leprous cunt of an obscene ass!

the pure sounds of your own spheres
in yr/own head cldnt keep you out of it—
no-one's cld . . .
a cacophony to make you neurotic; & yet
not harm that admirable black-erotica,
whose relation intertonally & within all
its outside form itself
we call blues
                    is more life than geriatrics;
more living than chemical-biology &
more often laid than all of Princeton;
cooler than the whole of Princeton;
of an interior-Chinese startling foreign policy;
than all the tremendous Atomical-deaths
whose numbers,
                    comparatively,
                              are minor &
insignificant—(tho we'll still blow the whole world
into an impenetrable cosmic-dust one of these
—let us say—geophysical years!)

& what an unholy communion with noise
that criminally-maniacal execution of
utter malice & hell-embarrassing evil/
will, of its own necessity, be . . .
                              (that be, indeed,
tho we be & behold, be not!
be that as it may:
i have heard it already/
but live yet . . .
we shall *never* know it together,
simultaneous—only
the Gods hear that . . .

but/Harold,
in the meanwhile, blow . . .
take all yr/solos
everywhere you go,
yr/too soon gone & hardly nobody hears

when you do—
                    but i do,
Harold;
            i am listening now;
in the dormitory afternoons
we manslaughtered with our own beauty
(& Maybe at the *cost* of that beauty! Yet
i *remember* yr/beauty, Harold . . . i think,
i recall & i reflect—
i can describe it, pronounce it,
praise it & not ever want to take it away from you;
i am safe & saved in my own—

                        / man's sad & beautiful warmth we
                        all own / our selfs / whose maturity
                        will grow to cost the same as yours,
                        & all of them do . . .
                        in the end . . . ah, you know;
                        & no trouble at all,
                        out there . . .
                        in that void, to yr/peers,
                        to the moon . . .
                        to science, (to ornithology
                        in particular) to nothing
                        , O, nothing at all

but an undiscovered discographer's craft
whose secret applications
are impressed on the heart
as clumsy as Ignu
so only another'd
know . . .
them who listen / who's ears /
but to hear . . . come & go / now
                    blow now / Harold;
                            take yr/solo . . .

STERLING A. BROWN

Cabaret

(1927, Black & Tan Chicago)

Rich, flashy, puffy-faced,
Hebrew and Anglo-Saxon,
The overlords sprawl here with their glittering darlings.
The smoke curls thick, in the dimmed light
Surreptitiously, deaf-mute waiters
Flatter the grandees,
Going easily over the rich carpets,
Wary lest they kick over the bottles
Under the tables.

The jazzband unleashes its frenzy.

> *Now, now,*
> *To it, Roger; that's a nice doggie,*
> *Show your tricks to the gentlemen.*

The trombone belches, and the saxophone
Wails curdlingly, the cymbals clash,
The drummer twitches in an epileptic fit

> Muddy water
> Round my feet
> Muddy water

The chorus sways in.
The 'Creole Beauties from New Orleans'
(By way of Atlanta, Louisville, Washington, Yonkers,
With stop-overs they've used nearly all their lives)
Their creamy skin flushing rose warm,
O, le bal des belles quarterounes!
Their shapely bodies naked save
For tattered pink silk bodices, short velvet tights,
And shining silver-buckled boots;
Red bandannas on their sleek and close-clipped hair;
To bring to mind (aided by the bottles under the tables)
Life upon the river—

> Muddy water, river sweet

(Lafitte the pirate, instead,
And his doughty diggers of gold)

    There's peace and happiness there
    I declare

(In Arkansas,
Poor half-naked fools, tagged with identification numbers,
Worn out upon the levees,
Are carted back to the serfdom
They had never left before
And may never leave again)

    Bee—dap—ee—DOOP, dee—ba—dee—BOOP

The girls wiggle and twist

    Oh you too,
    Proud high-stepping beauties,
    Show your paces to the gentlemen.
    A prime filly, seh.
    What am I offered, gentlemen, gentlemen. . . .

    I've been away a year today
    To wander and roam
    I don't care if it's muddy there

(Now that the floods recede,
What is there left the miserable folk?
Oh time in abundance to count their losses,
There is so little else to count.)

    Still it's my home, sweet home

From the lovely throats
Moans and deep cries for home:
Nashville, Toledo, Spout Springs, Boston,
Creoles from Germantown;—
The bodies twist and rock;
The glasses are filled up again. . . .

(In Mississippi
The black folk huddle, mute, uncomprehending,
Wondering 'how come the good Lord
Could treat them this a way')

23

shelter
Down in the Delta

(Along the Yazoo
The buzzards fly over, over, low,
Glutted, but with their scrawny necks stretching,
Peering still.)

I've got my toes turned Dixie ways
Round that Delta let me laze

The band goes mad, the drummer throws his sticks
At the moon, a *papier-mâché* moon,
The chorus leaps into weird posturings,
The firm-fleshed arms plucking at grapes to stain
Their coralled mouths; seductive bodies weaving
Bending, writhing, turning

My heart cries out for
M U D D Y   W A T E R

(Down in the valleys
The stench of the drying mud
Is a bitter reminder of death.)

Dee da dee D A A A A H

Ma Rainey

(Ma Rainey, "Mother of the Blues," 1886–1939)

1

When Ma Rainey
Comes to town,
Folks from anyplace
Miles aroun'
From Cape Girardeau,
Poplar Bluff,
Flocks in to hear
Ma do her stuff;
Comes flivverin' in,

24

Or ridin' mules,
Or packed in trains,
Picknickin' fools . . .
That's what it's like
Fo' miles on down,
To New Orleans delta
An' Mobile town,
When Ma hits
Anywheres aroun'.

2

Dey comes to hear Ma Rainey from de little river settlements,
From blackbottom cornrows and from lumber camps;
Dey stumble in de hall, je' a-laughin' an' a-cacklin',
Cheerin' lak roarin' water, lak wind in river swamps.

An' some jokers keeps deir laughs a-goin' in de crowded aisles,
An' some folk sits dere waitin' wid' deir aches an' miseries,
Till Ma comes out before dem, a-smilin' gold-toofed smiles,
An' Long Boy ripples minors on de black an' yellow keys.

3

O Ma Rainey,
Sing yo' song;
Now you's back
Whah you belong,
Git way inside us,
Keep us strong . . .
O Ma Rainey,
Li'l an' low,
Sing us 'bout de hard luck
Roun' our do';
Sing us 'bout de lonesome road
We mus' go . . .

4

I talked to a fellow, an' the fellow say,
'She jes' catch hold of us, somekindaway.
She sang Backwater Blues one day:
—'IT RAINED FO' DAYS AN' DE SKIES WAS DARK AS NIGHT,
  TROUBLE TAKEN PLACE IN DE LOWLANDS AT NIGHT.
  THUNDERED AN' LIGHTENED AN' THE STORM BEGIN TO ROLL

THOUSAN'S OF PEOPLE AIN'T GOT NO PLACE TO GO.
DEN I WENT AN' STOOD UPON SOME HIGH OL' LONESOME HILL,
AN' LOOKED DOWN ON THE PLACE WHERE I USED TO LIVE.

'An' den de folks, dey natchally bowed dey heads an' cried,
Bowed dey heavy heads, shet dey moufs up tight an' cried,
An' Ma lef' de stage, an' followed some of de folks outside.'

Dere wasn't much more de fellow say:
She jes' gits hold of us dataway.

New St. Louis Blues

MARKET STREET WOMAN

Market Street woman is known fuh to have dark days,
Market Street woman noted fuh to have dark days,
Life do her dirty in a hundred onery ways.

Let her hang out de window and watch de busy worl' go pas',
Hang her head out de window and watch de careless worl' go pas',
Maybe some good luck will come down Market Street at las'.

Put paint on her lips, purple powder on her choklit face,
Paint on her lips, purple powder on her choklit face,
Take mo' dan paint to change de luck of dis dam place.

Gettin' old and ugly, an' de sparks done lef' her eye,
Old an' ugly an' de fire's out in her eye,
De men may see her, but de men keeps passin' by—

Market Street woman have her hard times, oh my Lawd,
Market Street woman have her hard times, oh my Lawd,
Let her git what she can git, 'fo dey lays her on de coolin' board.

RICHARD BURNS

The Song of the Yellow Star

I sing you the song of the yellow star,
   The six point star of Manichee
That rose through skies when hell's apple was torn
   From the first rose-garden tree.

And night fell down to hide Dad's sorrow
   And the moon waltzed out on the sky,
Lilting and wandering, iced to bone-marrow,
   Lily craters filling her eye.

And her yellow turned blue-bird, and opened wings,
   And the blind harper's eyes flashed wide
As he plucked out a song from the Moon's apron strings
   For his daddy-O Sun who had died.

But then the childhood springtime came
   And the tree blossomed out in white,
And a lynched child cried, "I am he with no name
   Come to swing your moonsong to light."

They strung the child with the tattooed arm
   On a high tree-cross, as he laughed in his pain.
But he rose in the gas with a silent psalm
   That his blue star would flame in yellow again.

And now we wait weaving in fields of dull green,
   And our fact'ry smoke pours in the seas,
While the yellow star sings in the dark man's blues,
   We pray for the rose, on our knees.

So I sing you the song of the yellow star
   That the six points will sprout to a seven,
And the frei-making work gates will be pushed ajar
   To a road which spirals to heaven.

He comes, he's reborn in five continents,
   The brown one, with hair like a lion.
He has loins of gold, riding the elements
   Over fields of tobacco and cotton.

27

So sing out the song of the yellow star
  And the six points will peal to a nine,
The nine pregnant seeds of the first garden tree.
  Twelve roses soon will be mine.

HAYDEN CARRUTH

Paragraphs

[Sections 11, 26, 27, 28]

11

Oh I loved you Pete Brown. And you were a brother
to me Joe Marsala. And you too sweet Billy Kyle.
You Sid Bechet. And Benny Carter.
And Joe Jones. Cozy Cole.
Cootie Williams. Dicky Wells. Al Hall. Ben Webster.
Matty Matlock. Lou McGarity. Mel Powell. Fats Waller.
Freddie Green. Rex Stewart. Wilbur & Sid
de Paris. Russ Procope. And Sister Ida
Cox dont forget her. And Omar Simeon. Joe Smith.
Zutty Singleton. Charlie Shavers.
Specs Powell. Red Norvo. Vic Dickenson. J.C.
    Higginbotham.
Nappy Lamare. Earl Hines. Buck Clayton.
Roy Eldridge, Pops Foster. Johnny Hodges. Ed Hall.
Art Tatum. Frankie Newton. Chu Berry. Billy Taylor.
And oh incomparable James P. Johnson.

    Brothers I loved you all.

26

A day   very solid   February 12th, 1944
cheerless in New York City
                 (while I kneedeep
elsewhere in historical war
was wrecking Beauty's sleep
and her long dream)

28

a day (blank, gray) at four
in the afternoon, overheated in the W.O.R.
Recording Studios. Gum wrappers *and* dust
and a stale smell. A day. The cast
was Albert Ammons, Lips Page, Vic Dickenson,
Don Byas, Israel
Crosby, and Big Sid Catlett. (*And* it was Abe Linkhorn's
birthday.) And Milt Gabler
presided over the glass with a nod, a sign. Ammons
counted off

a-waaaaan,,,   *tu!*

and went feeling
his way on the keys gently,
while Catlett summoned

27

the exact beat from—
say from the sounding depths, the universe . . .
When Dickenson came on it was all established,
no guessing, and he started with a blur
as usual, smears, brays—Christ
the dirtiest noise imaginable
belches, farts
curses
but it was music
music now
with Ammons trilling in counterpoise.
Byas next, meditative, soft/
then Page
with that tone like the torn edge
of reality:
and so the climax, long dying riffs—
groans, wild with pain—
and Crosby throbbing *and* Catlett riding stiff
yet it was music   music.
(Man, doan
fall in that bag,
you caint describe it.)
Piano & drum,
Ammons & Catlett drove the others. *And* it was done
and they listened *and* heard themselves
better than they were, for they had come

high above themselves. Above everything, flux, ooze,
loss, need, shame, improbability/   the awfulness
of gut-wrong,   sex-wrack,   horse & booze,
the whole goddamn mess,
And Gabler said "We'll press it"   *and* it was
    "Bottom Blues"
BOTTOM BLUES   five men knowing it well   blacks
    & jews
yet music, music   high
in the celebration of fear, strange joy
of pain: blown out, beaten out
                a moment ecstatic
in the history
of creative mind *and* heart/   not singular, not the rarity
we think, but real and a glory
our human shining, shekinah . . .   Ah,
             holy spirit, ninefold
I druther've bin, a-settin there, supernumerary
cockroach i' th' corner, a-listenin, a-listenin,,,,,,,
    than be the Prazedint ov the Wuurld.

CYRUS CASSELLS

Strange Fruit

The wailing of a clarinet,
And then the wounding voice
Of the woman with the fulgent
Gardenia in her hair:
"Southern trees bear a strange fruit,
Blood on the leaves,
And blood at the root . . ."
How can I tell you?
As a boy,
I was frightened by Billie's song,
The way a child is frightened,
Begins to fathom his own
Capacity for mourning,

Learning a grief
That is racial,
Cached in the soul
From generations of suffering
—Everything in our people
That is strangulated, stillborn,
Welling up
In a song,
In a child's pure sadness
I came to identify
By its bitter taste
As "strange fruit."
In school I heard about Emmett Till,
The boy who was lynched
For "eyeball rape."
And then the strange fruit was given
A face, a body like my own—
Tonight I am listening
To what haunted me as a child:
Lady Day evoking
Fear's murderous harvest, a boy's body
Swinging from a tree.
And I'm dreaming the death of fear,
That one word, if we could grasp it,
Which might stop a child from becoming strange fruit.

MAXINE CASSIN

Three Love Poems by a Native

I. New Orleans

You have to be almost on top of the Mart
to know it's really a crescent,
even though all your life
you have never understood
how parallels become perpendicular
and streets that run for miles without meeting
suddenly encounter each other at their far reaches.

II. Bastille Day

What do we do when the fanfare ends?—
when the last of the musicians
is bathing his feet in the fountain
and the tuba lies abandoned on the grass,
dull and mute.
The band drifts across the square
in pursuit of tones
that rise above the cathedral
and disappear.
The French horn clamors for wine
in a darkened corridor
beside the Presbytere.

III. Jazz Funeral

As they cut the body loose,
he whose footsteps falter
can no longer keep time
to the staccato rain
or the umbrella's tarantella.
Our pulse is the drumbeat;
the brass band—the sun—
in this city that plans
all its celebrations
under the sky,
taunting Jupiter.

GRACE CAVALIERI

The Liberation of Music

When someone brought
Anthony Braxton flowers
He didn't frown and
He didn't ask if
They were
Picked off a tree.

Like this tear
On my eye

Becoming a circle
Which I flick off my cheek
Just like that
With my nail

Removing the last flaw
Which holds my life together.

FRED CHAPPELL

The Highest Wind That Ever Blew:
Homage to Louis

> *Music is the world over again.*
> —Schopenhauer

Ever, ever in unanimous voice we drift:
But not you, baby, not you, Satchel-Gator-
Dippermouth. Punch them pepper lead-notes,
Louis. Ride it, fiercemeat, yon and hither.
Birthday morning I put the record on.
Hot Five, hot damn. What a way to never
Grow old! I couldn't count how many times
You saved my life.
                    Tuning my tiny Arvin,
I'd gasp to glimpse through the mindless crackle one gleamiest
Corner of a note you loosed. Once more tell us
About Black Benny and Mary Jack the Bear;
Red-Beans-and-Ricely Ours, *all ours,*
Let's hear the Good News about Fats Waller.
"You got millions in you and you spend
A nickel": that's what the Message is, okay,
I hear you, shall I ever understand?

What's in that Trumpet is the Tree of Life,
The branches overfreight with cantaloupes,
Peacocks, mangoes, and nekkid nekkid women.
And all around the tree a filigree halo
Like a silver lace mantilla. And limb to limb
Zip little silver birds like buckshot dimes,
Kissing and chucking each other under the chin.

33

Curst be he who worships not this Tree,
Cause you S.O.L., baby   I mean
You   outtaluck . . . It's summertime forever,
Believe to your soul; and this is the River of Jordan.
Everyone was born for a warmer climate
And a jug of wine. You born for it, sweet mama,
And me, and even the blackbox boxback preacher,
He born for it. Up on the Mountain of Wind
I heard in the valley below a lonesome churchbell
Calling home, home, home, home,
And the last swell of the hymn dying at sunset.
Everywhere in your trumpet I heard that.
I'll follow it like a fire in air, I will,
To the purple verge of the world.
                              Rain aslant the wind,
The cozy lovers wind their wounds together.
The weepy eaves peep down into the rooms.
Wind and water drive against the windows
Like a black blind moth in the dark. They sigh
And settle and snuggle. A lemon-colored sun
Warms their innermosts, memory
Of the trumpet-bell uplifted like a sun
Where they'd paid a buck to see the greatest man
Who ever lived, man playing with fire
In air, pursuing his soul in a hovering sun;
Had a tune would melt the polar cap to whiskey.
This dreamshot sun the mellow lovers dream,
It warms them amid each other, the rain goes cozy.

And me too, man, I had me a woman livin
Way   back o' town.
Would wait till the blue-gray smoke of five o'clock
Came down and fetch my bourbon and Beechnut chewing gum
Along the cindery railroad track, counting
The chemical raw smells the paper mill
Dumped into the Pigeon, and the railroad ties.
From tie to tie I whistled *Potatohead Blues,*
Even the clarinet part. It made me happy.
It made me nostalgic for that present moment.
I could have walked like that forever, I could
Have snagged the ballhoot freight to New Orleans
And clung to the windy boxcar singing, *singing.*
I could have lugged my trombone and learned to learn . . .
I learned, anyhow . . . There's something in the woman

More than in the horn to teach you the blues.
Yet still you need the tune, it fixes a pride
On the joy of Traveling Light, there's courage in it.
Father Louis had told me all already.

What's whiskey without the jazz?
Nothin but gutache, nothin to look back on.
Whiskey alone don't fill you that honeysuckle
Sunlight in your vein, it ain't the gin
That makes you shine. It's the man in the cyclone of flame
Who keeps on saying *Yes* with a note that would light
Up the Ice Ages. He's the silver sunrise
In the pit of the body, dawnwind jiving the trees.
Thoreau was right: morning is moral reform,
Gimme a shot. And please play *West End Blues,*
I need to hear the wistful whippoorwill,
To hear the railroad ties hauling the lovers
As they walk down the line, walk down the line
With nineteen bottles of whiskey in each hand,
Going to meet the woman and hear the man.

I've had the warm May nights in the feathery grasses,
Wind poling woozy clouds across the moon,
And the glare light slicing out of the honky-tonk,
Oblong light with a frizzly shape of woman
Troubling its center, one hand on her slouch hip,
Trumpet-flutter in the jukebox behind her
Like a pinwheel of copper fire. She watched the moon.
She too knew that something pulled between them,
The moon and trumpet revolved on a common center
Of gravity which was—where? who? when? how?
Which was *some*where and some*thing,* mystical
But surely palpable, a hungry force
Obtaining as between sharpeyed lovers.

Fire's in the blood, my father told me; wind
Whips it forward, seizing every atomy
In the veins till bloodfire, bloodfire takes the body
Whole, jerks the form of a man along
On that windriver bloodfire, helplessly
A new creature in the Planet of Green Night,
Half funky animal, half pure music,
Meat and spirit drunk together under
The cotton moon. And not one man alone,

35

Ever, but everyone in reach of the trumpet:
An armada of fireships destroying themselves
To essence pure as wind in the fever nighttime.
Papa Louis Armstrong has refashioned us
For our savage reverend assault upon the stars.

WANDA COLEMAN

At the Jazz Club He Comes on a Ghost

remember? we were here once. love was a new cut
of meat, the sweat of fresh blood. into each other's eyes
falling. a closeness of breath. a toast. two glasses. reflection
his knee courting mine. i thought wrong. thought maybe

flesh time. widowed sheets. a memory of a half flushed toilet.
the smell of him lingers just at the edge of my nose. a pressed
carnation stains the paper of our lives. pages to lock away
in a chest of disquiet

where are they all now? the ones who listened so rapt to our
rhetoric? the spirits that mirrored my enthusiasm/lust for adventure?
the window that promised escape in case the smoke became too thick

a prayer catches me unaware. religiosity is something other than
dogma. the stink of our love losing potence between applications of
pine sol and i'm burning for him/bacon on a hot greasy grill

the singer sets a mood. what more can we do, we cemented in bond of
flesh, eager to get there, never tiring of the ritual: detergent and
bleach. the sun burning kisses on the tips of my fingers pressed against
safety glass. sometimes his touch comes through with the urgency of
a dying race: my heart beneath his shoe

we whispered overthrows, speculated on the egyptian book of the dead
soul train and liberation. whatever happened to the brown-eyed
me, a mini-skirted wound weeping soft red candle light? she
reappears occasionally behind motel doors, takes her
lover's wallet while he sleeps and steals away

CLAIRE COLLETT

Midsummer

Dad would turn up the stereo
sit on the back steps
to smoke and drink gin.
He'd play
Jack Teagarden and Lady Day—
talking to himself
as if my mother was still
there to disagree.
Unnoticed, I'd balance
on a thin window ledge,
watch the one constant
light on Fairwood common.
I'd listen to my father
argue himself silent
then pour another drink,
Billie's voice rising
cool, bitter as magnolia,
thick in the gaining dark.

LEO CONNELLAN

Mommy's Hubby

We were drinking buddies in high old time town
womb warm with Billie songs and Bird jazz,
so I put you up when you asked me now, but
you blew it when I filled the refer Ale full against my wife's frown.

She has seen me like we are
and my marriage cartwheeled for a minute.

Hey, buddy, the wind avoids
flashing his cape of zest at me.

How come you think the chicks still die downstairs for Jackie Levine!?
Jackie Levine has shot his last load into a young head.

> Jackie, Jackie Levine, Captain U.S. Cavalry
> Falling all over the Pacific, leaving his wife
> to finger herself, with a glue hairdo
> up in perpetual pin curlers,
> America's love starved sweetheart dried up like a prune
> being true to Jackie Levine, dashing warrior.

And the mandolins were playing for hard-nose Fisk.
his red nose shines a medal from all the whiskey companies,
but the bottles are all broken in city dumps
full of Seagulls and stink.

> Our youth went out in tapped beer-keg blasts,
> spread-legged chicks where are you, wives of
> upstate doctors taking it on your sun decks
> behind shrubbery concealing freeways?

> You liked it in an East Side dump
> giving your cries to old men
> through cockroach paper-thin walls.

And I am Willis Fisk again
creeping streets to my job and crawling home.

> It gets over sometime, when?
> why do we wait!

> We wait waiting to find out what we waited for,
> then we're quite willing to leave.

Hey, buddy, you remember that sweet young thing
come into Johnny Romero's on Minetta with oranges for a nice
tight little ass so pot high she didn't know who you was next
morning after we both banged her so drunk we never knew if
we got off or not and she looked at us through her shades
like we were creeps.

Hey, buddy, remember Jerry's on the Bowery
where I'd get a three-day kick washin' dishes and after
fly for Thunderbird and Fanny'd come by with a bottle of
green gin and maybe money to blot out horrible Sunday and
you'd turn on your charm talkin' until finally dawn . . .

I remember, sure I do.
I lie awake seeing it
in the snore dark of marriage.

Now, you come to my house as though Billie was still singin' "Easy
    Living",
The Bird still blowin' in high old time town.
        In the face of my old lady who saw me through
        all the galloping hee-hee's,
        well, Jackie Levine, I have to say so long.

                    Yes, it's Fisk tellin' you split.
            Imagine it, Fisk tellin' you leave!

Because now I'm Mommy's Hubby and we've got our coffins picked out
            plots and perpetual flowers.

GILLIAN CONOLEY

The One

*Given two women
you'd love the one who doesn't exist*
—Nicanor Parra

Along the alleys I can hear the love songs
come out of jukeboxes like dying embers,
the songs played when lovers
walk away from each other speechless
and the singer opens her mouth wide
to the scat that is the scandal
of the unlanguaged birds overhead.

Beneath that music, those birds,
in the stagger of my forming
I walk as though I have no hips,
as though when I sight proof of myself
my heart doesn't gallop
nor my footsteps scald the snow.

Though the cinema is huge with me,
and murderers of my thoughts lurk

in the whole realm of possibility
that carries me like a mother,
I think I'm drifting off the icon stand,
I think I'm just another saint in a housedress.

Or the sparrow who nests low to the pond,
in love with her disturbing double,
because when I walk out of the love song
I fall in love too, like the pedestrian
waiting for the echo of my shoes to die down
as I step on the bus and hold the rail
like a captive, like a captive on a ribbon of road
stirred by the voices of travelers,
the cup I too hold in my throat atremble.

I don't know if this is life
or someone else's myth etched into my palm,
if this is wishful, or unutterable beauty,
but I have to drag my heel through the dust
then back off angrily
before returning to rain or night, fatigue
or hope for the lovers who beseech into each other's arms
with my fate in their hands,
while in other rooms of smoke and lament,
professors turn blank pages
looking for me.

CLARK COOLIDGE

The Great

The Greatness of Music
   and it won't hold still since only you heard it
     that mind doubles itself faster than seconds
Perfect Rate
   brightening wasting ears that nothing will disturb it
     brains are burnished on what Bud threw away
Batter sea and he heard it
   laughing in the teeth on edge of shuddered building
     straight shaft as shunt as Monk draped in the belows
I only want to make midnight mast to my song

in shivered and tracing words in other words
    the Miles off further from the phantom he is blow back
And I preach to January, that's who, that's all, a
    Webcor Holiday floating ice
We Reach, a new anthem, as Carla's in minor
    better than whether and snatch back the coat
      Lester laid down, so pulled
Music not to stain you but never escape its frame
    there are windows in it all the copey while, oh yeah
Blues in a muscle fit, such strain goad mind that it'll fit
    no nod off fray of blessing ridge
Two dates of pound cake and one of fray horn
    that missing sunspot, period of Ornette
I see a great skully sea afringe with horn
    and missing dice and house grace of stub hands, Tatum there
And I hear
    what's missing there
      music is core of the missing
        the code of fly time
On Parchman's floor there are sendings
    and at Cecil's bar the heights
In all the sections the cats drop their mutes
    aghast at robey sky appear in ceiling tile dive
Confirmation
    of Bud's Bubble
      when Bird Food
        and Blue Aria in a brewing luminous
I turn over my hands more times than are thought
    and sheathe of the all
      the seething things
      a breathing star

GREGORY CORSO

For Miles

Your sound is faultless
    pure & round
      holy
    almost profound

Your sound is your sound
    true & from within
    a confession
    soulful & lovely

Poet whose sound is played
    lost or recorded
    but heard
    can you recall that 54 night at the Open Door
    when you & bird
    wailed five in the morning some wondrous
    yet unimaginable score?

JAYNE CORTEZ

Into This Time

(for Charles Mingus)

Into this time
of steel feathers blowing from hearts
into this turquoise flame time in the mouth
into this sonic boom time in the conch
into this musty stone-fly time sinking into
the melancholy buttocks of dawn
sinking into lacerated whelps
into gun holsters
into breast bones
into a manganese field of uranium nozzles
into a nuclear tube full of drunk rodents
into the massive vein of one interval
into one moment's hair plucked down into
the timeless droning fixed into
long pauses
fixed into a lash of ninety-eight minutes screeching into
the internal heat of an ice ball melting time into
a configuration of commas on strike
into a work force armed with a calendar of green wings
into a collection of nerves
into magnetic mucus

42

into tongueless shrines
into water pus of a silver volcano
into the black granite face of Morelos
into the pigeon toed dance of Mingus
into a refuge of air bubbles
into a cylinder of snake whistles
into clusters of slow spiders
into spade fish skulls
into rosin coated shadows of women wrapped in live iguanas
into coins into crosses into St. Martin De Porres
into the pain of this place changing pitches beneath
fingers swelling into
night shouts
into day trembles
into month of precious bloods flowing into
this fiesta of sadness year
into this city of eternal spring
into this solo
on the road of young bulls
on the street of lost children
on the avenue of dead warriors
on the frisky horse tail fuzz zooming
into ears of every madman
stomping into every new composition
everyday of the blues
penetrating into this time

This time of loose strings in low tones
pulling boulders of Olmec heads into the sun
into tight wires uncoiling from body of a strip teaser on the table
into half-tones wailing between snap and click
of two castanets smoking into
scales jumping from tips of sacrificial flints
into frogs yodeling across grieving cults
yodeling up into word stuffed smell of flamingo stew
into wind packed fuel of howling dog throats slit into
this January flare of aluminum dust falling into
laminated stomach of a bass violin rubbed into red ashes
rubbed into the time sequence of
this time of salmonella leaking from eyeballs of a pope
into this lavender vomit time in the chest into
this time plumage of dried bats in the brain into
this wallowing time weed of invisible wakes on cassettes into
this off-beat time syncopation in a leopard skin suit

43

into this radiated protrusion of time in the desert into
this frozen cheek time of dead infants in the cellar
into this time flying with the rotten bottoms of used tuxedos
into this purple   brown   grey   gold minus zero time trilling into
a lime stone crusted Yucatan belching
into fifty six medallions shaking
into armadillo drums thumping
into tambourines of fetishes rattling
into an oil slick of poverty symbols flapping
into flat-footed shuffle of two birds advancing
into back spine of luminous impulses tumbling
into metronomes of colossal lips ticking
into a double zigzag of callouses splitting
into foam of electric snow flashing into this time
of steel feathers blowing from hearts
into this turquoise flame time in the mouth into
this sonic boom time in the conch
into this musty stone fly time sinking into
the melancholy buttocks of dawn

Rose Solitude

(for Duke Ellington)

I am essence of Rose Solitude
my cheeks are laced with cognac
my hips sealed with five satin nails
i carry dreams and romance of new fools and old
flames
between the musk of fat
and the side pocket of my mink tongue

Listen to champagne bubble from this solo

Essence of Rose Solitude
veteran from texas   tiger from chicago   that's me
i cover the shrine of Duke
who like Satchmo   like Nat (King) Cole
will never die because love they say
never dies

I tell you from stair steps of these navy blue nights
these metallic snakes
these flashing fish skins
and the melodious cry of Shango
surrounded by sorrow
by purple velvet tears
by cockhounds limping from crosses
from turtle skinned shoes
from diamond shaped skulls and canes
made from dead gazelles
wearing a face of wilting potato plants
of grey and black scissors
of bee bee shots and fifty red boils
yes the whole world loved him

I tell you from suspenders of two-timing dog odors
from inca frosted lips
nonchalant legs
i tell you from howling chant of sister Erzulie
and the exaggerated hearts of a hundred pretty
women
they loved him
this world sliding from a single flower
into a caravan of heads made into ten thousand
flowers

Ask me
Essence of Rose Solitude
chickadee from arkansas that's me
i sleep on cotton bones
cotton tails
and mellow myself in empty ballrooms
i'm no fly by night
look at my resume
i walk through the eyes of staring lizards
i throw my neck back to floorshow on bumping goat
skins
in front of my stage fright
i cover the hands of Duke who like Satchmo
like Nat (King) Cole will never die
because love they say
never dies

Solo Finger Solo

When evening goes down into its jelly jelly jelly
into drain pipe cuts and stitches and vaccinations
protruding from arms

And spirit of the five by five man pushes
his sweet potatoes in the air
feather daddy leaps into a falcon of tropical bird squats
rubber legs swing into off-beat onijos onijos
then into your solo finger solo
the blues chantress jumps up and
repeats her nasal volcanic chant calling

Count Basie   Count Basie   Count Basie

And Count Basie
you burn through this timbale of goose flesh rhythms
a drop of iodine on your starfish lips
the intonation of your kiss of melodica trilling
into a labyrinth of one o'clock jumps
into corpuscle flashes of the blues torpedo
the erupting volcano of the blues shouters chanting your name

Count Basie   Count Basie   take em to Chicago Count Basie

And Count Basie
you punctuate this strong bourbon mist of gamma globulin breath
a mixture of chords like serpentariums coiling
from the deep everglades of your body
and when the luscious screams of three headed root doctors split
Kansas City reeds in unison with this triple tapping
double stopping   slow grinding   loosey butt night swinging
with the blues chantress
erupting volcano of the blues torpedoes chanting your name

Count Basie
you reach through the bottom of the music
way down beneath cross rhythm vamps
below air stream of the lowest octave
into depths of a sacred drum
and Count Basie   Count Basie   Count Basie
how powerful and dignified and exquisite and direct and sharp
your solo finger solo is

Tapping

(for Baby Laurence, and other tap dancers)

When i pat this floor
  with my tap

when i slide on air
  and fill this horn intimate with
the rhythm of my two drums

   when i cross   kick
scissor   locomotive

  take four for nothing
four we're gone

when the solidarity of my yoruba turns
join these vibrato feet
  in a Johnny Hodges lick
a chorus of insistent Charlie Parker riffs

   when i stretch out for a chromatic split
together with my double X
   converging in a quartet of circles

when i dance my spine in a slouch
  slur my lyrics with a heel slide
arch these insteps in free time

   when i drop my knees
when i fold my hands
   when i decorate this atmosphere
with a Lester Young leap and

   enclose my hip like snake repetitions
in a chanting proverb
  of the freeze

I'm gonna spotlite my boogie
  in a Coltrane yelp

echo my push in a Coleman Hawkins whine

i'm gonna frog my hunch in a Duke Ellington strut

quarter stroke my rattle
  like an Albert Ayler cry

i'm gonna accent my march in a Satchmo pitch

  triple my grind in a Ma Rainey blues

i'm gonna steal no steps

  i'm gonna pay my dues

i'm gonna 1   2   3

  and let the people in the Apple
go hmmmp   hmmmmp   hmmmmmp

ROBERT CREELEY

The Bird, the Bird, the Bird

for Charles

With the spring flowers I likewise am.
And care for them. That they have odor.

We are too garrulous (Brugm. i. §638), we
talk not too much but too often.

And yet, how otherwise to oblige the
demon, who it is, there

implacable, but content.

Broken Back Blues

O yr facing reality now—
& yr in the same beat groove—

you try to get up—
& find you just can't moo-oove
                    (take it take it
uncle john
we can play it all nite long . . .

        I got them things in my head—
no sounds will ever solve
                    (heh heh heh, heh heh heh . . .)

So yr bent in yr middle—
yr face is on the floor—
they take a great big club—
& beat you out the doo-oor
                    (watch it watch it

mr man
we're going to get you if we can

        that I'm alive today, I want to say, I want to say—
that I'm alive today
                    (heh heh heh, heh heh heh . . .)

I havent got a nickle—
I havent got a dime—
I havent got a cent—
I dont have that kind of time
                    (all rite for you, friend
                    that's the most
                    we herewith
                    propose a toast:
It's a hopeless world.

TOM DENT

After Listening to Monk

(for Ralph Edwards)

Too much the city's cacophonous noise and light
Too long the clash of death-streets
Too much the blood of masked dances

dance, dance away the day
watch the sun dance

Too many giggles, too many earthquakes, too much derision
Too often "he must be weird, or somethin"

dance, dance away the day
watch the sun dance

Too much
Death just around the corner
Of midnight.

For Lil Louis

(for Louis Armstrong)

Louis i'm trying to understand what you were
here
how you left this place
how you gave the people bravura music
how you could survive it all
even bucket-a-blood
where the frustration of our people
            boiled into daily slaughter
but then New O is an old place for that:

                don't you think it's a moon-town
                where the imagination of violence
                sparks easily to life?
                what festers in the minds
                of the grandchildren of the
                people you knew who languish
                now in the projects?
                bucket-a-blood was demolished
                its people banished to the project
                your old town
                the city's new progress
                your old house
                gone for the city's new jailhouse
                such the way it is the city
                tells you what they think of you

50

& everyone like you & still the
people dance & progress looks on afraid . . .

Louis i'm trying to understand what you were
really like
in the dark moments away from the stage.
rumors have it you were not pleasant
to be around,
the shit-eating grin nowhere to be found:

       did the moon-blood intrude
       the sleep of your nights
       even sleep of your days
       did you carry moon-blood
       memories to the grave?

Louis i'm trying to understand but never
mind
it's enough that you said don't bury me in
New Orleans
& it's enough to hear your trumpet
laughing at it all
it's enough that you played de-truth-de-truth-beeeeeeeee

& the sweaty handkerchief
honest enough   honest
it's enough
it's enough
but Lou/est

       someday the dancers will explode
       and all this little history
       will shatter as the
       shit-eating masks fall . . .
       & only the moon will understand

Lou/is.

OWEN DODSON

Yardbird's Skull

(for Charlie Parker)

The bird is lost,
Dead, with all the music:
Whole sunsets heard the brain's music
Faded to last horizon notes.
I do not know why I hold
This skull, smaller than a walnut's,
Against my ear,
Expecting to hear
The smashed fear
Of childhood from . . . bone:
Expecting to see
Wind nosing red and purple,
Strange gold and magic
On bubbled windowpanes
Of childhood. Shall I hear?
I should hear: this skull
Has been with violets
Not Yorick, or the gravedigger,
Yapping his yelling story,
This skull has been in air,
Sensed his brother, the swallow
(Its talent for snow and crumbs).
Flown to lost Atlantis islands,
Places of dreaming, swimming lemmings.
O I shall hear skull skull.
Hear your lame music,
Believe music rejects undertaking,
Limps back.
Remember tiny lasting, we get lonely:
Come sing, come sing, come sing sing
And sing.

GEORGE ECONOMOU

33⅓ RPM

for John Coltrane

One plays the saxophone
another the stereo
and writes poems
listening to the other one
dead now, playing
as if he were alive
and remembers
he heard the one who plays the saxophone
playing it alive
but nothing more of that performance
dead now, for them both
one of whom plays the saxophone
as if he were alive
the other of whom writes poems
listening to the other one
dead now, playing the saxophone
leaving it behind

RICHARD ELMAN

Chet's Jazz

The jamming together of fragments
puffed through a failing wind
reiterates such sounds as can extenuate
the hurt lips on the caved-in face.
"If you could see me now."
sings the ghost of pretty boy Chet,
faintly flirtatious, and when he blows again
he goes up and down on tip toes
as if reaching for distortions
that are the ghosts of melodies he started
20 years ago with Gerry Mulligan.

Strange feedback now to spook
his old sidekick with these noises
which announce they were never there
in the first place, and then to declare,
"that's one we call *Broken Wing.*"
The titles tell one story of a talent
broken, strung out, in jail more times than he has
notes left in his mouthpiece, but the tunes
aren't grim. Behind Chet's clerical specs
a death's head blows frivolous trills
on a brass horn, blue notes so oblique
his group can only vamp and vamp and
vamp again a rhythm like applause.
Chet's got it tonight. He's on!
Even his sweetest clinkers encourage
us to believe in inspired errors.

Driving Home

for Alice

Radiant blue grey
clouds above the cold
earth remind me of
the sounds of Fats Navarro
blowing inside the car.
As this vamping wind
shivers my fenders
Long Island seems
sanctified and clear:
holy the earth, these
trees silver and gold
with leaves like ingots
kernelled on their boughs,
this sudden glistening solid
state which static interrupts
metallic bliss. These sounds
are light, inside is out, the
glow as real as any
images of pain he may have
ever known: this hard Bop light . . .
Today along the Parkway

54

Fats pierced the Fall of
all of Heaven with his
trumpet sword of delight;
a brand new gusting first snow
darkened the air as silver
dust that, tarnished, split
the frozen hills it touched
like soft ripe orange melons.

JOHN ENGELS

In the Palais Royale Ballroom in 1948

for Zimmer, most marvelous ofay

Just at the end of the first set I step out
in my white tux, my white shoes
onto the sequined dais at center,
into a golden spot, another focused overhead

onto the spinning, mirrored ball,
spills and whirls of gold light everywhere,
like stars, like comets hurtling across
the blue cloth ceiling of the Palais Royale Ballroom

in South Bend. And I wait,
Kenton and the boys riffing quietly behind me,
Milt Bernhart disconsolate among the brasses,
June Christie waiting, even June, for this

is mine to do alone, and everyone
knows it; and everyone
is waiting. And then
I see out there beyond the light

the dancers begin to take notice, to turn,
to gather themselves into a circle around me,
arms linked, swaying, others, little
eager knots of them, hurrying to get back,

55

the word having spread, even
unto the streets. And they gather around me and wait,
knowing what is to come, the air growing dense
with the fragrances of gardenias, camellias, carnations,

the light that is like stars and comets
careening over the ceiling of the Palais Royale Ballroom.
They wait, and suddenly I raise to my lips
the red-gold Olds trombone,

and hit high G so clean, so sweet, so un-
endurably sustained, that the girls
I am remembering myself to have loved beyond desire
go faint with desire,

and the song is "Summertime," and I am alone with it,
and play it out, drive through
to the last sweet resolution of the last phrase.
And then, my solo finished, the great band

riding it out behind me, the song diminishing
forever into the sky beyond the starry sky
which was the ceiling of the Palais Royale Ballroom in 1948,
my lips still numb from the embouchure, I think of it

as if in fact it might have been,
as if those dancers to whom too late and far too late
I have thought to offer this as a memory
might truly have gathered themselves around

and have remembered such a thing: the song
held in its starry, high, unlikely register,
the surging of their bodies to that song:
that fragrance of light again.

CLAYTON ESHLEMAN

Un Poco Loco

Bud Powell's story is never complete.
The image of a man playing blues
who earlier that day

56

sipped lunch on all fours
is rudimentary turning, crawling
chorus after chorus, lifting I Covers,

to view simmering Waterfront splinters,
he is visiting fist shacks,
the sipped milk becomes a dug root,

he bites into the horizon
wearing keyboard braces, he winds within
the steel cord all

who have pulled through mother recall
as the bastard spirit beyond her strength.

FATISHA

From Star to Sun We Are Going

(for Miles Dewey Davis)

The out-sane men have walked
    already on the face of God &
    felt color/they have been
    intrinsic placements who blew
    through their navels & curved
    life's usage to fit the dreams
    of perpetual strokers . . .
    they stilled the river so
    the faithless could cross

We have been in the by-ways
    together/we have talked &
    indulged in useless fucking
    & run our separate way up
    the same paceless vision to
    look ominous into the face
    of Sun & ask for Chance to
    do us over different in the
    next surrender—to let
    promise be more than remembered—
    to be fulfilled.

57

What can be more emptied &
    drained than the speechless heart
    & the iron tongue that surrounds us?
    a lover's eyes look during the
    pragmatic sessions/they do not
    talk or sing or cut these knives
    pinioned in your spirit

    so you go to each one looking
    for the love-hands that will
    release you from dreams
    that have become your bondage

    they can do it from a horse
    or a wagon or sitting on the
    steps parked in long cars
    having their vanity flattered—

Styles and costumes/periods
    that definitely end can all
    be of your choosing if you
    just know that our drowning
    & saving is the ancient ritual
    in karmic lore/and it is our
    time to live again—to move
    our habitat into the SUN!

SASCHA FEINSTEIN

Buying Wine

His alto leaks steam, a radiator of sound,
frozen breath shining on the bell. He's good,
and I can't help but lean against the bus stop

and watch: someone's blue cotton hat with
a Yankees sticker not doing shit for heat,
cut-open gloves to finger the horn, a shiny

coat from the Salvation Army, and two blocks up
some fellow stuffed in a Santa suit clangs
for donations. There's a yellow haze

from the local food mart, carts for bags no doubt
full with fatty hams and cranberry relish,
sweet potatoes, flour for the thick gravy

and scones, tubs of butter, peaches, fresh
cream. The wheels scrape icy concrete, clatter
quickly by him, somehow blending with an off-

minor run so hip I yell to him, *Do it, do it.*
A hunched figure sorts his change, drops coins
that vaguely catch the light. I've got

seven bucks for a Chianti, bills twisting
in my pocket. When I return with a bottle
he's playing "Blue Monk," slow for the mood,

just up enough for circulation. I empty
what's left so fast he knows I can't be
counting, knows it can't be much,

but pulls the sax from his mouth to thank me.
Wonderful holiday to you, sir. I wave,
and only when I reach the apartment

do the sounds disappear completely. You're
basting a roast, and my ears fill with blood.
We kiss, I pour the wine, and of course

it's delicious. *I'm so glad you went out
for this,* you say. *Everything's just perfect.*

Monk's Mood

One-fingering my way through
   the New York white pages
      I stopped upon *T.S. Monk*

still listed there even for me
   just turned on to jazz with you
      as a hero. I dialed

and when a voice deeper
   than mine would ever get said
      Yeah I said nothing

59

for several seconds.
 I've blocked out my nervous
  words—something about

digging your music,
 until a laugh said, "Hey,
  friend—you talkin' 'bout

my father." Thelonious Sphere Monk,
 Junior. I didn't even know
  you *had* a son.

You were in retirement then,
 dying before I could see you
  though I've heard so many gigs

in my mind: it's late, you look past
 the whole room, your silence
  inviting everyone into

your world like the talk
 we never had, or those months
  when performing didn't matter.

It's how I see you even now: not wanting
 to play, just nudging that piano
  like a rush-hour New Yorker—

hit a stray note, stare at it, wait
 for the leftover sound to tell you
  what tune to fall into, or who'll

survive your patience, who will leave—
 wait for some polyester jacket to say,
  Mr. Monk, it's really time to begin—

Those were the moods that kept
 us keyed into you more
  than the elbow dances off

the stand. Because so much
 decision pressed itself into each
  small move, because we wanted to say

we're listening, man, we've got the night,
    and you, with your black fez & shades darkening
        everything you didn't play.

LAWRENCE FERLINGHETTI

Sometime During Eternity . . .

Sometime during eternity
                    some guys show up
and one of them
            who shows up real late
                        is a kind of carpenter
    from some square-type place
                    like Galilee
        and he starts wailing
                    and claiming he is hip
        to who made heaven
                        and earth
                            and that the cat
            who really laid it on us
                        is his Dad

    And moreover
        he adds
            It's all writ down
                    on some scroll-type parchments
        which some henchmen
            leave lying around the Dead sea somewheres
            a long time ago
                        and which you won't even find
    for a coupla thousand years or so
                        or at least for
    nineteen hundred and fortyseven
                            of them
            to be exact
                    and even then
        nobody really believes them
                    or me
                        for that matter

61

You're hot
            they tell him

And they cool him

They stretch him on the Tree to cool

        And everybody after that
                            is always making models
                    of this Tree
                            with Him hung up
and always crooning His name
                        and calling Him to come down
                    and sit in
                            on their combo
            as if he is *the* king cat
                            who's got to blow
    or they can't quite make it

        Only he don't come down
                        from His Tree

Him just hang there
                on His Tree
looking real Petered out
                and real cool
                            and also
            according to a roundup
                            of late world news
    from the usual unreliable sources
                            real dead

CALVIN FORBES

Drum Crazy

The year of the drummer
He fell into a coma.

Sulking he couldn't turn his
Cotton into silk.

62

All he remembered were
The drummer's hands, the thin

Fabric, delicate
As a chin, the speed and precision

Of each hit tightening
His stomach like hunger or worry.

But still he was greedy enough
To ask for more.

Until tongue tied
Shuddering like a cold motor

He found a chair
And dozed off full of shock,

Delirious, dreaming
Of his bout against the drums.

ALICE FULTON

You Can't Rhumboogie in a Ball and Chain

(for Janis Joplin)

You called the blues' loose black belly lover
and in Port Arthur they called you pig-face.
The way you chugged booze straight, without a glass,
your brass-assed language, slingbacks with jeweled heel,
proclaimed you no kin to their muzzled blood.
No chiclet-toothed Baptist boyfriend for you.

Strung-out, street hustling showed men wouldn't buy you.
Once you clung to the legs of a lover,
let him drag you till your knees turned to blood,
mouth hardened to a thin scar on your face,
cracked under songs, screams, never left to heal.
Little Girl Blue, soul pressed against the glass.

63

That voice rasping like you'd guzzled fiber-glass,
stronger than the four armed men behind you.
But pale horse lured you, docile, to heel:
warm snow flanks pillowed you like a lover.
Men feared the black holes in your body and face,
knew what they put in would return as blood.

Craving fast food, cars, garish as fresh blood,
diners with flies and doughnuts under glass,
formica bars and a surfer's gold face,
in nameless motels, after sign-off, you
let T.V.'s blank bright stare play lover,
lay still, convinced its cobalt rays could heal.

Your songs that sound ground under some stud's heel,
swallowed and coughed up in a voice like blood:
translation unavailable, lover!
No prince could shoe you in unyielding glass,
stories of exploding pumpkins bored you
who flaunted tattooed breast and hungry face.

That night needing a sweet-legged sugar's face,
a hot, sky-eyed Southern comfort to heal
the hurt of senior proms for all but you,
plain Janis Lyn, self-hatred laced your blood.
You knew they worshipped drained works, emptied glass,
legend's last gangbang the wildest lover.

Like clerks we face your image in the glass,
suggest lovers, as accessories, heels.
"It's your shade, this blood dress," we say. "It's you."

CHRISTOPHER GILBERT

Horizontal Cosmology

[Sections 1, 4]

1. *The Backyard*

Suddenly this voice is calling
when I go to the backyard.
The garden leaves cut the wind to singing

and their bodies, the perfect green
instruments for what they do.

The tree next door whose leaves
are phrases falling
where the wind is blowing,
the arpeggio of the Charlie Parker tune—
an impossible flight of notes.
And I'm humming to myself.

I will work the day out here, singing.
It makes me a gift with myself.
Something to make the yard bigger.
My hands fall at my sides, octaves apart,
How far? Clear enough for my friends
who look for me to feel between them.

4. *Saxophone*

My bell is Charlie Parker's
hatband. So few of you who
come to touch me understand
my feeling,
only this black voice.
I am a temple and he comes
to speak through me. I am the dream
lip because
I say what you're afraid of
facing, *Living is intense.*

I am bad from note to note
like god's nostril, I connect
living to what lies ahead
by breath.
You want to know how to feel
in this world, the technology
bigger than the ear? Listen,
I can't tell you what to hear.
I have no message waiting
for you: you must be-
hold enough to play.

Resonance

In a back room
upstairs crouched over crystal
set, the dark headphones a cap
worn to finish the circuit.

Touching the quartz, a wave
would roll its clear tongue
against the windows, the dark
midwest faces come looking into—
spaces struck deep in the bone.

And I pulled the cat's whisker,
rolled the coil in hope,
from my hands a phoenix fluttered—
the lid of teenage body
a throbbing shell at sea.

Listening, I could hear
the whole Black house was music;
my brother playing Wes Montgomery downstairs
on the turntable, a lost double
octave rolling round through the air.

DANA GIOIA

Bix Beiderbecke (1903–1931)

January, 1926

China Boy. Lazy Daddy. Cryin' All Day.
He dreamed he played the notes so slowly that
they hovered in the air above the crowd
and shimmered like a neon sign. But no,
the club stayed dark, trays clattered in the kitchen,
people drank and went on talking. He watched
the smoke drift from a woman's cigarette
and slowly circle up across the room
until the ceiling fan blades chopped it up.

A face, a young girl's face, looked up at him,
the stupid face of small-town innocence.
He smiled her way and wondered who she was.
He looked again and saw the face was his.

He woke up then. His head still hurt from drinking,
Jimmy was driving. Tram was still asleep.
Where were they anyway? Near Davenport?
There was no distance in these open fields—
only time, time marked by a farmhouse
or a barn, a tin-topped silo or a tree,
some momentary silhouette against
the endless, empty fields of snow.
He lit a cigarette and closed his eyes.
The best years of his life! The Boring 'Twenties.
He watched the morning break across the snow.
Would heaven be as white as Iowa?

ELTON GLASER

Elegy for Professor Longhair

Over the low lope of the bass, the highhat's chatter,
I'll always hear that upright
Stutter and sway—the Professor's playing
His bareknuckle rhumba boogie on Rampart Street!
Stand back now, it's the crawfish love call,
It's the wild bell ringing for resurrection,
It's the ghost of hambones in Congo Square,
Voodoo by Jesus out of Jelly Roll!

I'll take my place in the second line,
Do the zulu strut
Where the brothers sweat through the streets,
Slow drag and blues—oh the bottom
Done drop out the big drum and the horn's
All empty, but the tourists still
Step off the train, some hi-fi squalling
Get yo' ticket in yo' hand, you wanna go to New Orleans!

I've come back and you've gone.
No gospel or gris-gris
Could keep you here, however much
You loved the jukejoints pouring out
Bourbon and a smokey beat, the palm trees
Lashing their green rhythm down Elysian Fields.
These words are for the wide river
That spreads forever south, and that black box

You rode like a raft into heaven.

VINCE GOTERA

Hot Club de France *Reprise on MTV*

—Django Reinhardt, 1910–1953

A rock video, and there you were.
Only two good fingers on your left hand
hammering note after rapid note from an old guitar,
unheard beneath a rush of heavy metal.

Was it Whitesnake? Def Leppard?
The rock group's lead guitarist couldn't believe it.
He stepped from his Ferrari into a fast-food
sushi bar, opened chrome doors and found himself

50 years back in time: a Paris cafe, smoke,
and you jammed against the beat. Winking at him,
in your wide-brimmed, black floppy hat,
you slipped out the side door and he followed.

A will-of-the-wisp chase through
cobbled streets, the lure of a velvet cloak.
He finally caught up with you, passed out in some alley.
And I wanted to shout, "No, that's not how it was."

I wanted my son watching videos 2000 miles away
to know the real Django.

I wanted MTV to send a time machine
to Saturday, February 23, 1935,

the night Coleman Hawkins detonates Django
and the Hot Club Quintet upon Paris. The joint
jumping as the Hawk trades riffs on sax
with Stephane Grappelli on violin.

The videocam would focus on your hands,
welding a solo from jive licks and magic octaves,
swirling the air with chords in harmonic spirals.
Dancers jitterbug while hepsters pat their feet.

I could call my son long-distance, tell him
to watch for you on the tube: your fingers lit up
by your crimson tie, like some artificial flower, like
a blossom of flame blooming from a gypsy caravan.

LEE MEITZEN GRUE

Billie Pierce's Jazz Funeral

> *You can keep up to date*
> *and learn all the new numbers*
> *if you want to, but what the*
> *people like best is just a gang*
> *of good old blues.*
> —Billie Pierce

Billie Pierce used to sing to me
when it was hot, when I couldn't get sleep.
She sang *Algiers Hoodoo Blues*
and *Nobody Wants You When You're Down and Out;*
A gold cornet curved around
those long hard blues.

Yesterday, I second-lined her
to the St. Louis cemetery
with a bunch of school children
holding hands for Billie dead.

69

The Olympia Brass Band played
slow beautiful;
a bright skinned man
stiff-armed a derby hat,
gimp-legged, but moving fine for Billie dead.

There were people taking pictures,
as if you could,
too many cars underfoot,
and in a long car, Billie dead.

It was a long way there and sad;
the music crying and us crying,
children needing a bathroom bad
so we went while the music was down.

I never got to hear them
bringing it back happy for Billie dead
so I'm still grieving.

Jazzmen

Mister, your eyes are bright blue numbers
rimmed in white enamel.
I like to look at your
diamond crackle
when you middle finger
your bright-lipped horn.
You pour music into my upturned face
I'm so happy
I can't stop laughing.
Old Sly-face, the piano player,
half-masks his eyes   smug cat
says:
How do you like that?
I like it.
I like men who play music
who bind me in their fine conspiracy.
My man says: STOP IT.
You give yourself to the piano player
the bass   the horn   the thin
reed of the clarinet

I can't listen to his talk
when there's music.
This music. I like
men who make music.
There's never been anything so good
as that note.
Oh, you're sly, piano man,
his eyes say:
I know it   I know it
then the cornet takes it somewhere up
and the horn,
the horn is an astronaut
saying mundane things at heights profound
promising me walks in space
trips at the end of a live wire,
landings   landings,
but it stops somewhere
midair
he puts down his horn
shakes out a cigarette
lights it   nods.
Oh, God, Alice,
I know how it feels to
fall.
The man takes my arm
says: Let's go now.
Instruments float the bandstand,
the bus tour pulls out in waves
foaming
tables   chairs strew the floor.
He pays the check
wades me past tables,
half-pulled out chairs,
musicians smoking on the stair.
We walk into a street
empty with let down glare
and distant buoys that bell in the night.

MARILYN HACKER

Elegy

for Janis Joplin

Crying from exile, I
mourn you, dead singer, crooning and palming
your cold cheeks, calling you: You.
A man told me you died; he was
foreign, I felt for the first time, drunk, in his car, my
throat choked: You won't sing for me
now. Later I laughed in the hair between
his shoulder-blades, well enough
loved in a narrow
bed; it was
your Southern Comfort
grin stretching my
mouth. You were in me
all night,

shouting our pain, sucking off
the mike, telling a strong-headed
woman's daily beads to dumb kids
creaming on your high
notes. Some morning at wolf-hour
they'll know.
Stay in my
gut, woman lover I never
touched, tongued, or sang to; stay
in back of my
throat, sandpaper
velvet, Janis, you
overpaid your
dues, damn it, why are you dead?

Cough up your whisky gut
demon, send him home howling
to Texas, to every
fat bristle-chinned
white motel keeper on
Route 66, every half-
Seminole waitress with a

72

crane's neck, lantern-jawed
truck driver missing a
finger joint, dirt-farmer's
blond boy with asthma and sea dreams,
twenty-one-year-old
mother of three who got far
as Albuquerque once.

Your veins were
highways from
Coca-Cola flatland,
dust and dead
flies crusting the
car window till it rained.
Drive! anywhere
out of here, the
ratty upholstery smelling
of dogpiss and cunt,
bald tires swiveled and
lurched on slicked macadam
skidding the funk in your mouth
to a black woman's tongue.

Faggots and groupies and
meth heads loved you, you
loved bodies and booze
and hard work, and more
than that, fame. On your
left tit was a tattooed
valentine, around your
wrist a tattooed filigree; around
your honeycomb brain webbed
klieg lights and amp circuits screamed
Love Love and the booze-
skag-and-cocaine baby twisted your
box, kicked your
throat and the songs came.

I wanted to write your
blues, Janis, and put my
tongue in your mouth that way.
Lazy and grasping and
treacherous, beautiful
insomniac freaking the ceiling,

73

the cold smog went slowly blue, the cars
caught up with your heartbeat, maybe you were not
alone, but the ceiling told you
otherwise, and skag said:
You are more famous than anyone
out of East Texas, your hair is a
monument, your voice preserved
in honey, I love you, lie down.

I am in London and
you, more meat than Hollywood
swallowed, in Hollywood, more
meat. You got me through
long nights with your coalscuttle
panic, don't be scared
to scream when it hurts
and oh mother it hurts, tonight
we are twenty-seven, we are
alone, you are dead.

MICHAEL S. HARPER

"Bird Lives": Charles Parker

Last on legs, last on sax,
last in Indian wars, last on *smack*,
Bird is specious, *Bird* is alive,
horn, unplayable, before, after,
right now: it's heroine time:
smack, in the melody a trip;
smack, in the Mississippi;
smack, in the drug merchant trap;
smack, in St. Louis, Missouri.

We knew you were through—
trying to get out of town,
unpaid bills, connections
unmet, unwanted, unasked,
Bird's in the last arc
of his own light: *blow Bird!*

74

And you did—
screaming, screaming, baby,
for life, after it, around it,
screaming for life, *blow Bird!*

What is the meaning of music?
What is the meaning of war?
What is the meaning of oppression?
Blow Bird! Ripped up and down
into the interior of life, the pain,
Bird, the embraceable you,
how many brothers gone,
smacked out: blues and racism,
the hardest, longest penis
in the Mississippi urinal:
Blow Bird!

Taught more musicians, then forgot,
space loose, fouling the melodies,
the marching songs, the fine white
geese from the plantations,
syrup in this pork barrel,
Kansas City, the even teeth
of the mafia, the big band:
Blow Bird! Inside out Charlie's
guts, *Blow Bird!* get yourself killed.

In the first wave, the musicians,
out there, alone, in the first wave;
everywhere you went, Massey Hall,
Sweden, New Rochelle, *Birdland,*
nameless bird, Blue Note, Carnegie,
tuxedo junction, out of nowhere,
confirmation, confirmation, confirmation:
Bird Lives! Bird Lives! and you do:
Dead—

Cannon Arrested

Somethin' Else and
Kind of Blue
bleed back to back

75

as the Cannon arrests,
his V-shaped heart
flowing in glycerine
compounds of fixed signs
stabilized in his going:
who helps him as he softshoes
starstreamed joculars across
each throated arch of song,
stylings of separation?

His fat silent reed
beds down in Gary,
shanked by Stevie Wonderful's
moment of silence,
these mosquito whinings
near the liter can of gas
I pour into Buick 59.

In some unmarked Floridian grave
another ancestor shakes
to your damnation,
her son perhaps pulling a giant
sailboat behind his Cadillac
to sporty Idlewild, Michigan,
sanctified in attitudes
of 'Dis Here' on this side of the road,
'Dat Dere' *going over* on that side,
and the boat docks before me
in distant transformed banks
of you transporting this evil
woman's song pianola-ed
on Interstate 80, cardiac bypass
road-turn you didn't make,
your fins sailing over boundaries,
lined fingertips in a reefered house,
a divided storehouse near a black
resort town, this sweet alto-man
wickered in vestibule, drifting away.

Dear John, Dear Coltrane

a love supreme, a love supreme
a love supreme, a love supreme

Sex fingers toes
in the marketplace
near your father's church
in Hamlet, North Carolina—
witness to this love
in this calm fallow
of these minds,
there is no substitute for pain:
genitals gone or going,
seed burned out,
you tuck the roots in the earth,
turn back, and move
by river through the swamps,
singing: *a love supreme, a love supreme;*
what does it all mean?
Loss, so great each black
woman expects your failure
in mute change, the seed gone.
You plod up into the electric city—
your song now crystal and
the blues. You pick up the horn
with some will and blow
into the freezing night:
a love supreme, a love supreme—

Dawn comes and you cook
up the thick sin 'tween
impotence and death, fuel
the tenor sax cannibal
heart, genitals and sweat
that makes you clean—
a love supreme, a love supreme—

Why you so black?
cause I am
why you so funky?
cause I am

why you so black?
cause I am
why you so sweet?
cause I am
why you so black?
cause I am
a love supreme, a love supreme:

So sick
you couldn't play *Naima,*
so flat we ached
for song you'd concealed
with your own blood,
your diseased liver gave
out its purity,
the inflated heart
pumps out, the tenor kiss,
tenor love:
a love supreme, a love supreme—
a love supreme, a love supreme—

Elvin's Blues

Sniffed, dilating my nostrils,
the cocaine creeps up my
leg, smacks into my groin;
naked with a bone for luck,
I linger in stickiness,
tickled in the joints;
I will always be high—

Tired of fresh air,
the stone ground bread,
the humid chant of music
which has led me here,
I reed my song:

"They called me the black
narcissus as I devoured
'the white hopes'
crippled in their inarticulate
madness,

Crippled myself,
Drums, each like porcelain
chamber pots, upside down,
I hear a faggot insult my
white wife with a sexless grin,
maggots under his eyelids,
a candle of my fistprint
breaks the membrane of his nose.
Now he stutters."

Last Thursday, I lay with you
tincturing your womb
with aimless strokes I could not feel.
Swollen and hard the weekend,
penitent, inane
I sank into your folds,
or salved your pastel tits,
but could not come.

Sexless as a pimp
dying in performance
like a flare gone down,
the tooth of your pier
hones near the wharf.
The ocean is breathing,
its cautious insomnia—
driven here and there—
with only itself to love.

Here Where Coltrane Is

Soul and race
are private dominions,
memories and modal
songs, a tenor blossoming,
which would paint suffering
a clear color but is not in
this Victorian house
without oil in zero degree
weather and a forty-mile-an-hour wind;
it is all a well-knit family:
a love supreme.

Oak leaves pile up on walkway
and steps, catholic as apples
in a special mist of clear white
children who love my children.
I play "Alabama"
on a warped record player
skipping the scratches
on your faces over the fibrous
conical hairs of plastic
under the wooden floors.

Dreaming on a train from New York
to Philly, you hand out six
notes which become an anthem
to our memories of you:
oak, birch, maple,
apple, cocoa, rubber.
For this reason Martin is dead;
for this reason Malcolm is dead;
for this reason Coltrane is dead;
in the eyes of my first son are the browns
of these men and their music.

HOWARD HART

Ben Webster and a Lady

Did you call?
At seven or eight
I was out
But I met in the hall
An old man with a red cough
Who said passing my apartment
He heard the phone ringing and ringing

Did you?

I didn't call you
Because I had to play
And went out to this little place

Holland is strange
Sometimes I play tenor all night
The water here
It does something to my blood

I've been practising scales of Czerny
                    and playing as much
                    of the night as I can

You know the number of the pool parlor
                    the best yes in Amsterdam

Call there

Sonny Greer

I remember nights you carried
the whole Duke Ellington orchestra
on your back
            across Jim Crow swamps

I was amazed
            a kid unable to believe
That your right hand could handle
            all those drums those cymbals
While your left picked flowers out of the horns
            of Ben Webster Rabbit Harry Carney
And each time Duke played
            you put a ring on each finger
                              of his hand
                              and a bell on his toe.

ROBERT HAYDEN

Homage to the Empress of the Blues

Because there was a man somewhere in a candystripe silk shirt,
gracile and dangerous as a jaguar and because a woman moaned
for him in sixty-watt gloom and mourned him Faithless Love
Twotiming Love Oh Love Oh Careless Aggravating Love,

She came out on the stage in yards of pearls, emerging like
a favorite scenic view, flashed her golden smile and sang.

Because grey laths began somewhere to show from underneath
torn hurdygurdy lithographs of dollfaced in heaven;
and because there were those who feared alarming fists of snow
on the door and those who feared the riot-squad of statistics,

She came out on the stage in ostrich feathers, beaded satin,
and shone that smile on us and sang.

Soledad

(And I, I am no longer of that world)

Naked, he lies in the blinded room
chainsmoking, cradled by drugs, by jazz
as never by any lover's cradling flesh.

Miles Davis coolly blows for him:
O pena negra, sensual Flamenco blues;
the red clay foxfire voice of Lady Day

(lady of the pure black magnolias)
sobsings her sorrow and loss and fare you well,
dryweeps the pain his treacherous jailers

have released him from for awhile.
His fears and his unfinished self
await him down in the anywhere streets.

He hides on the dark side of the moon,
takes refuge in a stained-glass cell,
flies to a clockless country of crystal.

Only the ghost of Lady Day knows where
he is. Only the music. And he swings
oh swings: beyond complete immortal now.

DAVID HILTON

Blind Saxophonist Dies

"blind saxophonist dies"
small photo & caption make
him a circus act

"age 41, noted
for playing three
horns at one time"

when he was two
in columbus ohio
a nurse dosed his eyes

with some bad
medication "at that
moment i felt

the whole world
become an
inflated tear" & much later

he warned "the boogie-
electric
is out to get us"

left-brain died first
served two more years
as a prop

while right-brain
sang out & celebrated
serene realm of

rhymeless poetry
all music sudden total
vision in

a dream *rahsaan*
it came yellow stars
wheeling across the

blue midnight ceiling
of the jammed club
shouting *rahsaan rahsaan*

rahsaan now a chant
now praise *rahsaan*
roland kirk

roland kirk
rahsaan roland kirk
rahsaan & the frail man

black tophat
supported by singer
& trombonist moves

off the stage
when asked about his
massive stroke he said

"that happened
that's over with
that's done

now bright moments
bright moments
everyone"

EVERETT HOAGLAND

Jamming

It was that rainy summer night
when Bobby Green was playing at The Pub.
He took out his horn
did his *thang*
and poured blue
milk into her ear.

She leaned near
and whispered to me.
It was the vaporous voice
of sax.

We picked up on the jam session
and danced home
to do it to death:

a duet to Life.

We sang all songs.
We danced all dances
until dawn came

up like song
on Sunday.

Dawn had a rainbow
wrapped around its waist,
and the pot
at the end of the rainbow
spilled over with

The alto rain of sax
and the baritone love-moan
of a saxophone:

The Music

after reading, *All God's Dangers* :
the life of Nate Shaw

Your archival voice,
our long blues song,
life's story
coughed up
the blood-soaked cotton
gag. Blue blood
blues.

Book-long
blue steel guitar blues.

Your Smith and Wesson
.32 gun metal voice.
Six strings.

What did they call you
when you didn't yield?

"If you were a :
white man : principled
mule : stubborn
nigger : *crazy"*

You were a blue steel guitar

and your wife was
a fiddle and a tambourine.
Hannah. Soft as cotton
and as strong.

And your wife was
a fiddle and a tambourine
and we your sons are
banjos
and we your daughters
cane fifes,

playing your gun metal voice,

playing your blue steel
guitar book-long song
Crazy!

ANDRE HODEIR

Outside the Capsule

[Excerpt]

by salt and by mercury
by asbestos and by phosphor
by sulphur and by silica
by the Okootoos and by the Allus
by the Voodoos and by the Zulus
by the In Cubi and by the Sub Cubi
by the inexorable figures
by the unconjurable and inexorcisable names
of Ecarerioh and Molahc-Molahc
of Armstroth and Dominavaroth
of Asmodsen and Baileyal
of Amba-Jadal and Leveyathan
of Error Nergal and Murmurossia
by the Choreae of E'Ridan
by the Ellingchtonian Lollards
by the Basielics of the Big Appeal
by the antagonistic figures of Llabnonnac and Ettenro
by the unpronounceable names of Bbewkcihc and Xibekcebrediable

and by the unclean shadow of Arpàd the depraved child the gallinacean child

hitherto follows an exegetical examination also termed analysis

of a phonotype fragment lately unearthed in a post-Christian crypt (Yelb! Yelredda! Yenracyrrah! Come!)

the object similar in this respect to all other phonotypes previously unearthed and duly described in archeological/catalogues

is black of color flat and circular in shape and its surface is graven with countless barely perceptible anfractuosities

many of which have been destroyed by the centuries but while damage suffered by the phonotype is most deplorable

its exceptional and well worth considering destiny resides in its being found outside the capsules which the Ancients meant for the preservation of their objects of worship (Snilloc! Enartloc! Elocyzoc! Hurry up!)

from which it may be deduced that it is an object of worship of the second degree or else

an object belonging to a form of worship (Relya! Rolyat! Get here!) prior to what is known as the capsule period and already discarded by then

for it is proven that at that time men attached an absolute moral value to capsulation

what was *in* being regarded as sacred and what was not *in* as sinister

such was the way of post-Christian beliefs (Crisscrollinstitt! Quick!)

notwithstanding which the archeologist whose function it is to make sense out of the insignificant

applied himself to classifying comparing describing examining and cataloguing this object

on whose surface a few fragmentary numbers and letters may still be read (MILES STAR MICROGROOVE BA[S]GROOVE 44 50)

he next entrusted it to the experts of the Foundation for Bioparapsychic Identification

sole possessors of an ancient machine the praying wheel whose artifice is still a source of wonderment today

as it is capable of restituting through gyration and the steady circular abrasion of a wooden stylus the invocations contained in the phonotype

now upon such contact the object produced clearly intelligible sounds in the middle section of its reverse side exclusively

allowing F.B.I. experts to extrapolate the complete and definitive analysis hitherto appended

ANALYSIS BY THE F.B.I.

Preamble
the musical substance condensed in the hollows of this phonotoype by a process of inscrutation

closely related to what the Ancients called a synthetic industry

is of especial interest in that it offers no resemblance whatsoever to the musical samples condensed into phonotypes discovered in capsulae

the word groove which appears twice first associated with the Latin prefix bas suggesting depth

then with the Hellenic prefix micro suggesting minuteness

is a Saxon term used by the Ancients as a doublettery for furrow

this detail reveals that the phonotype carries music for sowing-time

small seeds buried deep in accordance with the customs of the day

such as mary-jane which nourished industrial man and was sown in rows and broadcast

hence there is little justification in relating however remotely this sowing music as certain so-called experts nevertheless have done

either with the Singleton phonotype (*cf.* capsule 585) also known as opus 59 3 and 74 whose substance is bow-hunting music

as expressly stated in the inscription string quar clearly to be read on one of its sides quar being an abbreviation for quarrel a scholarly term for arrow

or with the Berrigan phonotype (*cf.* capsule 858) known as Ebony Con and which carries in its interstices an invocation to Staviski god of the forests (Bellibissie! Elsaraahl! Arrive!)

already celebrated in other invocations known to archeologists as Renard and the Bird and the Fire

all clear examples of hunting music in which the wood rather than the string which it carries is symbolically magnified

while the sowing-music found outside the capsules is dedicated to the god Miles-Selim (A-lou-qha! Suinoleth! Make haste!) no doubt a telluric power

as suggested by the sequence of isometric strophes representing the seasons' periodical return and the regular succession of sounds signifying the fall of life-giving rain

these sounds were produced by an apparatus of archaic type probably a big harpy

which because of its sound volume and above all the superior depth of its register is cast throughout the fragment under analysis in a role of overwhelming preponderance

whence the infallible certitude that this is also true of the inaudible parts of the phonotype under consideration

which big harpy is nevertheless subjected to the obtrusive proximity of other pieces of apparatus difficult to identify pursuing parallel invocations

the first of these being a light and very mobile drone heard only briefly in the audible fragment

and in like manner the last a kind of stable dense flute which appears on the verge of the destroyed section of the phonotype and is therefore doomed to annihilation between them however is heard an apparatus already known to archeologists as a chopin by reference to a phonotype (*cf.* capsule 855) which made possible its classification

this apparatus has the special feature of emitting several sounds simultaneously and is characteristic in this respect of the cacophonic tendencies of the civilization which brought it forth (Shedim! Shedims! Amdukscias! Adramelewk! Andiam!)

thus we must forgo noting its musical substance shapeless and irregular in any case

whose function is perhaps to emphasize the rigor of that produced by the principal apparatus

each sound from the big harpy is reinforced by a paraphernalia of drums and cymbals fairly modern in that it resembles those used by the priests of Ecarerioh in the damnation ceremony

and the brevity and isolation of these sounds arranged like feet in a line of verse

enabled F.B.I. experts after a thorough investigation of this substance and a comparison of each sound with the supreme standard

namely the great bell at the Abbey of Neo Porto (Bac! Lac! Tac! Don't delay!) said in an ancient text to sound a dominant B-flat

to reconstruct the strophic structure of the principal invocation

at the same time avoiding the powerful temptation to assimilate this sowing-music with the symphonic poems of the Ancients

for by a stroke of infernal luck the B-flat rhyme that persistently terminates each strophe is a strong reminder

that other texts of the period make much of an invocation called B-flat blues

whose lines were dodecaphonous in other words composed of twelve sounds as by notable coincidence is the fragment under study

now reference is made to this blues in the famous Shamanic manuscript known as the Collection (Lozit! Nosnhoj! Yajyaj! Sito and Situo and Suessy-do! Here!)

torn page number 000 of a book fallen to dust

found in the so-called Chaptal Square Crypt on the site of ancient Paris (Lalos! Rapsaj! Ognajd! Ytnop! Shake it up!)

this text possibly cryptographic in the ultimate sense has so far eluded most minute structuralistic analyses

yet clearly stipulates the existence of three-and-twenty species-of B-flats hereafter enumerated in consideration of the fact that in those times distinctions between B-flats were drawn accordingly as they were

(quotation)

1) for tuning purposes
2) long, drawn out

3) vibrant, too vibrant
4) played by Mezz Mezzrow
5) written with the left hand
6) in eight-note triplets at 120 = a quarter note
7) heard correctly
8) spoken by the critics
9) called A-sharp by ignoramuses
10) high B-flats disguised by transposition to the lower octave (the rarest piece)
11) sounded at 477 vibrations per second
12) recorded at too low a level
13) keys to the B-flat blues
14) doubled in unison by the trombone III and the saxophone IV
15) lasting two and two-thirds beats
16) occurring in the 3rd bar of the 12th chorus of the 55th piece
17) meant to be played at 3:12:55 AM
18) played with the right hand
19) different from the previous ones
20) called B by German scholars
21) called F by Frenglish horn players
22) easily taken for E by ears with absolute pitch gone haywire
23) like all other B-flats

(end of quotation)

GARRETT HONGO

Roots

I.

There are seven steps to heaven,
and enlightenment stares me in the face
every morning when I shave.

I know this much because
I've walked up and down the spine of my soul,
searching for a name in the country
my ancestors had called their own.
Every mountain was a shrine there,
and had spires of cindercone pine
that could snag a cloud or crane,

and bring it down to the human throat
in a throb of religious song.
I learned there was a signature to all things
the same as my own, and that my own sight
sanctified streetlights and stalled cars
the same as ceremonies in solitude.

When I came back to California,
to the foothills stubbled with wild oat
and valleys ragged with housing tracts,
I appreciated the joy of street slang and jive,
the thrill of girl-watching
without guilt or conniving,
and sensed I had come to own my face
in whatever state or prefecture,
in whatever place.

II.

These days an old man hangs over my sleep,
mumbling behind a screen of dreams,
painting a landscape of sandspits,
fishing shacks, and terraced hills
struggling for space on a wave-hewn coast.
He walks on the sound of a snore,
the renegade sage and sorcerer,
laughing and laughing from his place
in the corner of that scroll.
It is his signature that scratches
across my unconscious life,
that leaves the luminous stamp of the moon
on every month of my memory.
It is for him I take the *shakuhachi*
to the desert's dead shore
and conjure up a melody of bamboo reeds,
cryptomeria, or blue lotus flowers
from the pastel silences of Mojave sage and lupine.
It is for him I learn a buffalo dance,
step out the trace of a dry wash,
and speak the grammar of a trance.
So now I study spells in Sanskrit
and memorize a tenor sax lick,
knowing my Self to be my faith,
my life to be my mate.

92

One day soon, the old man and I
will go off together toward the Sierra,
squat on the brow of a sculptured hill,
tip the cup of sky to our lips,
drink a *saké* of cactus juice,
and wait for the moon to rise
over the salt flats near Manzanar.

And so, my sutra comes around midnight,
and I chant it to the tune of "A Love Supreme":

> MAKA HANYA HARAMITA SHIN GYO
> A LOVE SUPREME
> A LOVE SUPREME
> SUPREME, SUPREME
> A LOVE SUPREME
> GYA TE GYA TE
> HA RA GYA TE
> HARA SO GYA TE
> SOWA KA
> HAN NYA SHIN GYO

When I pace the seven steps of the shrine in my soul,
the old man of my dreams will be me,
leaning into the wind blowing off the Mojave,
over Sierra passes and stands of sequoia,
circling around L.A. to spin out past Catalina
across the Pacific all the way to Asia,
and heritage will be an ancient flute
throbbing from its place in my heart
where his heart has found its roots.

LANGSTON HUGHES

Dream Boogie

Good morning, daddy!
Ain't you heard
The boogie-woogie rumble
Of a dream deferred?

Listen closely:
You'll hear their feet
Beating out and beating out a—

You think
It's a happy beat?

Listen to it closely:
Ain't you heard
something underneath
like a—

What did I say?

Sure,
I'm happy!
Take it away!

Hey, pop!
Re-bop!
Mop!

Y-e-a-h!

Jazzonia

Oh, silver tree!
Oh, shining rivers of the soul.

In a Harlem cabaret
Six long-headed jazzers play.
A dancing girl whose eyes are bold
Lifts high a dress of silken gold.

Oh, singing tree!
Oh, shining rivers of the soul!

Were Eve's eyes
In the first garden
Just a bit too bold?
Was Cleopatra gorgeous
In a gown of gold?

Oh, shining tree!
Oh, silver rivers of the soul!

In a whirling cabaret
Six long-headed jazzers play.

Morning After

I was so sick last night I
Didn't hardly know my mind.
So sick last night I
Didn't know my mind.
I drunk some bad licker that
Almost made me blind.

Had a dream last night I
Thought I was in hell.
I drempt last night I
Thought I was in hell.
Woke up and looked around me—
Babe, your mouth was open like a well.

I said, Baby! Baby!
Please don't snore so loud.
Baby! Please!
Please don't snore so loud.
You jest a little bit o' woman but you
Sound like a great big crowd.

The Weary Blues

Droning a drowsy syncopated tune,
Rocking back and forth to a mellow croon,
    I heard a Negro play.
Down on Lenox Avenue the other night

By the pale dull pallor of an old gas light
    He did a lazy sway. . . .
    He did a lazy sway. . . .
To the tune o' those Weary Blues.
With his ebony hands on each ivory key

He made that poor piano moan with melody.
    O Blues!
Swaying to and fro on his rickety stool
He played that sad raggy tune like a musical fool.
    Sweet Blues!
Coming from a black man's soul.
    O Blues!
In a deep song voice with a melancholy tone
I heard that Negro sing, that old piano moan—
    "Ain't got nobody in all this world,
    Ain't got nobody but ma self.
    I's gwine to quit ma frownin'
    And put ma troubles on the shelf."
Thump, thump, thump, went his foot on the floor.
He played a few chords then he sang some more—
    "I got the Weary Blues
    And I can't be satisfied.
    Got the Weary Blues.
    And can't be satisfied—
    I ain't happy no mo'
    And I wish that I had died."
And far into the night he crooned that tune.
    The stars went out and so did the moon.
    The singer stopped playing and went to bed
    While the Weary Blues echoed through his head.
    He slept like a rock or a man that's dead.

LYNDA HULL

Hollywood Jazz

Who says it's cool says wrong.
    For it rises from the city's
        sweltering geometry of rooms,

fire escapes, and flares from the heels
    of corner boys on Occidental
        posing with small-time criminal

intent—all pneumatic grace. This
   is the music that plays at the moment
      in every late-night *noir* flick

when the woman finds herself alone, perfectly
   alone, in a hotel room before a man
      whose face is so shadowed as to be

invisible, one more bedroom arsonist
   seeing nothing remotely
      cool: a woman in a cage

of half-light, Venetian blinds.
   This is where jazz blooms, in the hook
      and snag of her zipper opening to

an enfilade of trumpets. Her dress
   falls in a dizzy indigo riff.
      I know her vices are minor: sex,

forgetfulness, the desire to be someone,
   anyone else. On the landing, the man
      pauses before descending

one more flight. Checks his belt. Adjusts
   the snap brim over his face. She smoothes
      her platinum hair and smokes a Lucky

to kill his cologne. And standing there
   by the window in her slip, midnight blue,
      the stockings she did not take off,

she is candescent, her desolation
   a music so voluptuous I want
      to linger with her. And if I do not

turn away from modesty or shame,
   I'm in this for keeps, flying with her
      into fear's random pivot where each article

glistens like evidence: the tube of lipstick,
   her discarded earrings. When she closes
      her eyes, she hears the streetcar's

nocturne up Jackson, a humpbacked sedan
rounding the corner from now
to that lavish void of tomorrow,

a sequence of rooms: steam heat, modern,
2 bucks. Now listen. Marimbas.
His cologne persists, a redolence

of fire alarms, and Darling,
there are no innocents here, only
dupes, voyeurs. On the stairs

he flicks dust from his alligator
shoes. I stoop to straighten
the seams of my stockings, and

when I meet him in the shadows
of the stairwell, clarinets whisper
Here, take my arm. Walk with me.

LAWSON FUSAO INADA

Plucking Out a Rhythm

Start with a simple room—
a dullish color—
and draw the one shade down.
Hot plate. Bed.
Little phonograph in a corner.

Put in a single figure—
medium weight and height—
but oversize, as a child might.

The features must be Japanese.

Then stack a black pompadour on,
and let the eyes
slide behind a night of glass.

The figure is in disguise:

slim green suit
for posturing on a bandstand,
the turned-up shoes of Harlem . . .

Then start the music playing—
thick jazz, strong jazz—

and notice that the figure
comes to life:

sweating, growling
over an imaginary bass—
plucking out a rhythm—
as the music rises and the room is full,
exuding with that rhythm . . .

Then have the shade flap up
and daylight catch him
frozen in that pose

as it starts to snow—
thick snow, strong snow—

blowing in the window
while the music quiets,
the room is slowly covered,

and the figure is completely
out of sight.

KEN IRBY

Homage to Coleman Hawkins

for John Moritz

—still hearing the Hawk in his region
following his season

across the Northeast shorelines, heart
                                    strike

of the horn, dive
bomber of the home

front porches

that there have to be porches
in the heat of

—he raised his horn
across the Missouri fault

as sure as the rise and now the fall of sap

the rubber plant
and geranium of affection

from Washburn from St Joe
following the tornado

jazz hounds direction

yoke of going somewhere else
to find out home

—so fall the leaves
in Massachusetts

settling home, a longing
for all Northeast corners everywhere

the pressure upon the body
of the Pacific mental

of the Atlantic visual
of the Canadian

anterior elemental

—so falls the warm November
Medford rain

as fine as winter
California
pooling the brain

having no known direction, even
. . . only the open road

the eyes closed, leaning forward into
the only riches

the great souls
solo

ROD JELLEMA

Four Voices Ending on Some Lines from Old Jazz Records

(1)   *any little woman*

The red neon sign
makes jumps like knuckles
and I almost forget how blood
moves soft inside.
Hearing it now, the beat,

I don't care a dime
how they can shoot and rock out
all the lights in the street
long as I sit here alone.
The walls lean firm and big

and I hear the long trucks
slipping west out highway twenty-two
to nowhere I've ever seen
but know the land's tucked flat
and I ain't going

already been where I'm going
one man after another

I've hit enough good times
and listen, *I can stand more trouble
than any little woman my size.*

(2)   *riffin'*

They tell me to settle down
like mellow is a job
I have to retire from.
It's like they want to give me
a gold watch on a chain
a railroad watch
one I can rise and set
in & out of a dark vest pocket
rocking on a porch
thinking the track really ends
where I see the two rails pinch
long before they hit old Memphis town.
Hell, I been there, plenty.
But right here I got a woman
in a headlights-yellow blouse,
two friendly shoes that lay a shine
on every street they walk *and boy
if I ain't riffin' tonight I hope sumthin'.*

(3)   *get the hell off my note*

Out in the smoke of every gig I play
I pinpoint orange specks
of their cigarettes, focus on how
ice and splinters of gin
cut through fog.

I'd paint if my hand didn't shake.
Tonight is what—
the sound is what these blinks
and shapes are for
and Maxie's cornet holds

a phrase just straight enough
for me to lean in lights
and work it out
and look out Brunis
get the hell off my note.

(4)   I wouldn't be a Methodist

This morning
before it was sky
was a far child
back of the trees
shy in a pale green dress.
Now my kitchen's full
of yellow, yes Lord,
and the spoon fits my hand,
Jesus cares and the branches
clap along rivers of light
and *I wouldn't be a Methodist*
to save me.

the sources:

(1) Mama Yancey
(2) Louis Armstrong
(3) Pee Wee Russell
(4) Fats Waller

Stop-time

Paul Stewart from the college was black (was the point)
and washing the yellowing ceiling in our kitchen.
I played old jazz records from my room
while a droning fan pumped slow electric air,
air that said King Oliver's *Dippermouth Blues* and *Riverside*
Blues, Morton's *Black Bottom Stomp,* air that said
wow there's a negro right there in the kitchen.

Fifteen and trying to jive without a horn. Maybe he knew.
Somehow through a Tommy Ladnier stop-time cornet run
"hey" he called, "that's great, kid like you
diggin that kind of jazz!" But then the talk wouldn't swing,
couldn't ride at all like Spanier, hot past white,
jamming with Bechet on *China Boy.* We stalled.

The needle drumming clinkers in the reject-groove,
maybe he sensed my mother's wanting to hear some *Old Black Joe*
but anyway he was talking bright and fast Bix Beiderbecke
and Bunny Berigan (whites), how they died young for art

103

and had I read Dorothy Baker's *Young Man with a Horn?* Yes—
and he was whitening walls. I kept the door open,

and all these years, Paul Stewart, first black
I ever knew, through all these years gone yellow as the news,
between the scratchy hours of my old records
you've been a wacky, mellow, low-down stop-time horn
in a blues I improvise that says
man I didn't mean it when I made you lie to me.

(for Sterling Brown)

TED JOANS

Jazz Is My Religion

JAZZ is my religion   and it alone do I dig   the jazz clubs are
my houses of worship   and sometimes the concert halls   but some
holy places are too commercial (like churches)   so I dont dig the
sermons there   I buy jazz sides to dig in solitude   Like man/Harlem,
Harlem U.S.A. used to be a jazz heaven where most of the jazz
sermons were preached   but now-a-days due to chacha cha and
rotten rock'n'roll alotta good jazzmen have sold their souls   but jazz
is still my religion   because I know and feel the message it brings
like Reverend Dizzy Gillespie/ Brother   Bird and Basie/ Uncle
Armstrong/ Minster Monk/ Deacon Miles Davis/ Rector Rollins/
Priest Ellington/ His Funkness Horace Silver/ and the great Pope
John,John COLTRANE   and Cecil Taylor   They Preach A Sermon
That Always Swings!!   Yeah jazz is MY religion   Jazz is my story
it was my mom's and pop's   and their moms and pops from the
days of Buddy Bolden who swung them blues to Charlie Parker and
Ornette Coleman's extension of Bebop   Yeah jazz is my religion
Jazz is a unique musical religion   the sermons spread happiness and
joy   to be able to dig and swing inside   what a wonderful feeling
jazz is/YEAH BOY!!   JAZZ is my religion and dig this: it wasnt for
us to choose because they created it for a damn good reason   as   a
weapon to battle our blues!JAZZ is my religion   and its
international   all the   way   JAZZ is just an Afroamerican music
and like us its here to stay   So remember that JAZZ is my religion
but it can be your religion too but JAZZ is a truth that   is always

black and blue   Hallelujah I love JAZZ so   Hallelujah I dig JAZZ so
Yeah J A Z Z   I S   MY   R E L I G I O N

Jazz Must Be a Woman

to all the jazzmen that I fail to include

Jazz must be a woman because its the only thing that
Albert Ayler Albert Ammons Albert Nichols Gene Ammons Cat
Anderson Louis Armstrong Buddy Bolden Ornette Coleman Buster
Bailey Ben Bailey Benny Harris Ben Webster Beaver Harris Alan
Shorter Coleman Hawkins Count Basie Dave Bailey Dexter Gordon
Danny Barker Wayne Shorter Duke Ellington Jay Macshann Earl Hines
Tiny Grimes Barney Bigard Sahib Shihab Sid Catlett JELLY ROLL
Morton Nat King Cole Johnny Coles Lee Collins John Collins Sonny
Rollins Pete Brown Jay Jay Johnson Dickie Wells Vic Dickenson Ray
Nance Junior Mance Sonny Parker Charlie Parker Leo Parker Lee
Morgan Mal Waldron Ramsey Lewis John Lewis George Lewis Pops
Foster Curtiss Fuller Jimmie Cleveland Billy Higgins John Coltrane
Cozy Cole Bill Coleman Idries Sulimann Hank Mobley Charlie
Mingus Dizzy Gillespie Lester Young Harney Carney Cecil Payne
Sonny Payne Roy Haynes Max Roach Thelonious Monk Wes
Montgomery Johnny Dodds Johnny Hodges Kenny Drew Kenny
Durham Ernie Wilkins Ernie Royal Babs Gonzales McCoy Tyner
Clifford Brown Shadow Wilson Teddy Wilson Gerald Wilson Wynton
Kelly Huddie Leadbelly Big Bill Bronzy Cannonball Adderly Bobbie
Timmons Sidney Bechet Sonny Criss Sonny Stitt Fats Navarro Ray
Charles Benny Carter Lawrence Brown Ray Brown Charlie Moffett
Sonny Murray Milt Buckner Milt Jackson Miles Davis Horace Silver
Bud Powell Kenny Burrell Teddy Bunn Teddy Buckner King Oliver
Oliver Nelson Tricky Sam Nanton Buber Miley Freddy Webster
Freddy Redd Benny Green Jackie Maclean Art Simmins Art Blakey
Art Taylor Cecil Taylor Billy Taylor Gene Taylor Clark Terry Don
Cherry Sonny Terry Joe Turner Joe Thomas Ray Bryant Freddie
Greene Freddie Hubbard Donald Byrd Roland Kirk Carl Perkins
Morris Lane Harry Edison Percey Heath Jimmy Heath Jimmy Smith
Willie Smith Buster Smith Floyd Smith Johnny Smith Pinetop Smith
Stuff Smith Tab Smith Willie 'the Lion' Smith Roy Eldridge Charlie
Shavers Eddie South Les Spann Les Macann Speckled Red Eddie
Vinson Mr. Cleanhead Rex Stewart Slam Stewart Art Tatum Erskine
Hawkins Cootie Williams Lionel Hampton Ted Curson John Tchicai
Joe Thomas Lucky Thompson Sir Charles Thompson T-Bone Walker

Fats Waller Julius Watkins Doug Watkins Muddy Waters Washboard
Sam Memphis Slim Leo Watson Chick Webb Frank Wess Denzil Best
Randy Weston Clarence Williams Joe Williams Rubberlegs Williams
Spencer Williams Sonnyboy Williams Tampa Red Jimmy
Witherspoon Britt Woodman Leo Wright Jimmy Yancey Trummy
Young Snooky Young James P Johnson Bunk Johnson Budd
Johnson Red Garland Erroll Garner Jimmy Garrison Matthew Gee
Cecil Gant Walter Fuller Roosevelt Sykes Slim Gaillard Harold Land
Pete Laroca Yusef Lateef Billy Kyle John Kirby Al Killian Andy Kirk
Freddie Keppard Taft Jordan Duke Jordon Louis Jordan Cliff
Jordan Scott Joplin Willie Jones Wallace Jones Sam Jones Rejnald
Jones Quincy Jones Philly Jo Jones Jimmy Jones Hank Jones Elvin
Jones Ed Jones Claude Jones Rufus Jones Curtiss Jones Richard
Jones Wilmore 'slick' Jones Thad Jones and of course me . . . . . TED
JOANS/yes JAZZ must be a WOMAN because its the only thing
that we Jazzmen want to . . . . B L O W!!

Lester Young

Sometimes he was cool like an eternal
    blue flame burning in the old Kansas
    City nunnery
Sometimes he was happy 'til he'd think
    about his birth place and its blood
    stained clay hills and crow-filled trees
Most times he was blowin' on the wonderful
    tenor sax of his, preachin' in very cool
    tones, shouting only to remind you of
    a certain point in his blue messages
He was our president as well as the minister
    of soul stirring Jazz, he knew what he
    blew, and he did what a prez should do,
    wail, wail, wail. There were many of
    them to follow him and most of them were
    fair—but they never spoke so eloquently
    in so a far out funky air.
Our prez done died, he know'd this would come
    but death has only booked him, alongside
    Bird, Art Tatum, and other heavenly wailers.
Angels of Jazz—they don't die—they live
they live—in hipsters like you and I

JOE JOHNSON

Cecil Taylor

[Excerpt]

conga li bombo gri gri
bombo canga li bombo
burned blood blast down black
on boy's dark life cut with night's gun blood
bombo conga li bombo
child's lip jacked up to kiss stars silent
li li bombo li li
dead medicine of boy's heart heat burst
child's eyes are dirty rags, child's lips are frail
child down up on stone with blood still
gri gri bombo li li
bursting centipede sounds circling fire's   burst
bam bam bullets fuck space train up on life and stiff
dick it silent
conga li bombo li li
conga li bombo
pale hand laying red on leather in lost loose tribe silent
spotting shiny eye, thick lip prey breaking still
words club and balk barking down on flesh burst
blue mother blind grind your stone black hip crushing
through heart's black
while your child drown on steel: what was his last word
in life, blood?
blood thick spear lash bone through blood child
conga li bombo gri gri
bombo conga li bombo
night hold this scolding passion motherfucking silence
slipping still silent,
I wander and kill paper and wind my heart through wired
blood,
now cop mad heat whitens and locks my blood
chaining door with stone flowers and grinding still lips
still
mad fingers smoke, bruised visions choke on steel lost
in mama black
eternity, deep thick in come of life lift burst
conga li bombo gri gri
bombo conga li gri gri

107

this dance is the dance of blood
                    bombo
this dance is blood burst
                    bombo li li bombo
this dance is with child
this dance is silent
this dance is black
                    bombo li li bombo
child blood bursting silent
                    gri gri silent
this is the dance of blood's black slipping still black
                    bombo li li bombo

STEVE JONAS

One of Three Musicians

The first time I heard Ornette
Coleman I thought
about Picasso's
          Three Musicians
          w/ their neo-
                    classical in-
struments: cigarboxes w/
          soft line strains drawn
across barrel staves, tin

                    cans thrown
(or kicked) in Congo Square
                    these "fakers"
with jaw bone percussions out of dead
          horses & instruments from
                    the child's hand
They reproduce the spasms, the screams
the outbursts of dark religious ex-
          orcisms. these are not the

shoed peasant feet out of Brueghel's
          painting *The Kermess,* these are
bare black feet pounding

                        delta clay
        the wire & steel singing over
                        broken barrel staves,
    saying a theatre is any place
                        free associates come in
        to play.

BOB KAUFMAN

Bagel Shop Jazz

Shadow people, projected on coffee-shop walls.
Memory formed echoes of a generation past
Beating into now.

Nightfall creatures, eating each other
Over a noisy cup of coffee.

Mulberry-eyed girls in black stockings,
Smelling vaguely of mint jelly and last night's bongo
    drummer,
Making profound remarks on the shapes of navels,
Wondering how the short Sunset week
Became the long Grant Avenue night,
Love tinted, beat angels,
Doomed to see their coffee dreams
Crushed on the floors of time,
As they fling their arrow legs
To the heavens,
Losing their doubts in the beat.

Turtle-neck angel guys, black-haired dungaree guys,
Caesar-jawed, with synagogue eyes,
World travelers on the forty-one bus,
Mixing jazz with paint talk,
High rent, Bartok, classical murders,
The pot shortage and last night's bust.
Lost in a dream world,
Where time is told with a beat.

109

Battle Report

One thousand saxophones infiltrate the city,
Each with a man inside,
Hidden in ordinary cases,
Labeled FRAGILE.

A fleet of trumpets drops their hooks,
Inside at the outside.

Ten waves of trombones approach the city
Under blue cover
Of late autumn's neo-classical clouds.

Five hundred bassmen, all string feet tall,
Beating it back to the bass.

One hundred drummers, each a stick in each hand,
The delicate rumble of pianos, moving in.

The secret agent, an innocent bystander,
Drops a note in the wail box.

Five generals, gathered in the gallery,
Blowing plans.

At last, the secret code is flashed:
Now is the time, now is the time.

Attack: The sound of jazz.

The city falls.

Walking Parker Home

Sweet beats of jazz impaled on slivers of wind
Kansas Black Morning/ First Horn Eyes/
Historical sound pictures on New Bird wings
People shouts/ boy alto dreams/Tomorrow's
Gold belled pipe of stops and future Blues Times
Lurking Hawkins/ shadows of Lester/ realization
Bronze fingers—brain extensions seeking trapped sounds

Ghetto thoughts/ bandstand courage/ solo flight
Nerve-wracked suspicions of newer songs and doubts
New York altar city/ black tears/ secret disciples
Hammer horn pounding soul marks on unswinging gates
Culture gods/ mob sounds/ visions of spikes
Panic excursions to tribal Jazz wombs and transfusions
Heroin nights of birth/ and soaring/ over boppy new ground.
Smothered rage covering pyramids of notes spontaneously
      exploding
Cool revelations/ shrill hopes/ beauty speared into
      greedy ears
Birdland nights on bop mountains, windy saxophone
      revolutions
Dayrooms of junk/ and melting walls and circling vultures/
Money cancer/ remembered pain/ terror flights/
Death and indestructible existence

In that Jazz corner of life
Wrapped in a mist of sound
His legacy, our Jazz-tinted dawn
Wailing his triumphs of oddly begotten dreams
Inviting the nerveless to feel once more
That fierce dying of humans consumed
In raging fires of Love.

War Memoir

Jazz—listen to it at your own risk.
At the beginning, a warm dark place.

(Her screams were trumpet laughter,
Not quite blues, but almost sinful.)

Crying above the pain, we forgave ourselves;
Original sin seemed a broken record.
God played blues to kill time, all the time.
Red-waved rivers floated us into life.

(So much laughter, concealed by blood and faith;
Life is a saxophone played by death.)

Greedy to please, we learned to cry;
Hungry to live, we learned to die.

111

The heart is a sad musician,
Forever playing the blues.

The blues blow life, as life blows fright;
Death begins, jazz blows soft in the night,
Too soft for ears of men whose minds
Hear only the sound of death, of war,
Of flagwrapped cremation in bitter lands.

No chords of jazz as mud is shoveled
Into the mouths of men; even the blues shy
At cries of children dying on deserted corners.
Jazz deserted, leaving us to our burning.

(Jazz is an African traitor.)

What one-hundred-percent redblooded savage
Wastes precious time listening to jazz
With so much important killing to do?

Silence the drums, that we may hear the burning
Of Japanese in atomic colorcinemascope,
And remember the stereophonic screaming.

War Memoir: Jazz, Don't Listen to It at Your Own Risk

In the beginning, in the wet
Warm dark place,
Straining to break out, clawing at strange cables
Hearing her screams, laughing
"Later we forgot ourselves, we didn't know"
Some secret jazz
Shouted, wait, don't go.
Impatient, we came running, innocent
Laughing blobs of blood and faith.
To this mother, father world
Where laughter seems out of place
So we learned to cry, pleased
They pronounced human.
The secret jazz blew a sigh
Some familiar sound shouted wait

112

Some are evil, some will hate.
"Just Jazz, blowing its top again"
So we rushed and laughed.
As we pushed and grabbed
While Jazz blew in the night
Suddenly we were too busy to hear a sound
We were busy shoving mud in men's mouths,
Who were busy dying on living ground
Busy earning medals, for killing children on deserted
    streetcorners
Occupying their fathers, raping their mothers, busy humans
    were
Busy burning Japanese in atomicolorcinescope
With stereophonic screams,
What one-hundred-percent red-blooded savage would waste
    precious time
Listening to Jazz, with so many important things going on
But even the fittest murderers must rest
So we sat down on our blood-soaked garments,
And listened to Jazz
                  lost, steeped in all our dreams
We were shocked at the sound of life, long gone from our own
We were indignant at the whistling, thinking, singing, beating,
    swinging
Living sound, which mocked us, but let us feel sweet life again
We wept for it, hugged, kissed it, loved it, joined it, we
    drank it,
Smoked it, ate with it, slept with it
We made our girls wear it for lovemaking
Instead of silly lace gowns,
Now in those terrible moments, when the dark memories come
The secret moments to which we admit no one
When guiltily we crawl back in time, teaching away from
    ourselves
We hear a familiar sound,
Jazz, scratching, digging, bluing, swinging jazz,
And we listen
And we feel
And live.

SYBIL KEIN

Jazz

(pour Vernel Bagneris)

De Storyville, Vaudeville, Cabarets et Tonks,
Nous joue Les Blues, Marches, Chansons religiéux, et Rags
Et nous quitte fardeau-là de
Maître, esclave, et bâtard;
Nous metté li dans un syncopé insolent.
La Viéux Nouvelle-Orléans dansé
Les Quadrilles, Rumbas, Shimmes, et Grinds.
Et nous quitté fardeau-là.
Jassbo et Jassebelle.
Les tambours Congo et chansons Créole.
Nous quitté fardeau-là
Pas besoin d'étudier la guerre encore.
Quand Saint-ça-yé rentre apé marcher,
Nous va êt dans bande-là.
Satchmo et Jelly Roll,
L'ébène et l'ivoire
Apé jouer harmonie doux
"UN FOIS PLUS"!

Jazz

(for Vernel Bagneris)

From Storyville, Vaudeville, Cabarets, and Tonks,
We played Blues, Marches, Spirituals, and Rags,
And we laid down that burden of
Massa, slave, and bastard.
We laid it down in sassy syncopation.
Old New Orleans danced with
Quadrilles, Rhumbas, Shimmies, and Grinds.
We laid that burden down.
Jassbo and Jassebelle,
Congo drums and Creole songs,
We laid that burden down.
No need to study war no more;

When those saints go marching,
We will be in that number:
Satchmo and Jelly Roll,
The ebony and the ivory,
Playing sweet harmony
"ONE MO' TIME"!

JACK KEROUAC

221st Chorus

[From *Mexico City Blues*]

Old Man Mose
Early American Jazz pianist
Had a grandson
Called Deadbelly.
Old Man Mose walloped
    the rollickin keyport
    Wahoo wildhouse Piany
    with monkies in his hair
    drooling spaghetti, beer
    and beans, with a cigar
    mashed in his countenance
    of gleaming happiness
    the furtive madman
    of old sane times.

Deadbelly dont hide it—
    Lead killed Leadbelly—
Deadbelly admit
    Deadbelly modern cat
Cool—Deadbelly, Man,
Craziest.
        Old Man Mose is Dead
        But Deadbelly get Ahead
        Ha ha ha

239th Chorus

[From *Mexico City Blues*]

Charley Parker Looked like Buddha
Charley Parker, who recently died
Laughing at a juggler on the TV
after weeks of strain and sickness,
was called the Perfect Musician.
And his expression on his face
Was as calm, beautiful, and profound
As the image of the Buddha
Represented in the East, the lidded eyes,
The expression that says "All is Well"
— This was what Charley Parker
Said when he played, All is Well.
You had the feeling of early-in-the-morning
Like a hermit's joy, or like
                    the perfect cry
Of some wild gang at a jam session
"Wail, Wop" — Charley burst
His lungs to reach the speed
Of what the speedsters wanted
And what they wanted
Was his Eternal Slowdown.
A great musician and a great
                  creator of forms
That ultimately find expression
In mores and what have you.

ETHERIDGE KNIGHT

For Eric Dolphy

on flute
spinning   spinning   spinning
love
thru/ out
the universe

i
know
exactly
whut chew mean
man

you like
titi
my sister
who never expressed LOVE
in words (like the white folks always d
she would sit in the corner   o
and cry   i
everytime   n
ah   g
got a whuppin

Jazz Drummer

MAX ROACH
    has fire and steel in his hands,
    rides high, is a Makabele warrior,
    tastes death on his lips, beats babies
    from worn out wombs,
                  grins with grace,
    and cries in the middle of his eyes.

MAX ROACH
    thumps the big circle in bare feet,
    opens wide the big arms,
    and like the sea
                calls us all.

KENNETH KOCH

The History of Jazz

1

The leaves of blue came drifting down.
In the corner Madeleine Reierbacher was reading *Lorna Doone*.

The baby's water helped to implement the structuring of the garden hose.
The envelope fell. Was it pink or was it red? Consult *Lorna Doone*.
There, voyager, you will find your answer. The savant grapeade stands
Remember Madeleine Reierbacher. Madeleine Reierbacher says,
"If you are happy, there is no one to keep you from being happy;
Don't let them!" Madeleine Reierbacher went into the racing car.
The racing car was orange and red. Madeleine Reierbacher drove to Beale
Street.
There Maddy doffed her garments to get into some more comfortable clothes.
Jazz was already playing in Beale Street when Madeleine Reierbacher
arrived there.
Madeleine Reierbacher picked up the yellow horn and began to play.
No one had ever heard anything comparable to the playing of Madeleine
Reierbacher.
What a jazz musician! The pianist missed his beats because he was so
excited.
The drummer stared out the window in ecstasy at the yellow wooden trees.
The orchestra played "September in the Rain," "Mugging," and "I'm Full
of Love."
Madeleine Reierbacher rolled up her sleeves; she picked up her horn; she
played "Blues in the Rain."
It was the best jazz anyone had ever heard. It was mentioned in the news-
papers. St. Louis!
Madeleine Reierbacher became a celebrity. She played with Pesky Sum-
merton and Muggsy Pierce.
Madeleine cut numerous disks. Her best waxings are "Alpha Beta and
Gamma"
And "Wing Song." One day Madeleine was riding on a donkey
When she came to a yellow light; the yellow light did not change.
Madeleine kept hoping it would change to green or red. She said, "As long
as you have confidence,
You need be afraid of nothing." Madeleine saw the red smokestacks, she
looked at the thin trees,
And she regarded the railroad tracks. The yellow light was unchanging.
Madeleine's donkey dropped dead
From his mortal load. Madeleine Reierbacher, when she fell to earth,
Picked up a blade of grass and began to play. "The Blues!" cried the work-
men of the vicinity,
And they ran and came in great numbers to where Madeleine Reierbacher
was.
They saw her standing in that simple field beside the railroad track
Playing, and they saw that light changing to green and red, and they saw
that donkey stand up
And rise into the sky; and Madeleine Reierbacher was like a clot of blue

In the midst of the blue of all that sky, and the young farmers screamed
In excitement, and the workmen dropped their heavy boards and stones
in their excitement,
And they cried, "O Madeleine Reierbacher, play us the 'Lead Flint Blues'
once again!"

O railroad stations, pennants, evenings, and lumberyards!
When will you ever bring us such a beautiful soloist again?
An argent strain shows on the reddish face of the sun.
Madeleine Reierbacher stands up and screams, "I am getting wet! You are
all egotists!"
Her brain floats up into the lyric atmosphere of the sky.
We must figure out a way to keep our best musicians with us.
The finest we have always melt into the light blue sky!
In the middle of a concert, sometimes, they disappear, like anvils.
(The music comes down to us with sweet white hands on our shoulders.)
We stare up in surprise; and we hear Madeleine's best-known tune once
again,
"If you ain't afraid of life, life can't be afraid for you."
Madeleine! Come back and sing to us!

2

Dick looked up from his blackboard.
Had he really written a history of the jazz age?
He stared at his television set; the technicolor jazz program was coming
on.
The program that day was devoted to pictures of Madeleine Reierbacher
Playing her saxophone in the golden age of jazz.
Dick looked at his blackboard. It was a mass of green and orange lines.
Here and there a red chalk line interlaced with the others.
He stared attentively at the program.

It was a clear and blue white day. Amos said, "The calibration is finished.
Now there need be no more jazz."

In his mountain home old Lucas Dog laughed when he heard what Amos
had said.
He smilingly picked up his yellow horn to play, but all that came out of
it was steam.

119

YUSEF KOMUNYAKAA

Elegy for Thelonious

Damn the snow.
Its senseless beauty
pours a hard light
through the hemlock.
Thelonious is dead. Winter
drifts in the hourglass;
notes pour from the brain cup.
Damn the alley cat
wailing a muted dirge
off Lenox Ave.
Thelonious is dead.
Tonight's a lazy rhapsody of shadows
swaying to blue vertigo
& metaphysical funk.
Black trees in the wind.
Crepuscule with Nellie
plays inside the bowed head.
"Dig the Man Ray of piano!"
O Satisfaction,
hot fingers blur
on those white rib keys.
Coming on the Hudson.
Monk's Dream.
The ghost of bebop
from 52nd Street,
footprints in the snow.
Damn February.
Let's go to Minton's
& play "modern malice"
till daybreak. Lord,
there's Thelonious
wearing that old funky hat
pulled down over his eyes.

February in Sydney

Dexter Gordon's tenor sax
plays "April in Paris"

inside my head all the way back
on the bus from Double Bay.
Round Midnight, the '50's,
cool cobblestone streets
resound footsteps of Bebop
musicians with whiskey-laced voices
from a boundless dream in French.
Bud, Prez, Webster & The Hawk,
their names run together
like mellifluous riffs.
Painful gods jive talk through
bloodstained reeds & shiny brass
where music is an anesthetic.
Unreadable faces from the human void
float like torn pages across the bus
windows. An old anger drips into my throat,
& I try thinking something good,
letting the precious bad
settle to the salty bottom.
Another scene keeps repeating itself:
I emerge from the dark theatre,
passing a woman who grabs her red purse
& hugs it to her like a heart attack.
Tremolo. Dexter comes back to rest
behind my eyelids. A loneliness
lingers like a silver needle
under my black skin,
as I try to feel how it is
to scream for help through a horn.

RICHARD KOSTELANETZ

STRINGFOUR

for Ned Sublette

Stringfourselvestrymandolingerbillowbrowboatmealtimetablemi-
shapelessencephalogrampagentangleefulcrumpushoverballerinadverten-
thralligatoreadorablessingletonsilverwarehouselesssayisthmustarden-
throneselfingernailmentallowancestoragencyclopedialysisternumbilical-

endartifactotumultransomewhatnoticebergothiccupolaryngitissue-
delweissuancestryoutlinefficientertainmentorpidginghamstermite-
mizenmastounderpassassingularderangelatinseltzerotickettledrum-
pleasantimacassarsaparilladvisedimenterprisenatornadoptometryin-
grownershippotamusclericalculustrylistickingestabilishmenthusi-
astronautobiographysicalculatorriderivationosphereafterriblend-
eavortextinguishermitigatewaylaymankindependentombudsman-
drillustriousstereophonicotinelegantipathymusseldominantebellumber-
yardormanticipatenteemingredienterracetracknowledgerryman-
deriveterandomestickerchieftaintervalianticlimaximummerchanti-
thesisalvagendangermanestheticklepтomaniacinnamonarchangeld-
erogatekeepersimmonsterlingrainedibleachievermorelayoverte-
braceletterheadachestnutmegaphonestrangerunderneathletickero-
senemancipatorpornographylumbarbershopefulsomelethallucino-
genitalkalinertiarabesquestrogenocidenticaliperoxideathwar-
timekeeperpendicularkspurpleafletup

STRINGFIVE

Stringfiveterancideridafencerebrumblendivestablishmentertaininteger-
underwritemperamentorthographysicisternumericalibereavesdropen-
ervoustermagantonymphomaniacinemaciatediousnessencephalitissue-
demasculatecyclopedictumoribunderseashellipsesamendemicropho-
nemesisterhoodluminescepterminextricableederailmentrapproche-
mentrenchantihistaminestroneroustaboutiqueasymptotempower-
ectilinearachemistryoutboardorsalonesomenopauseufulfillogicallow-
downerverackingottenementouragendangerminalienableathereafter-
rapineappleaseldomesticategoricalumetaphorticulturemiasmartenta-
cleavagentlemanpowerewolfhounderdevelopederastylustereophonick-
namendmentrainbowlingerbillboardinghouselessonnethermosteopathe-
tickerosenemanatingleefulcrumpetticoatheisthmusculargessaying-
redientrancestorrentalismanslaughterrifictionospheretickettledrum-
plethoracleverticaliconoclastrayonderiversidenticalliopeningrained-
ibleachievergladentifricebounderlinexactornadoptimalaproposter-
rainfalligatorquellipticalendarticlergymanumitigatewayfarerun-
towardentalentrusticaterpillargestimaterialistendencyclicalipermanent-
ranthropocentrichinosisalamanderogatekeepersimmonosyllables-
sedatlinesmandolinchpinnacleavernacularderangelatinderboxcarpetbag-
germanemoneselfinalexandrinexhautibleardrummerchanticlimax-
imalevolentomboycotterracetylenervate

122

ART LANGE

Blues Five Spot

Charlie Parker played havoc
—Peter Kostakis

A last item a found object
          a lost item
a refrain of rain, wordstruck,
                              birdlike
              to conjure with
borrowings new and "savage"
delicate forms in blue green orangish-yellow white
sonorities scream or "sigh as you stroke it"
          growing softer and given
to a purple lyricism
                    startling, in tandem
          elliptical and perfect as a planet a
very sophisticated night life we go very early
into the home of a lyrically articulate gorgeous artifact
whose
      names are merely different bits of a whole
a blown landscape of event
                        where we
now be, legitimate
              -ly

Monk's Dream

I welcome though
the things I have
not written but

can remember
by way of sleeping of
feeling   "too much"
"too much"

enough for now to be here

123

Monk's Point

What's this all about
                    the cool the sinister
on the phone my sister
                            assumptions
many loves

                    (of)

mood
                            through a throng
                                        wading

one once
            what
        one wants

                                        body count
    it's a pleasure
                    under
a sarong
                your song
completely gone (what is)

I mean
                    completely gone, no other

PHILIP LARKIN

For Sidney Bechet

That note you hold, narrowing and rising, shakes
Like New Orleans reflected on the water,
And in all ears appropriate falsehood wakes,

Building for some a legendary Quarter
Of balconies, flower-baskets and quadrilles,
Everyone making love and going shares—

Oh, play that thing! Mute glorious Storyvilles
Others may license, grouping round their chairs
Sporting-house girls like circus tigers (priced

Far above rubies) to pretend their fads,
While scholars *manqués* nod around unnoticed
Wrapped up in personnels like old plaids.

On me your voice falls as they say love should,
Like an enormous yes. My Crescent City
Is where your speech alone is understood,

And greeted as the natural noise of good,
Scattering long-haired grief and scored pity.

PHILIP LEVINE

On the Corner

Standing on the corner
until Tatum passed
blind as the sea,
heavy, tottering
on the arm of the young
bass player, and they
both talking
Jackie Robinson.
It was cold, late,
and the Flame Show Bar
was crashing
for the night, even
Johnny Ray
calling it quits.
Tatum said, Can't
believe how fast
he is to first. Wait'll
you see Mays
the bass player said.
Women in white furs
spilled out of the bars

and trickled toward
the parking lot. Now
it could rain, coming
straight down. The man
in the brown hat
never turned his head up.
The gutters swirled
their heavy waters,
the streets reflected
the sky, which was
nothing. Tatum
stamped on toward
the Bland Hotel, a wet
newspaper stuck
to his shoe, his mouth
open, his vest
drawn and darkening.
I can't hardly wait, he said.

LARRY LEVIS

Whitman:

*I say we had better look our nation searchingly
in the face, like a physician diagnosing some
deep disease.*
                                        —Democratic Vistas

Look for me under your bootsoles.

On Long Island, they moved my clapboard house
Across a turnpike, & then felt so guilty they
Named a shopping center after me!

Now that I'm required reading in your high schools,
Teenagers call me a fool.
Now what I sang stops breathing.

And yet
It was only when everyone stopped believing in me
That I began to live again—
First in the thin whine of Montana fence wire,

126

Then in the transparent, cast-off garments hung
In the windows of the poorest families,
Then in the glad music of Charlie Parker.
At times now,
I even come back to watch you
From the eyes of a taciturn boy at Malibu.
Across the counter at the beach concession stand,
I sell you hot dogs, Pepsis, cigarettes—
My blond hair long, greasy, & swept back.
In a vain old ducktail, deliciously
Out of style.
And no one notices.
Once, I even came back as *me*,
An aging homosexual who ran the Tilt-a-Whirl
At county fairs, the chilled paint on each gondola
Changing color as it picked up speed,
And a Mardi Gras tattoo on my left shoulder.
A few of you must have seen my photographs,
For when you looked back,
I thought you caught the meaning of my stare:

Still water,
Merciless.

A Kosmos. One of the roughs.

And Charlie Parker's grave outside Kansas City
Covered with weeds.

Leave me alone.
A father who's outlived his only child.

To find me now will cost you everything.

LYN LIFSHIN

Alberta Hunter

you could hear
Bessie Smith
from here to
49th St

127

I've got the first
record I made
on Black Swam   ran

away from home
away from Beale St
working at a night
club called Dream
land   brother Louis
Armstong up to
play 2nd trumpet
his first wife
collapsed   died
at her husband's
funeral   I love

church but until
they put that sand
and dirt in my face
ladies and gentle
man I've had enough

N. J. LOFTIS

Black Anima

[Section 9]

Spiked cadillacs with silver teeth
Miss Black America
in blond wig
     waves at us
from chauffeured limousine

Stereos blasting behind closed
     loan shop windows
Black volcanic rhythms
Black music
     Black soul
into sterile cocaine heaven

O think think
'bout what you tryin'
to do to me

Cruising through Harlem in a gypsy cab
    for the other taxis
    were on strike that year
the darkness syncopating
turning, writhing, stretched
on a cross of lassitude.

    Half watts of celluloid
    dread whistling down
    to you

Aretha is at the Apollo
Black soul sister
whose Veiled tribal sounds
    shattered the mask
    of Athena
Aretha is at the Apollo
screening on a shield
the dreadful prospects of tomorrow

    You'd better
    think, think
    O you'd better
    think

Her euphoric therapy
    only appeasing distress
even between her breaths
    hearts fluttering
    in calcified cavity
the panic in the abdomen
the Negro syndrome
revives again
    squads of heroin
    under long-sleeved shirts
circulate through the arteries
    faster than
    the IRT

129

Is it you, Federico Garcia
walking these mean streets
    where a skyful
    of visionary birds
strike at you
along the corners of fear
You who taught us to sing
the poet among his people
    the multitude
    with its king
beautiful, graceful, Garcia
your sex transfixed into a flower's

Your rumor reaches me
Your rumor reaches me

It is the hour of the wolf

I am going away
I am going away

the airport nearly deserted
the city unmasked
by a barrage of lights
lies naked

swing low sweet cadillac
swing low sweet cadillac

It is time to begin again, Mrs. Epstein
you who are perishing
the revolution is at hand
    I, Diamond Katambo
    leading linguist
at the Institute for Black Speech
see the mirror cracked
    in the hallway
and the blood upon the wall
I see the ruin of all space
    and hear the sound
    of crumbling masonry
    Listen!

Now once again with feeling
"Baby"
No, no, your voice sounds too deceiving
"Ba-By"
Ah, Mrs. Epstein, Mrs. Epstein
you see being a nigger's
    not as easy as it seems
We who were dead are now living
You who were living
    are now dying

       Boom! Boom! Boom! Boom! Boom!
       drop,   drop,   drop,   drop,   drop
       Boom! Boom! Boom! Boom!
       drop,   drop,   drop,   drop,
       Boom! Boom!
       drop,
       drop

Bing! Bing! *No smoking please*
the bell in the interior
releases the night mares
    from the post
the plane climbing skyward
leaves the dead concerns
of the earth behind

     swing low sweet cadillac
     I'm going away and ain't
     never coming back

Pen my suit-coat pocket,
ring gleaming, burning, gleaming
    ordering the air around it
the plane unbuttoning the sky
    the void jetting by.

JOHN LOGAN

Chicago Scene

(for Roger Aplon)

At the bar called
        Plugged
Nickel in Chicago
red, blue and yellow hammers
on its honky tonk piano
easily make their hits.
A boyish drummer ticks
his brush
       and pushes
back
   a shock
        of brown hair.
He draws lightly from his glass of beer.
A heavy scholar of the sax
mounts his giant bass
and together they begin
to snort,
      smoke,
         and carry on
like a Saint George with dragon.
This certain beat
pulses to the puff of Bobby Connally's cheek.
And now the sweet and sour sauce
of the old New Orleans Jazz
potent as our father's jizz
permeates the air,
seems to knock us in the ear
and starts
       melancholy thoughts
(it is too loud to talk).
Behind the bar,
       oracular,
a bushy bearded (black)
and muscled man
        works
and broods. No one has ever seen
his face!

132

For he's gone,
                    proud,
     to the dark side
                    of the plugged moon.

MINA LOY

The Widow's Jazz

1.

The white flesh quakes to the negro soul
Chicago!   Chicago!

An uninterpretable wail
stirs in a tangle of pale snakes

to the lethargic ecstasy of steps
backing into primeval goal

White man quit his actin' wise
colored folk hab de moon in dere eyes

Haunted by wind instruments
in groves of grace

the maiden saplings
slant to the oboes

and shampooed gigolos
prowl to the sobbing taboos.

An electric clown
crashes the furtive cargoes of the floor.

The pruned contours
dissolve
in the brazen shallows of dissonance
revolving mimes
of the encroaching Eros
in adolescence

The black brute-angels
in their human gloves
bellow through a monstrous growth of metal trunks

and impish musics
crumble the ecstatic loaf
before a swooning flock of doves.

2.

Cravan
colossal absentee
the substitute dark
rolls to the incandescent memory

of love's survivor
on this rich suttee

seared by the flames of sound
the widowed urn
holds impotently
your murdered laughter

Husband
how secretly you cuckold me with death

while this cajoling jazz
blows with its tropic breath

among the echoes of the flesh
a synthesis
of racial caress

The seraph and the ass
in this unerring esperanto
of the earth
converse
of everlit delight

as my desire
receded
to the distance of the dead

searches
the opaque silence
of unpeopled space.

NATHANIEL MACKEY

Ohnedaruth's Day Begun

—"bright light of shipwreck"—

There I sit afloat in
the Boat of Years, a thin ellipsoid
   breath against the roof of
my mouth pressed to modulate
   pitch, reed lipped across
   time to've been wormlike,
                              earth

to become a navigable sludge.
   Sixty-eight days to my
   forty-first year, this endless
      dwelling on air the key to
a courtyard filled with
   talkers, tongues in hand,
                        bush fled
      by birds whose wings burn, air
                              love's
   abrasive hush.

                  These bird-gods
   anoint me with camphor, escort me
thru each a more private room, the
   chronic juices of lust flood an
                        ended earth
   whose beckoned image
                  burns on.

   Still I see no light, no
letting go of my remorse come
   shining thru, this unruly wail a not
so thickly veiled prayer you
   Anubic sisters, not a harp no
      fingers pluck played on by
                           wind.

   First I'm told my false mask is
   "reformation," this horn my
                        heart's

135

undoing, eyes clouded with salt . . .
the bitter coat of my rebirth
I'll stitch of a cloth whose colors
run.

In the augur's full to bursting
overload of sense mix flirts with
meaning, says my divorced mother
daddied me to death, my road is
wet,
shows Century City against
a futuristic sun.

So there I sit outside the
Heartbreak Straits at twenty-seven,
sad blackened bat-winged angel, my
new day not of light but a watery
nest. My new day roots beneath
a basement of guts but also rises
in the flash of my falling there.
Though none
of its light comes down to me the ark of its
rising sails.

So again I see my-
self afloat inside this Boat of
Years,
a raft of tears as Elvin's
drumset pretends to break
down. At the upper reach of
each run I
reach earthward, fingers blurred
while Jimmy's wrist-action
dizzies the sun. I see my ears cocked
Eastward, eyes barely open,
beads
of sweat across my brow like rain.

Quivering
reed between implosive teeth, Nut's tethered son,
I groan the ache of Our Lady's earth-
encumbered arch, the bell of my axe
become a wall whose bricks I
dabble on in blood as if neediness

                                      fed us,
     the blemishless flesh of her bone-goddess
         body giving birth to gloom cursing,
                                          "Heal
dank world. Goodbye. I'm thru,"
                             all
       "three" of us breathless now,
     so abruptly unborn again.

                           But all such
     abortion compels me inward. With
         bleeding fist I paw this pelvic
     strath and straining ask myself to
what will Night carry me next? *ta'wil*
                                   to where?

         pray softly, *Breath be with me*
             always, bend me East of
             all encumbrance, heave the
             moist earth ecstatic under
                             grass.

         I grope thru smoke to glimpse New
York City, the Village Gate, late
     '65. I sit at the bar drinking scotch between
     sets, some kid comes up and says he'd
         like to hear "Equinox."

                           We play "Out of
         This World" instead, the riff hits
     me like rain and like a leak in my
         throat it won't quit. No reins whoa
             this ghost I'm ridden by and again
                                   I'm asking
         myself what "climb" will Nut ask of
             me next? *ta'wil* to where?
                             to what love
     turned into loss by my getting there
     as Night's reign whips on to where
                                   someday
         weaned of time's ghosted light we
     begin again, our Boat as was in
                             the beginning,
             the sea itself?

                      137

Next I'm sipping
wine while hearing my muse try to
tell me which door I came in thru.
Her thread of words a white froth at our
feet as I forget myself,
limbs as
though they were endlessly afloat,
a flood of
wreckage barters wood against incestuous
dust.

Her splintered ships clog the sea of new
beginnings. Beyond waking, walking
legless down where dreams unbottom our sleep,
soaked ruins of a raft on which
the world outlived itself to
bear the Heartbreak Church . . .
We sit
on pews cut from worm-infested wood.

The backs
of our necks caressed by African pillows,
the far side of her voice by
the flutter of birds blown out to sea . . .
While "each is both" we bask in
an air swept clean of all distance,

attended by bells . . .
Attended by
birds, in their beaks the hem of dawn's
lifted
skirts

CLARENCE MAJOR

Un Poco Loco

—for Bud

to start, I have to draw blood,
find the right weakness,
show my grief,

just to get things moving:
sweep a bit,
and since what I'm after
is so abstract, I bump
harder into chrome,
into the cluttered tables.

This one nearly killed me:
a lover I never wanted
to see again, a half empty
glass of wine, lipstick
stuck in its brass tube,
a Cupid nailed to a globe,
half of an apple.

To keep going, I think:
disconnected thoughts:
Riviera chatter.
Obvious horror. Magic passion.
Phoenicians. Redneck chew-tobacco.

To keep going I watch
my grandmother hold the chicken
by its legs: bauk bauk bauk!
Walter this time.
Bar-be-cue bed on a china
platter? Cluck-cluck went
last Sunday. It was a start.

Keep going: the work
is the person: Peter
standing there like that,
silent, before two hundred
people. Yes, that's the answer,
the work itself: everyone
else missed. We reflect. He is.
There's no time to stop.

On the other hand, my uncle
cut the chicken's throat: let
the blood gush: Baaaaauk!

There's no time to stop:
for sickness or Dine or clever
lines or the upshot or the right note.

No time to remember precisely:
two glasses left on the floor
beside two of us, gone
down to the level of plant
life, where we look
so mysterious and lovely
nobody's going to give
one good scream
whether we sprout
next spring or not. This is
the problem with a complete thing!
Praise its respect for life,
but you can't lead it away
from the water
it wants to drink.
It'll kick your brains out!

Nazis drew blood a certain way.
They started something
they couldn't finish:
they nailed cupids to crosses
and fed apples to snakes,
raped on the Riviera
and kicked holes through
the dance motion of abstract
paintings I expected to see
later in Budapest, where leaves
on trees, birds on skies, blew
Bird and whispered Monk intimacies.
The Nazies, like the Ku Klux Klansmen,
had no means for appreciating
the squatting Pawnee at the edge
of Blue Lake.

The Pawnee is not going
to get nailed into a frame
of the Great American West.
Custer points his six-shooter
at the Indian's back: only
white space, the page's margin
between them: gun goes off:
a fluke of nature: I bleed.

To start again? I try
for egalitarian freakiness:

to go on: the light has to be
just right. I'm going to shoot
the scene before me: here:
Phyllis with that calculating
smile, slightly leaning over.
Just like that!
And perhaps your brother
at the piano with polished finger-
nails: making bobwhite sounds,
Pawnee whistles: starting
always from scratch.

Take one. Take two. Dis-
connect and start over:
Okay: there are no miracles.
Being a little crazy
isn't the result of a
volcanic eruption. Being
a little off, places you
in touch with Jene Ballentine's
"Born Free, 1968," with
Whistler's gray and pink, with
lava and its flow.

Let's do it again: from the top:
It's not Art Deco, not loco-
motives of brilliant returns
from sparkling cities,
the polished nipples
perched atop Byzantine temples;
no, no, no: it's the return
to the unanticipated start
that continues to count:
one two three: go! I press
on—to build, to swirl up,
sibilant, oscillating,
without government support.

Dangling occasionally. Sure.
I'm electric. Colors remain
pure. The columns won't shift.
Variety keeps the boats adrift.
Blue Lake absorbs the blood
and flows on, still blue.

141

DIONISIO D. MARTINEZ

Three or Four Shades of Blues

(after Charles Mingus)

These days in Europe no one is safe.
The terrorist who works at the newsstand
will tell you his country's government
is like a jazz band that improvises badly
and too often. His accomplice will say
the Prado museum is not a good shelter:
if someone walks in with a saxophone full
of explosives, Guernica will burn again.
He has figured out what it will take
to blow up the canvas, to bring down
every building in Madrid. The streets
will swallow you like night rain.
These days the European rain falls
through the roofs of the jazz clubs,
but no one seems to notice: no one leaves
before the last note of *Cryin' Blues* is
dead and the last wine glass broken.
Then they all go out for walks, thinking
that the streets are only streets. They
pass the museum and make plans to go in
someday. A woman says she's well acquainted
with an architect who assures her that
those walls will survive every jazz musician
in the continent. One of them overhears
this and says he's not convinced.
He wants to hock his five trombones and
move to Mexico before the next night rain.

Three or Four Shades of Blues (2)

If the revolution stops
we'll have to find work.
—Dialogue from a silent movie

The stress of Gijón are wider in the dark.
The tourists in the sidewalk cafés reach
for the stars that hang like overripe fruits
from the trees by their tables and squeeze
them until your music comes out of their hands.
Charlie, they know the titles better than the
names of their own children. They know that
the newsstand is dangerous, but they'll go
like pilgrims to buy yesterday's edition
of *The Herald Tribune* as if it were a relic.
Everybody knows it's published in Paris,
but it's the closest thing to home.
They'll read for the first time about
the jazz festival and the drummer whose house
blew up one morning while he slept or listened
to an old composition you might have played.
Even music is dangerous. On any wall along
these streets, behind the posters advertising
next week's concert, there are political
slogans. I'm like the drunk I met in Madrid
who kept telling me he didn't care who
ran the country as long as he was free to
sell his poetry and buy a few beers. But
I'm intrigued by anyone who tries to cover
up an ideal on a wall, intrigued by anyone
who wants to make us forget a date, say
4 October 1934. Charlie, even music
is political out here. They pitched a
circus tent on a square, showed silent movies
all night long and played your records instead
of an old piano. I imagined you behind
the screen, laughing at us, knowing that
the revolution isn't over until the last
mercenary spends all his blood money at the
jazz club like a recently divorced tourist.

143

WILLIAM MATTHEWS

Alice Zeno Talking, and Her Son George Lewis the Jazz Clarinetist in Attendance

Now if all of you were gone
I could sing those songs in a row
without stopping, but since you're here
they've all flown out of my head
like that many birds. It makes her
so happy to say this she won't laugh.
She began in Creole French and didn't
switch to English until her son came in,
sixty, in a rumpled suit, and sat,
his long-fingered hands not so much at rest
in his lap as asleep. *I believe I know*
this genneman here. Her interviewer's glad
to drop his paltry French and Ft. Wayne
accent. There's whisper and scuffle
and somebody goes out for Cokes.
My great-grandmother came over
from Senegal when she was eight,
and her mother's name was Zaire.
She hovers a second at *great* to get
the number of generations right.
Some of the songs go back that far.
This is great stuff, her interviewers
think—they're folklorists—but she
means something else. "Are any
of those songs about slavery?" *No,*
actually, but a lot of them
are about freedom. They're trying
to link her to a theory of the past.
Creole? Creole born from here.
Silence. They can be heard riffling
for a next question, and it's about
a song to which she knows and recites
the words. Her voice is low, as usual.
Her son's trumpeter for years, Kid
Howard, seldom played above the staff—
that was George-domain up there,

and George wound his loops and kerf
around the melody the band
had to tend so George could
curl and twine. The great Baptist hymns
he played straight as a Catholic boy,
ever a good guest to the earth, could arrange.
Even those hymns he played sexy,
she used to think but never say.
And isn't the clarinet strait as the gate?
That rain-soft tone, but urgent enough. . . .
In the low register the clarinet
can make you shiver and ripple
with goosebumps and can send
its breath-drenched messages
through arms and legs that show
no passing force inside or out, but hum
like telephone wires in wind.
I'm so old I can't remember a lot
and every day now I'm glad for,
I give something away the chirrun
will need later on. It's chirrun
the music is for, that's what I say.
George doesn't speak on this topic
but thinks how music is not to forget,
that music is about time
and not to be afraid of it,
but to deliver by hand raw meat
to the lion's mouth, and to praise
what is fearful. George shifts in his chair.
"Can you sing that song you just said
the lyrics to?" the interviewer asks.
A pause. *I did.* "No, Mama," says George,
and his voice could be drying a dish
after a holiday meal, "you didn't sing
it, you spoke it." *I did,* she says, and means
that's that. More silence. Love's been
keeping time all along and comes in on the beat,
explicit. She's loved that boy for sixty
years, and his brother, too. *Gracious knows*
I used to sing sing sing those boys
to sleep when they were only babies.

Blues for John Coltrane, Dead at 41

Although my house floats on a lawn
as plush as a starlet's body
and my sons sleep easily,
I think of death's salmon breath
leaping back up the saxophone
with its wet kiss.

Hearing him dead,
I feel it in my feet
as if the house were rocked
by waves from a soundless speedboat
planing by, full throttle.

Bmp Bmp

for James McGarrell

Lugubriously enough they're playing
Yes We Have No Bananas at deadpan
half-tempo, and Bechet's beginning
to climb like a fakir's snake,
as if that boulevard-broad vibrato
of his could claim space in the air,
out of the low register. Here comes
a spurious growl from the trombone,
and here comes a flutter of tourist
barrelhouse from the pianist's left hand.
Life is fun when you're good at something
good. Soon they'll do the *Tin Roof Blues*
and use their 246 years
of habit and convention hard.
Now they're headed out and everyone
stops to let Bechet inveigle his way
through eight bars unaccompanied
and then they'll doo dah doo dah doo
bmp bmp. Bechet's in mid-surge as usual
by his first note, which he holds, wobbles
and then pinches off to a staccato spat
with the melody. For a moment this stupid,
lumpy and cynically composed little money-

146

magnet of a song is played poor and bare
as it is, then he begins to urge it out
from itself. First a shimmering gulp
from the tubular waters of the soprano sax,
in Bechet's mouth the most metallic
woodwind and the most fluid, and then
with that dank air and airborne tone
he punches three quarter-notes
that don't appear in the song but should.
From the last of them he seems to droop,
the way in World War II movies
planes leaving the decks of aircraft carriers
would dip off the lip, then catch the right
resistance from wet air and strain up,
except he's playing against the regular disasters
of the melody his love for flight and flight's
need for gravity. And then he's up, loop
and slur and spiral, and a long, drifting note
at the top, from which, like a child decided
to come home before he's called, he begins to drift
back down, insouciant and exact, and ambles
in the door of the joyous and tacky chorus
just on time for the band to leave together,
headed for the *Tin Roof Blues.*

Bud Powell, Paris, 1959

I'd never seen pain so bland.
Smack, though I didn't call it smack
in 1959, had eaten his technique.
His white-water right hand clattered
missing runs nobody else would think
to try, nor think to be outsmarted
by. Nobody played as well
as Powell, and neither did he,
stalled on his bench between sets,
stolid and vague, my hero,
his mocha skin souring gray.
Two bucks for a Scotch in this dump,
I thought, and I bought me
another. I was young and pain
rose to my ceiling, like warmth,

147

like a story that makes us come true
in the present. Each day's
melodrama in Powell's cells
bored and lulled him. Pain loves pain
and calls it company, and it is.

Coleman Hawkins (d. 1969), RIP

As if that sax
were made of bone wrenched from his wrist
he urged through it dank music
of his breath. When he blew ballads
you knew one use of force:
withholding it.
This was a river of muscles.
Old dimes oily from handling,
eggs scrambled just right in a diner
after eight gigs in nine nights,
a *New Yorker* profile, a new Leica
for the fun of having one.
Gasps and twitches.
It's like having the breath
knocked out of me
and wearing the lost air for a leash.
I snuffle home.
I hate it that he's dead.

Listening to Lester Young

for Reg Saner

It's 1958. Lester Young minces
out, spraddle-legged as if pain
were something he could step over
by raising his groin, and begins
to play. Soon he'll be dead.
It's all tone now and tone
slurring toward the center
of each note. The edges that used to be
exactly ragged as deckle
are already dead. His embouchure

is wobbly and he's so tired
from dying he quotes himself,
easy to remember the fingering.

It's 1958 and a jazz writer is coming home
from skating in Central Park. Who's that
ahead? It's Lester Young! *Hey Pres,*
he shouts and waves, letting his skates
clatter. *You dropped your shit,* Pres says.

It's 1976 and I'm listening
to Lester Young through stereo equipment
so good I can hear his breath rasp,
water from a dry pond—,
its bottom etched, like a palm,
with strange marks, a language
that was never born
and in which palmists therefore
can easily read the future.

Unrelenting Flood

Black key. White key. No,
that's wrong. It's all tactile;
it's not the information
of each struck key we love,
but how the mind and leavened
heart travel by information.
Think how blind and near-
blind pianists range along
their keyboards by clambering
over notes a sighted man
would notice to leave out,
by stringing it all on one
longing, the way bee-fingered,
blind, mountainous Art
Tatum did, the way we like
joy to arrive: in such
unrelenting flood the only
way we can describe it
is by music or another
beautiful abstraction,

149

like the ray of sunlight
in a child's drawing
running straight to a pig's ear,
tethering us all to our star.

VICTORIA MCCABE

For Albert Ayler

> —*his works defied the norm.*
> —record blurb

You owned the surge and swill of water,
depths strange and murky as the Hudson.

Energy bash: honk and whirr: gut rhythms
of the ages.   Raucous snazz: now whine:
and boomboom hustled fine.   A crew of wolves
hovering in chorale: basic O's
thrashing through the horn in a black
fist: now *angst*:   now blast: the hushbomb
of some almost literal babe   fresh
into the human predicament: O
and it is painful, it is too
painful   Then: an old, chiding refrain
burppats the heart into journey: LIVE.
But O: the Nearly Unbearable Lucidity
of the river's silence, the stash of breath
done in, stopped.   by a sadsad neighbor
whose own wail this aylerman had stroked.
Ah whimper: ah bang: ah out, out, out:
cacophony of lovenoise   : blurt : of defiance——
O rage and understanding, more than worlds
ever allow.
            No wonder you died, unsung,
            your records unrealized, selling cheap.

KENNETH McCLANE

At the Bridge with Rufus

for James Baldwin

Once again the wind is howling and you, Rufus,
shall take that long shoreless journey back,
back into life, back where the alleys seem silent glaciers, the trees
bare indexes of themselves: Rufus, once again the wind howls
    and you remove yourself beyond any music:

Rufus, you hear the river: it calls
like some ill-fashioned gravity, a pact
honed when the stomach gnarled for bread—when you
(your own voice an accompaniment) forgot
    your family, forgot us, *forgot*
that we wrapped you in wind-tough sacrament, kept you
    (as we would others of prophecy):

But Rufus, you left us like a syphilitic:
you forgot the *beat,* the rich thump, the arpeggio
    which makes the knees jelly: Rufus,
        when the river called, you should have looked thither, let
the walls quake, the loneliness
    swim out some side window: But I understand

The river is strong at its source. Dangerous
it moves us past what we know.
I, too, have crept to that high place and looked outward.
Yes, it is hell. Yes, the voices open
like sweet music: and you, always you, the wind, the scream for blood:

And you, Rufus, the last symbol.

Rufus, heroes *live.*
And you, fulfilling that other exactitude (showing how the axis pulls
equally, plunges into worlds and afterworlds): Rufus, you showed us
not how to live but how mighty the cost:

Rufus, you gave yourself to the wind.
It howls.
You gave yourself.
And the rest of us must go back to the dark city.

COLLEEN J. MCELROY

The Singer

She sings, looks young
Carries visions of pop tunes
Better than the lines under her eyes.
Her freedom's fluid;
Moving with the length of a mike cord
And style that mellows with tears.
Liquid voice jazzing the standards;
No name in New York,
New name at some one name bar
Whose only light's a torch
Offered by a blind man
Picking up a dead whore.
Success stands at the door,
Drunk, asking her to sing
It blue just once more;
Play it slow
For his lost lover
And another drink.

Those lines around her nose
Frame her tunes.
She works the verse
With a virgin's touch,
Then snaps it like a tart.
Her dress caught in a bevel
Of light at waist and breast
Accent an empty house;
Another set, with the drummer
Struggling to follow her hips.
She pulls the next note
From her thighs,
Throws her shoulders high;
A star, balancing
Sex and song.
Eyes heavy lidded,
Full lips
Crooning for two more days
And food;
She pulsates on the last note,
Carrying the song like a crown.

HEATHER McHUGH

Sleep, after Ray Charles Show and Hurricane Report

A storm named for a woman
was born as a mild
disturbance off Africa.
It broke into interiors

of pianos, blew the tubes
of trees and went on
record with weed for its whistle.
Now, bystanding, I

come down with a blessed
attack of the dance. I am white
trash, brother, one more basket
case. You boss the winds

like nobody's business, but nobody
can bear or see himself.
Life is the mother
with murder in her eye, and we

are junked and treasured,
every one regardless.

JACK MICHELINE

Blues Poem

I got no smile cause I'm down
I carry a horn to blow in all these streets
A solo riff out of my head
How could you ever know I feel
So high on life and feet and ass and legs and thighs
That I can rise and dance with all the stars
And I can eat the moon and laugh and I can cry

153

The dark caves of cities hungry streets
The tired faces dark and dreary bent
and all the death it dies
I let it die
I lift my horn and blow some sounds
some soul for kids to come
Some unborn sun
in darker streets than mine
Magicians carry wings so they can fly
Let's blow a horn and love
Let's get on it and ride
and laugh and dance and jive
Let's shake the dead and let the downers die
The magic of the singers warms the earth
A song
A poem
Some paradise of mind
I got to smile now
I'm feeling good
The city street
The palace of my mind

VASSAR MILLER

Dirge in Jazz Time

for Sophie Tucker

Her voice forever match to dry wood
Since, a girl, she sang for a crust,
Her innocence even then understood
As a subtler word for lust
As in age her wisdom would mean delight—
Red-hot Mama who is cold tonight.

Her voice in the veins of every man
Like radiant fire would glisten
Till his body, tuned ear, did nothing else than
Keep cocked to her tones and listen.

But the lilt in his bones has taken flight,
Since Red-hot Mama is cold tonight.

"One of these days you'll miss me." Oh yes,
Though they couldn't credit it then
That she who had flashed in a sequined dress
And danced in the nerves of men
Should have given them this terrible slight,
Not Red-hot Mama grown cold tonight!

Turn the spotlight down on the nightclub floor.
Let the jazzmen muffle their drums
And their saxophones she will hear no more
Where winter forever numbs,
Where no one can warm her whose heart burned bright,
Where Red-hot Mama is cold tonight.

ROGER MITCHELL

For Stephane Grappelli

He got a rhythm in his wrist so quick
it sprinkles, if it doesn't thatfast jump
from here to here. I never thought a pump
motion could calibrate a wigglestick
so satisfyingly. And by what trick
of ear, or is it eye, can a slow slump
or swoop make noodle out of an old lump
of dough like this? I do not have the brick
with which to make my point, how flat or hard
or squared off, red, you name the property,
a thing can be and still be candy. Lard
is not more slick than butter, but it's three
to one the tootle of the hot club jarred
the jelly in the jam of his Paree.

JOHN MONTGOMERY

Snowmelt from Yesteryears

They said there were those who dig and those who blow;
These were the only ones; the rest was illusion
And Neal said if you want to live high, get high
And Jack wrote it plain as John Hancock and in
The effete East they said that wasn't
What Damrosch meant at all. And it took hold
And a groundswell from the nickel seats
Rose till they blew Philharmonic jazz at
The Metropolitan and in Moscow their metropolitan,
A cat in black spats wailed "dhzaz is cool, baby"
Long, long before Kissinger thought of playing
Them Mendelssohn on the black keys for white nights in tails

O much was entailed, even back to *Ou sont les nieges d'antan?*

The snows of yesteryear

Dylan Thomas wrote once, "The weather turned around".
21 years have turned since Dylan sang his last song,
Years of the beat generation. The poets of the campuses
Sound like Kerouac now; even Creeley
May come down from that eleven-year high . . .
Veteran young poets from the War to save the World
For Henry Miller are autographing collector's copies
For the dowager never dies But the weather turned around.
The beat generation marched and countermarched;
The poem about Jesus in Ferlinghetti's jive
Boiled trustees from Columbia to Chula Vista and Buddha
Fielded the puck; and battles, engagements, skirmishes,
Expeditions of sex against society still streak
Like the man against the sky, still unfurl
A new kind of Old Glory from Seattle Burlesque
To the topless towers of St. Petersburg on south.

 Envoi

Jack and Neal and Lew are gone; Kesey's pranksters
Are birling logs and boiling blueberries. Jets set

156

Soot on the snows of yesteryear. Major Corso,
Squadron Leader Holmes, like Benteen, are counting
                              the notches and scalps.

Envoi Encore

The hydro-surveyors of the grad schools
Have the snows of yesteryear in tube cores.
The wind off the snow is moaning low, dad or chick:
"The drums give a feeling of something present"
Whether your path a swath or strath,
Your Miller Glenn or Henry.

Et Encore une Fois

No one but you will generate where it was at, cat:
        watch your feet when your skull catches
                    the beat

JACK MUELLER

Death Jazz: A Review

*America has only given two arts to
the world: plumbing and jazz.*
—Anonymous

Stuck in a club with a group that calls itself
The USA Trio, I didn't mind because I was there
Before they set up, and besides, it's my neighborhood.

They introduced themselves as the three branches
Of government, a balance of powers. A few people giggled
And I kept on talking to Susu about Miles.

They played such sad, emasculated jazz
We walked away, muttering about a government
So out of touch with real people and their music,

Half-tamed and still in love.

157

LISEL MUELLER

January Afternoon, with Billie Holiday

for Studs Terkel

Her voice shifts as if it were light,
from chalk to parchment to oil.
I think of the sun this morning,
how many knives were flashed
through black, compliant trees;
now she has aged it with her singing,
turned it to milk thinned with water,
a poor people's sun, enough
knowledge to go around.

I want to dance, to bend
as gradually as a flower,
release a ball in slow motion
to follow in the marvelous path
of an unfolding jet streak,
love's expansive finger
across the cheek of the sky,
"Heaven, I'm in heaven . . ."

The foolish old songs were right,
the heart does, actually, ache
from trying to push beyond
itself, this room, the world,
all that can be imagined;
space is not enough space
for its sudden immensity

I am not what you think
This is not what I wanted

Desire has no object, it simply happens,
rises and floats, lighter than air—
but she knows that. Her voice scrapes
against the innocent words of the song;
tomorrow is something she remembers.

HARRYETTE MULLEN

Playing the Invisible Saxophone
en el Combo de las Estrellas

for Vangie

One of these days I'm gonna write a real performance poem.
A poem that can grab the microphone and sing
till voice becomes music, and music dance.
A boogie poem sparkled with star presence.

The way I'll score it, poem gonna dance into melody.
(Let me tell you, this poem can move!)
And the way I'll choreograph the words,
each sound be a musical note
that flies off the page like some crazy blackbird.

Yeah, gonna have words turning into dance,
bodymoving music,
a get-down poem so kinetically energetic
it sure put disco to shame.
Make it a snazzy jazzy poem extravaganza, with pizzazz.
Poem be going solo,
flying high on improbable improvisational innovation.
Poem be blowing hard!

Want to speak a wordsong that moves folks' minds
and gets em up dancing to their own heartbeats.
Poem, say some words that jump into the blood
and tapdance in the pulse like rainfall.
Gonna let the rhythm of this poem
soak through the skin like rain into earth.

Let me play musician magician,
growing out my sleeve a poem that raises cane,
Poem so sweet, be my magical musical instrument,
flashing back the spotlight's spectrum as meteoric shower.
And poem, shoot off sparks like comets with tails of fire
as I play the invisible saxophone *en el combo de las estrellas.*

159

Jazz Poem for the Girl Who Cried Wolf

just one too many times:
wolf at the cabin in the country
wolf on the subway wolf on the freeway
wolf at the station and wolf on the wagon
wolf on the whistle-stop tour
of the obscure geographies of her mind

and wolf on the way up-town
wolf on the way down-town
wolf when it was only the wind
that whined at our door.
Wolf like a note left on the window—
still I'M GOING OUT OF MY MIND.

Wolf in the pantry wolf on the porch
wolf as a weapon and wolf as a crutch
wolf as a seizure at 5 in the morning
wolf as a reason for not being there.
Crying wolf is a way not to be there.
Wolf when I came and wolf when I left

wolf when I walked out that whelmed up
inside her and tore at her fine clothes
and tore at her throat and tore at her hair
and ran to the windows and ran to the doors
and ran to the phone and ran to the basement
ran to the radio and out on the street below

and it was only the wind.
It was just being there.

Just being there.

Presenting Eustacia Beauchaud: Ward 3

Eustacia Beauchaud
combed her bozzo

red wig into the Frenchiest
of twists and never missed.
Shot down from Geriatrics
for alleged obscene advances
on a twice-stumped catatonic
she cousined all the kookies
on the spot and said her name
meant good and hot.

In faded brocade she flung
her years all seventy-six
down the echoless hall
of Acutely Disturbed.
With a fox-trot flutter
and a revlon wink
she gave us the word
that you're only as young
as you think   which lit
a few lima-bean eyes
dampened by months of therapy
who caressed the gift
incomprehensively
then let it drop.

With rouge as thick as licorice
and some lipstick oulala
and that slightly ompah strut
(her spirits all played tubas)
she told us she was Lady Levee
and had spooned with Old Man River—
a plantation queen she had been
aunt of the mayor of New Orleans:

       If I had my d'rathers
she sang
       I'd rather be down in old Louisiana.

The happy thump of her jazz piano
cured the bristly wino up the corridor
who gurgled her repertoire constantly
somewhere hot deep in his throat.

Evenings mounted like bordello
brawls down in Recreation Therapy.

161

A southern belle forgets like hell
I heard her hoot at the TV premiere
of *Hush . . . Hush, Sweet Charlotte*
as she was being helped to the toilet.

Always around Individual Lock Up
time she would tell the story ending
pull his tail the nigra told me
that's how you get a horse to work
and then slap herself into a giddy-up with
        We're just twenty-five minutes from Canal Street
        Let's go see the parade.
While orderlies jangled keys she finaled
by raising the beautiful varicose blue
of her leg to the keyboard to pick out Dixie
with her spiked heel of her pointed shoe
and then the black boys in white
would put her to bed
for the night.

FRANK O'HARA

The Day Lady Died

It is 12:20 in New York a Friday
three days after Bastille Day, yes
it is 1959 and I go get a shoeshine
because I will get off the 4:19 in Easthampton
at 7:15 and then go straight to dinner
and I don't know the people who will feed me

I walk up the muggy street beginning to sun
and have a hamburger and a malted and buy
an ugly NEW WORLD WRITING to see what the poets
in Ghana are doing these days
                I go on to the bank
and Miss Stillwagon (first name Linda I once heard)
doesn't even look up my balance for once in her life
and in the GOLDEN GRIFFIN I get a little Verlaine
for Patsy with drawings by Bonnard although I do

162

think of Hesiod, trans. Richmond Lattimore or
Brendan Behan's new play or *Le Balcon* or *Les Nègres*
of Genet, but I don't, I stick with Verlaine
after practically going to sleep with quandariness

and for Mike I just stroll into the PARK LANE
Liquor Store and ask for a bottle of Strega and
then I go back where I came from to 6th Avenue
and the tobacconist in the Ziegfeld Theatre and
casually ask for a carton of Gauloises and a carton
of Picayunes, and a NEW YORK POST with her face on it

and I am sweating a lot by now and thinking of
leaning on the john door in the FIVE SPOT
while she whispered a song along the keyboard
to Mal Waldron and everyone and I stopped breathing

KENNETH PATCHEN

Latesummer Blues

(In a Variety of Keys)

Well, the grass is a pleasant thing,
Blue of the sky against its green—
And the peaceful wind and water singing
Perhaps of an ancient queen
Who sleeps in another kingdom now;
And the sun, like a gentle hand, scattering
His gifts down on the peoples of this world
Who seem to have turned from all wonders now.

A battered hat, a torn shoe filled with gray sand . . .
Now that's where Gizzle Ruly went, down where the colder fishes stand.
I know, I know,
If it doesn't rain, the grass won't grow . . .
But have you heard
From Shammy Pistonrod and Kubber-Bubber Ned?
Huh! no word
Of that magic bird
Whose gland they thought would fetch the moxie back

163

When youth had fled?
What news of Lem the-Human-Toiletseat?
Remember his noon-day snack—
Two buckets of eels, six oyster pies, and a couple sides of beef?
He's on a diet now, you say?
I see, I see,
Silence in his banquet hall, and eyeless waiters
    making free.

  Hua, huua,—the grinning wind
      runs along the ground
  "Flesh"—"spoon"—what other word
      or any human sound
  Can make much difference now? in this black wound
  "Light" and "button" mean the same.

  What have you found that the world may use?
  Blackened grime on an idiot's shoes.
  But where is the trust in man's high aim?
  Darkness waits at the heart of the flame.

A pink tea-rose gown all squished into a bloody wad . . .
Now that's what Irma Shannon got to wear before her God.
I know, I know,
Some of us stay, while some of us go . . .
The proudest bastard and the sorriest whore, etc.,
All get a little less, who'd have a little more, etc., etc.
But, Jesus! where are these poor human rivers
        supposed to flow?
Just take the case of Susan Hooker,
Nobody's dope and a top-class looker—
Yeah, Jack, that come-and-take-me grin,
Her teasing eyes, and flaming walk . . .
She'll have the angels off that pin!
I'll bet she made St. Peter gawk—
For she got hit
By a lad who was lit
On goofer-dancing snow.
Ah, any time you listen, kid,
You can hear them bitter winds a-blow.
So mentioned this to Sulliman, Grote, and
         Easy-Fingered Syd;
Who've got a patent out for an indestructible man
That's made in the image of a Lorkadorcus squid,

With a detachable soulborator on the X-D-7 band.
But what of Hurk the-Woggling-Can
and Dan-o Groob, the last of the famous
                                        Pohunkett earls?
Where's Seraphane & Cathotex & Joanocoxi
& all the rest of Yaakibazzy's pretty factory girls?
—O flow peacefully my beautiful Lepiwammatoxee
And let them sleep, you filthy lousy poisoned sewer!
How come the lives of people are wasted like so much manure!
I know, I know,
The latest tommy-gun for little Alfy, and take
                                        the missus to a show.
Ah, let you be ever so noble, Mr. Foxey,
You can't stop them blackened winds that blow
                                        and blow and blow . . .

O love, how the scarlet leaves are falling,
Thrown to the earth by a cold hand.
In the gray woods, so still in the falling
Dusk, all the sadness of life is held.
Since it's up to God no longer, but to men—
Who knows? summer may never come again.
Fire by a monstrous hatred fanned.

What have you there for the world to see?
Bloody rags beneath the tree.
But where is the faith in man's great hope?
Tattered rot at the end of a rope.

ROBERT PINSKY

History of My Heart

[Section I]

One Christmastime Fats Waller in a fur coat
Rolled beaming from a taxicab with two pretty girls
Each at an arm as he led them in a thick downy snowfall

Across Thirty-Fourth Street into the busy crowd
shopping at Macy's: perfume, holly, snowflake displays.
Chimes rang for change. In toys, where my mother worked

Over her school vacation, the crowd swelled and stood
Filling the aisles, whispered at the fringes, listening
To the sounds of the large, gorgeously dressed man,

His smile bemused and exalted, lips boom-booming a bold
Bass line as he improvised on an expensive, tinkly
Piano the size of a lady's jewel box or a wedding cake.

She put into my heart this scene from the romance of Joy,
Co-authored by her and the movies, like her others—
My father making the winning basket at the buzzer

And punching the enraged gambler who came onto the court—
The brilliant black and white of the movies, texture
Of wet snowy fur, the taxi's windshield, piano keys,

Reflections that slid over the thick brass baton
That worked the elevator. Happiness needs a setting:
Shepherds and shepherdesses in the grass, kids in a store,

The back room of Carly's parents' shop, record-player
And paper streamers twisted in two colors: what I felt
Dancing close one afternoon with a thin blonde girl

Was my amazing good luck, the pleased erection
Stretching and stretching at the idea *She likes me,*
She likes it, the thought of legs under a woolen skirt,

To see eyes "melting" so I could think *This is it,*
They're melting! Mutual arousal of suddenly feeling
Desired: *This is it: "desire"!* When we came out

Into the street we saw it had begun, the firm flakes
Sticking, coating the tops of cars, melting on the wet
Black street that reflected storelights, soft

Separate crystals clinging intact on the nap of collar
And cuff, swarms of them stalling in the wind to plunge
Sideways and cluster in spangles on our hair and lashes,

Melting to a fresh glaze on the bloodwarm porcelain
Of our faces, Hey nonny-nonny boom-boom, the cold graceful
Manna, heartfelt, falling and gathering copious

As the air itself in the small-town main street
As it fell over my mother's imaginary and remembered
Macy's in New York years before I was even born,

And the little white piano, tinkling away like crazy—
My unconceived heart in a way waiting somewhere like
Wherever it goes in sleep.

STERLING D. PLUMPP

I Hear the Shuffle of the People's Feet

i am a name clanging
against circles

i go round
in what's been said and done
the old puts leashes
on my eyes
i go round
in tribal wisdom

men walking from the sea
as if it is dry land
enter my circle
put me in a straight line
from profit to death
i turn from now
back to the past
they fold my future
in their bank accounts

they take me from hands
to memory
i move from knowledge

to obedience
i plant tobacco
i train sugarcane
i yessir masters
i go straight from sunrises
to death
when i remember
i chant shango
i sing ogun
i dance obatala
i hum orishas

i am folded in work
i get up
i obey
i rebel
i runaway
they beat production
from my bones
and track up my mind
with their language

after one generation
i go round in silence
while my children work
without ever knowing tribal hands
they echo my songs
until whips dull their voices

i survive dungeons
by singing songs shaped by brutality:
i sing new necessities
in a strange band
my songs carry
rhythmic cries of my journey
and when i dance
yes, when i dance
i revive tribal possessions
the elders' hands
twist my eyes on right
and let my body go

true believer, the whip
tells my mind

what to dream
i feel the blood of africa
dripping down my back

though my pride rises
in what i do
to destroy the masters' blade
sinning against my skin
true believer, i survive
yes, i survive, i keep going
though they take everything away
i survive america

my name is written
in blood-wrapped days
untold centuries of cruelty
but i survive
come into the union
through a crack
my fist made
i had experienced
breaking freedom holes
by laying underground railroads
by plotting at night
by striking blows

they closed equality's door
before i could enter
they sent me bluesing towns
facing hostility
with open-eyed moans
i get my woman
from the master's bed
but lose her to his kitchen
learn every road
from all my searching
and not one of them end at opportunity
they send me bluesing towns

when I get the vote
terror drives me into fear
the tar, ropes, and evil men
scar my name with blood
they puke their fright and weaknesses

on me
instead of on those who own our bones
though they slaughter
still they cannot stop my efforts
i survive
following rivers to cities
putting my story on brass and winds

i live tyranny down
by swinging with jazz
but the white man's word
places hinges on my sky
from the shadows
i hear plantations talk
the civil war
sets me free from legal whippings
but not from lashes

when booker t prayed conformity
at backseat rites
i could hear lynchees scream
i could hear frightened men cry
i walked with DuBois
at Niagara
they jailed my reputation
in smelly epithets
yet i survive their onslaught
distance between freedom and chains
is measured by steps from backseats
to defiance

i move by going
where there ain't no fields
going where bondage is to production
to the factory's commands
in detroit
chicago
cleveland and milwaukee
away from hot suns
away from boll weevils
away from droughts
to a new world

my music affirms demons
barking resistance in my veins

and i sing ragtime gospels
hi-de-hi-hos hoochie coochies
my girls and temptation walks
in leaving the land
my legacy is transformed
in citified jive sayings

they take me to the work line
but leave my freedom at the station
listening to rails retell the places
i have not arrived at yet
i am still motherless
yet a hip-cat-rhinehart-zoot-suiting
malcolming wolf-waters shoeshine stone
i am a bigger bad trigger greedy
no-name boy prowling chitown
they put ethel in my waters
and she emerges lady day
pestering orchards of my soul
she-goddess of this strangeness
lady instrumentalized voice
tingling new sounds in new times

what the whip and lynchings
didn't get on the land
hard work, high prices, and the hawk
took away on these streets
they send me bluesing towns
"i ain't got nobody/got nobody
just me and my telephone"
i burn from exploitation
i empty my soul on fads
powdery substances Messiahs stand on

i mau-mau stampedes
against racist stalls
bellowing "for your precious love
means more to me
than any love can ever be"
the work songs rise
to become freedom anthems

the Supreme Court hears my lyrics
and its laws change beats
"separate but equal"

becomes "equality for all"
malcolm speaks/speaks so sweet
i hear the shuffle of the peoples' feet
we move in montgomery
we move in little rock
we move
we move at sit-in counters
we move on freedom rides
we move
we move in birmingham
we move on registration drives
we move
malcom speaks/speaks so sweet.

doin the riot/i fall from new bags
with a world fighting back
in viet nam
in angola
in mozambique
in the panther walks
poppa gotta rebellion thing
momma wears a freedom ring
freedom rings
from every alley and hole
brother, come here quick
take this struggle stick
freedom rings
the get black
burning too
take all the streets
do the boogaloo
freedom rings
feel so good
black out loud
dancing in the streets
with the fighting crowd

doin the riot
the burning too
throwing molotov cocktails
making black power new

we move
malcolm speaks/speaks so sweet.
i hear the shuffle of the peoples' feet

ISHMAEL REED

Poetry Makes Rhythm in Philosophy

Maybe it was the Bichot
Beaujolais, 1970
But in an a.m. upstairs on
Crescent Ave. I had a conversation
with K.C. Bird

We were discussing
rhythm and I said
"Rhythm makes everything move
the seasons swing
it backs up the elements
Like walking Paul-Chamber's fingers"

"My worthy constituent"
Bird said, "The Universe is a
spiralling Big Band in a
polka-dotted speakeasy,
effusively generating new light
every one-night stand"

We agreed that nature can't
do without rhythm but rhythm can
get along without nature

This rhythm, a stylized Spring
conducted by a blue-collared man
in *Keds* and denims

(His Williamsville swimming pool
shaped like a bass clef)
in Baird Hall
on Sunday afternoons
Admission Free!
All *harrumphs!* must be
checked in at
the door

I wanted to spin
Bennie Moten's
"It's Hard to Laugh or Smile"

173

but the reject wouldn't automate
and the changer refused to drop
"Progress," you know

Just as well
because Bird vanished

A steel band had
entered the room

KENNETH REXROTH

Written to Music

EIGHT FOR ORNETTE'S MUSIC

if the pain is greater
than the difference
as the bird in the night
or the perfumes in the moon
oh witch of question
oh lips of submission
in the flesh of summer
the silver slipper
in the sleeping forest
if hope surpasses the question
by the mossy spring
in the noon of harvest
between the pillars of silk
in the luminous difference
oh tongue of music
oh teacher of splendor
if the meat of the heart
if the fluid of the wing
as love
if birth
or trust as
love as love

is it dreaming falling in
the tangling light
calls the light
the small sharp wafers
in the whirlpool
on white plume
floating
in the sky the blades
nibbling the breasts
new trembling
discover honey
kiss kiss

She didn't say where

nobody home
they all left
lipstick letters stockings
torn
a star
on the sooty pane
deep in the far off forest
initials and hearts entwined
nobody ever comes back
night planes
over village sky rockets

the most wonderful one
we ever had
darling
in the drawer
the chambermaid
found 1000
counterfeit
$10 bills

then the waning
moon in young leaves
do you think of the old wounds
it is like Mykenai
with those terrible
dead kings with gold foil
over their faces
no animal or vegetable

anywhere
another landscape
with some people in a boat
sewn with needles or with thread
birds with dry human voices

who issues certificates
to whom it may concern:
the bearer is alive
turn on the sky
take off your dress
saw down the tree
climb the mountain
kiss the lips
close the eyes
speak low
open
come

time turns like tables
the indifferent and blissful Spring
saves all souls and seeds and slaves asleep
dark Spring
in the dark whispering human will
words spoken by two kissing tongues
hissing union
Eve's snake
stars come on
two naked bodies tumble
through bodiless Christmas trees
blazing like bees and rosebuds
fire turns to falling powder
lips relax and smile and sleep
fire sweeps
the hearth of the blood
on far off red double stars
they probate their own tied wills

the sea will be deep
the eye will be deep
the last bell has been deep

the iceberg has been cold
the nail has been cold
the hungry whore was cold

the jungle was fierce
the tooth was fierce
the poor bum's woman is fierce

the plate of tripe is shallow
the omelette in the pan is shallow
shallow as the wisdom of the ages

the hawk in the zenith knows
the mole under the spade knows
the curly brain knows too

don't you forget it

grey as the arctic
grey as the sea
grey as the heart
grey as the bird in the tree

red as the sun
red as the robin
red as the heart
red as the axe in the tree

blue as the star
blue as the gull
blue as the heart
blue as the air in the tree

black as the tongue
black as the vulture
black as the heart
black as the hanged girl in the tree

TWO FOR BREW AND DOCK

State and 32nd, Cold Morning Blues

A girl in a torn chemise
Weeps by a dirty window.
Jaws are punched in the street.

A cat is sick in the gutter.
Dogs bark up nightbound alleys.
There's nothing like the sorrow

177

Of the jukeboxes at dawn.
Dice girls going home.
Whores eating chop suey.

Pimps eat chile mac.
Drowsy flatfeet, ham and eggs.
Dawn of labor, dawn of life.

The awakening noises
Of the old sacrifices.
The snow blows down the bare street

Ahead of the first streetcar.
The lovers light cigarettes,
And part with burning eyes,

And go off in the daylight.

Married Blues

I didn't want it, you wanted it.
Now you've got it you don't like it.
You can't get out of it now.

Pork and beans, diapers to wash,
Too poor for the movies, too tired to love.
There's nothing we can do.

Hot stenographers on the subway.
The grocery boy's got a big one.
We can't do anything about it.

You're only young once.
You've got to go when your time comes.
That's how it is. Nobody can change it.

Guys in big cars whistle.
Freight trains moan in the night.
We can't get away with it.

That's the way life is.
Everybody's in the same fix.
It will never be any different.

KATE RUSHIN

The Black Back-Ups

This is dedicated to Merry Clayton, Cissy Houston, Vonetta Washington, Dawn, Carrietta McClellen, Rosie Farmer, Marsha Jenkins and Carolyn Williams. This is for all of the Black women who sang back-up for Elvis Presley, John Denver, James Taylor, Lou Reed, Etc. Etc. Etc.

I said Hey Babe
Take a Walk on the Wild Side
I said Hey Babe
Take a Walk on the Wild Side

And the colored girls say

Do dodo do do dodododo
Do dodo do do dodododo
Do dodo do do dodododo ooooo

This is for my Great Grandmother Esther, my Grandmother Addie, my Grandmother called Sister, my Great Aunt Rachel, my Aunt Hilda, my Aunt Tine, my Aunt Breda, my Aunt Gladys, my Aunt Helen, my Aunt Ellie, my Cousin Barbara, my Cousin Dottie and my Great Great Aunt Vene

This is dedicated to all of the Black women riding on buses and subways Back and forth to the Main Line, Haddonfield, N.J., Cherry Hill and Chevy Chase. This is for those women who spend their summers in Rockport, Newport, Cape Cod and Camden, Maine. This is for the women who open bundles of dirty laundry sent home from ivy-covered campuses

And the colored girls say

Do dodo do do dodododo
Do dodo do do dodododo
Do dodo do do dodododo ooooo

Jane Fox   Jane Fox
Calling Jane Fox
Where are you Jane?

My Great Aunt Rachel worked for the Foxes
Ever since I can remember

179

There was The Boy
Whose name I never knew
And there was The Girl
Whose name was Jane

My Aunt Rachel brought Jane's dresses for me to wear
Perfectly Good Clothes
And I should've been glad to get them
Perfectly Good Clothes
No matter they didn't fit quite right
Perfectly Good Clothes Jane
Brought home in a brown paper bag with an air of
Accomplishment and excitement
Perfectly Good Clothes
Which I hated

It's not that I have anything *personal* against *you* Jane

It's just that I felt guilty
For hating those clothes

I mean
Can you get to the irony of it Jane?

And the colored girls say

Do dodo do do dodododo
Do dodo do do dodododo
Do dodo do do dodododo ooooo

At school
In Ohio
I swear to Gawd
There was always somebody
Telling me that the only person
In their whole house
Who listened and understood them
Despite the money and the lessons
Was the housekeeper
And I knew it was true
But what was I supposed to say?

I know it's true
I watch them getting off the train

And moving slowly toward the Country Squire
With their uniform in their shopping bag
And the closer they get to the car
The more the two little kids jump and laugh
And even the dog is about to
Turn inside out
Because they just can't wait until she gets there
Edna Edna   Wonderful Edna
(But Aunt Edna to me, or Gram, or Miz Johnson, or Sister
Johnson on Sundays)

And the colored girls say

Do dodo do do dodododo
Do dodo do do dodododo
Do dodo do do dodododo ooooo

This is for Hattie McDaniels, Butterfly McQueen, Ethel Waters
Saphire
Saphronia
Ruby Begonia
Aunt Jemima
Aunt Jemima on the Pancake Box
Aunt Jemima on the Pancake Box?
AuntJemimaonthepancakebox?
auntjemimaonthepancakebox?
Ainchamamaonthepancakebox?
Ain't chure Mama on the pancake box?

Mama Mama
Get offa that damn box
And come home to me

And my Mama leaps offa that box
She swoops down in her nurse's cape
Which she wears on Sunday
And on Wednesday night prayer meeting
And she wipes my forehead
And she fans my face for me
And she makes me a cup o' tea
And it don't do a thing for my real pain
Except she is my Mama
Mama Mommy Mommy Mammy Mammy
Mam-mee Mam-mee

I'd Walk a mill-yon miles
For one o' your smiles

This is for the Black Back-ups
This is for my mama and your mama
My grandma and your grandma
This is for the thousand thousand Black Back-Ups

And the colored girls say

Do dodo do do dodododo
Do   do do   do   do
   Do   do
                              do
Do
                do

IRA SADOFF

At the Half-Note Cafe

for Gene Ammons

Once I heard him play
"Willow Weep for Me"
in a tone so full
and sentimental, I felt
a gap between my ribs
and lungs, a dearth of air
sorrow soon enough would fill.
I found the blues unfair
to boys like me who came to bars
unprepared for grief
that wasn't strictly personal

I told my girl
I knew all you had to know
about suffering and love, but when
I heard a woman drunk, cry out,
in front of everyone, "Don't go, Jug—

182

I'll give you all of what you want,"
my face went blank
and limp as an infant
when a stranger shakes
a rattle in his face. Later,
when he hit bottom,
the last broken chorus
of "Body and Soul," I collapsed in
my girl's arms, my composure crushed
by one note on the saxophone.
I couldn't think of what to tell her.
What the hell did she know anyhow?
We both came from the same suburban town.

It was a brittle winter night.
We had nowhere to go
except her parents' house,
so we drifted down Greenwich Ave.
hand in hand. I'd never seen
streets so crowded after dark—
with drunks, half-dead, and kids
who should have been in bed.
I'm shocked we made it out alive.
I know if I'd seen my stupid grin,
my wide-eyed stare, my gaping face,
I would have smashed it
just for the experience. We were lucky
though we didn't know it then. We ended up
parking in my mother's car. We kissed,
then stripped off her blouse,
grabbed her breast,
put her stiffened nipple in my mouth.

SONIA SANCHEZ

a/coltrane/poem

my favorite things
            is u/blowen
                        yo/favorite/things.

stretchen the mind
                        till it bursts past the con/fines of
solo/en melodies.
                            to the many/solos
of the
        mind/spirit.
            are u sleepen   (to be
            are u sleepen   sung
            brotha john   softly)
            brotha john
                        where u have gone to.
            no mornin bells
            are ringen here. only the quiet
aftermath of assassinations.
                        but i saw yo/murder/
the massacre
            of all blk/musicians. planned
in advance.
            yrs befo u blew away our passsst
    and showed us our futureeeeee
screech   screeech   screeeeech   screeech
a/love/supreme, alovesupreme a lovesupreme.
    A LOVE SUPREME
scrEEEccCHHHHH screeeeEEECHHHHHHH
    sCReeeEEECHHHHHH SCREEEECCCCHHHH
    SCREEEEEEEECCCHHHHHHHHHHHH
    a lovesupremealovesupremealovesupreme for our blk
    people.
        BRING IN THE WITE/MOTHA/fuckas
        ALL THE MILLIONAIRES/BANKERS/ol
    MAIN/LINE/ASS/RISTOCRATS (ALL
    THEM SO-CALLED BEAUTIFUL
    PEOPLE)
            WHO HAVE KILLED
    WILL CONTINUE TO
                KILL US WITH
    THEY CAPITALISM/18% OWNERSHIP
    OF THE WORLD.
                YEH. U RIGHT
THERE U ROCKEFELLERS. MELLONS
    VANDERBILTS
            FORDS.
                        yeh.
    GITem.

184

PUSHem/PUNCHem/STOMPem. THEN
LIGHT A FIRE TO
THEY pilgrim asses.
TEAROUT THEY eyes.
STRETCH they necks
till no mo
raunchy sounds of MURDER/
POVERTY/STARVATION

come from they
throats.
screeeeeeeeeeeeeeeeeeCHHHHHHHHHHH
SCREEEEEEEEEEEEEEECHHHHHHHHHH
screeEEEEEEEEEEEEEEEEEEEEEEEEE
EECCCCHHHHHHH
SCREEEEEEEEEEEEEEEEEEEEEEEEEEEEEE
EEEEEECHHHHHHHHHH
BRING IN THE WITE/LIBERALS ON THE SOLO
SOUND OF YO/FIGHT IS MY FIGHT
SAXOPHONE.
TORTURE
THEM FIRST AS THEY HAVE
TORTURED US WITH
PROMISES/
PROMISES. IN WITE/AMURICA. WHEN
ALL THEY WUZ DOEN
WAS HAVEN FUN WITH THEY
ORGIASTIC DREAMS OF BLKNESS.
(JUST SOME MO
CRACKERS FUCKEN OVER OUR MINDS.)
MAKE THEM
SCREEEEEEAM
FORGIVE ME. IN SWAHILI.
DON'T ACCEPT NO MEA CULPAS.
DON'T WANT TO
HEAR
BOUT NO EUROPEAN FOR/GIVE/NESS.
DEADDYINDEADDYINDEADDYINWITEWESTERN
SHITTTTTT
(softly   da-dum-da da da da da da da da da/da-dum-da
till it   da da da da da da da da da
builds   da-dum- da da da
up)   da-dum. da. da. da. this is a part of my
             favorite things.

185

```
                da dum da da da da da da
                da da da da
                da dum da da da da da da
                da da da da
                    da dum da da da da
                    da dum da da da da – – – – –
(to be      rise up blk/ people
sung                    de dum da da da da
slowly      move straight in yo/blkness
to tune                da dum da da da da
of my       step over the wite/ness
favorite    that is yesssss terrrrrr day
things.)    weeeeeeee are toooooooday.
(f          da dum
a           da da da (stomp, stomp) da da da
s           da dum
t           da da da (stomp, stomp) da da da
e           da dum
r)          da da da (stomp) da da da dum (stomp)
            weeeeeeeee (stomp)
                    areeeeeeeee (stomp)
                            areeeeeeeee (stomp, stomp)
toooooooday         (stomp.
        day             stomp.
        day             stomp.
        day             stomp.
        day                 stomp!)
(soft       rise up blk/people. rise up blk/people
chant)      RISE. & BE. What u can.
            MUST BE.BE.BE.BE.BE.BE.BE-E-E-E-E-BE-E-E-E-E-
                        yeh. john coltrane.
my favorite things is u.
                    showen us life/
                                liven.
a love supreme.
            for each
        other
    if we just
lissssssSSSTEN.
```

186

CARL SANDBURG

Jazz Fantasia

Drum on your drums, batter on your banjos,
sob on the long cool winding saxophones.
Go to it, O jazzmen.

Sling your knuckles on the bottoms of the happy
tin pans, let your trombones ooze, and go husha-
husha-hush with the slippery sand-paper.

Moan like an autumn wind high in the lonesome tree-
tops, moan soft like you wanted somebody terrible,
cry like a racing car slipping away from a motorcycle
cop, bang-bang! you jazzmen, bang altogether drums,
traps, banjos, horns, tin cans—make two people fight
on the top of a stairway and scratch each other's eyes
in a clinch tumbling down the stairs.

Can the rough stuff . . . now a Mississippi steamboat
pushes up the night river with a hoo-hoo-hoo-oo . . .
and the green lanterns calling to the high soft stars
. . . a red moon rides on the humps of the low river
hills . . . go to it, O jazzmen.

ROBERT SARGENT

Tin Roof Blues

In the 40's the Condon group made a "Tin Roof Blues"
for once and forever. Brunies was with them that day,
he'd played in the 20's, trombone,
with the New Orleans Rhythm Kings. Think for a moment
how it must have been as they sat around in the studio:
Brunies, Davison, Condon, Russell, Wettling,
Schroeder, and Casey, all for business,
nothing romantic. Condon, let's say, is talking:
"We gotta hold it to five choruses.

187

Start with the melody, you know," humming. "Now next,
by rights, comes the trumpet, the old Paul Mares solo.
Bill, what d'ye think? You know it, don't you?"
Davison sits there, frowning—it's not
that he doesn't know it—when he plays solo,
he wants it to be his. So Brunies speaks up,
"I'll play it, God, the times I've heard it,
I know it in my sleep." "Wait a minute, George,"
says Condon, "you got to play
your old chorus, that's why we picked this tune.
The one you keep hitting that low B-flat."
"I know," Brunies says. "I'll play Paul's with the mute,
then take it out for mine." "Well, that makes three,"
Condon says. "Then there's that free-for-all.
Can anybody hum it?" Somebody could, and did.
"Then back to the melody," Condon says.
"Slow down on the last four bars. Peewee,
give us a couple of notes to start with. Ready?"
The music begins, swinging slow and full.
What went into it, its perfection,
were simple things, six chords, twelve bars,
and an old New Orleans tune. But mainly
twenty years of learning to do it right.

Touching the Past

Uptown New Orleans, 1940,
And here was a man of the right color,
Old enough to have been there,

Who maybe heard. So I inquired
From the old man doing his yard work,
"Ever hear Buddy Bolden play?"

"Ah me," he said, stopping his work.
"Yes. But you mean *King, King* Bolden.
That's what we called him then."

He leaned on his rake a while, resting.
"Used to play in Algiers, played so loud
We could hear him clear 'cross the river."

He seemed listening. "King Bolden, now,
There was a man could play." We stood there,
Thinking about it, smiling.

MANDY SAYER

Choofa

One night before a gig
some musos picked up your beaten sax:
dented, scratched, split reed,
keys held together with rubber bands.
They flicked off the switch
and aimed a torch down the bell.
Pinholes of light escaped
from leaking pads,
from too much loving,
and no one could figure how
you could stand there each night
and push your soul through it.

Too much booze and all-night jam sessions
drove you down the South Coast,
and six months later, you were found
in a tent on a beach past Ulla Dulla
with only fresh barramundi to keep you alive.
They cleaned you up,
took you back to the Troc,
back to the radio shows,
back to where it was at but
you just picked up the advanced pay
and disappeared again.
The horn was your poultice,
and drew out too much too soon.

In '72 I saw you hunched over on a bed
with a flagon of Penfold's at your feet,
in a roach-ridden Woolloomooloo flat.
What had happened since '48
decomposed in a darkness

smelling of urine and decay.
I stood before you, Choof, knowing how
you could play a line til
pleasure peaked pain.
You looked up at me through half-light.
This last picture is unchanging:
the weight of your eyes
pressing into me like
that solo on "Nature Boy"
you used to blow.

ASGER SCHNACK

Aqua

[Excerpt]

let the poppy unfold itself let it intoxicate
itself in purple mascara by fits and starts as in a cue
for love soprano saxophone and equally wonderful
scent of lilac a late spring day an early summer day
in flying position like a piece of twilight

let us be here like a freedom an oblong
or oval dream-machine without stop or break
like a postcard sent with longing in blue lack
of reason or any earlier insight i.e.
hanging on the outside jingling like a handful of coins

without any knowledge of anything I move
into you without any knowledge of anything you
move into me like an elastic like an
elastic you move without any knowledge into
me I move without any knowledge into you

if anything if anything will ever stand and possibly
remain standing then this weeping feeling
of fulfillment of gauzebandage on the outside of crazy
kisses of ice-cold stone floor after shower with your tongue
on the outside of your body like a snail or a pearl

JAN SELVING

Dancing to Ellington

I found him downstairs
in the dark, eyes closed
bopping to *Money Jungle.*
A new hip dad, the red coal
of his cigarette trailing
the beat off Max Roach's drums,
Mingus' fingers sliding down the neck
in "Fleurette Africaine,"
wood breathing into his ear.

I'd learn to love this music
for myself, but that night
the city lights rose
out of the valley for Ellington
and my father, who years later
would tell me he couldn't bear
to have supper with us
after seeing a 17-year-old
patient with his skull caved in.

I never thought about it then,
how often my father brought death
home with him, locked himself
in his study till we'd gone to bed.
Now I listen to Coltrane's "Alabama,"
an elegy written on a train
for the girls who died
when their church was bombed.
And I remember those nights
I followed the sound of jazz
to the place I could watch
my father dance.

LÉOPOLD SÉDAR SENGHOR

Blues

The spring has swept the ice from all my frozen rivers
My young sap trembles at the first caresses along the tender bark.
But see how in the midst of July I am blinder than the Arctic winter!
My wings beat and break against the barriers of heaven
No ray pierces the deaf vault of my bitterness.
What sign is there to find? What key to strike?
And how can god be reached by hurling javelins?
Royal Summer of the distant South, you will come too late,
    in a hateful September!
In what book can I find the thrill of your reverberation?
And on the pages of what book, on what impossible lips taste your
    delirious love?

The impatient fit leaves me. Oh! the dull beat of the rain on the
    leaves!
Just play me your 'Solitude', Duke, till I cry myself to sleep.

New York

(for jazz orchestra: trumpet solo)

1

New York! At first I was confused by your beauty, by those great golden
    long-legged girls.
So shy at first before your blue metallic eyes, your frosted smile
So shy. And the anguish in the depths of skyscraper streets
Lifting eyes hawkhooded to the sun's eclipse.
Sulphurous your light and livid the towers with heads that thunderbolt
    the sky
The skyscrapers which defy the storms with muscles of steel and stone-
    glazed hide.
But two weeks on the bare sidewalks of Manhattan
—At the end of the third week the fever seizes you with the pounce of a
    leopard
Two weeks without rivers or fields, all the birds of the air
Falling sudden and dead on the high ashes of flat rooftops.

No smile of a child blooms, his hand refreshed in my hand,
No mother's breast, but only nylon legs. Legs and breasts that have no
sweat nor smell.
No tender word for there are no lips, only artificial hearts paid for in hard
cash
And no book where wisdom may be read. The painter's palette
blossoms with crystals of coral.
Nights of insomnia oh nights of Manhattan! So agitated by flickering lights,
while motor-horns howl of empty hours
And while dark waters carry away hygienic loves, like rivers flooded with
the corpses of children.

2

Now is the time of signs and reckonings
New York! Now is the time of manna and hyssop.
You must but listen to the trombones of God, let your heart beat in the
rhythm of blood, your blood.
I saw in Harlem humming with noise with stately colours and flamboy-
ant smells
—It was teatime at the house of the seller of pharmaceutical products—
I saw them preparing the festival of night for escape from the day.
I proclaim night more truthful than the day.
It was the pure hour when in the streets God makes the life that goes
back beyond memory spring up
All the amphibious elements shining like suns.
Harlem Harlem! Now I saw Harlem! A green breeze of corn springs up
from the pavements ploughed by the naked feet of dancers
Bottoms waves of silk and sword-blade breasts, water-lily ballets and
fabulous masks.
At the feet of police-horses roll the mangoes of love from low houses.
And I saw along the sidewalks streams of white rum streams of black
milk in the blue fog of cigars.
I saw the sky in the evening snow cotton-flowers and seraphims' wings
and sorcerers' plumes.
Listen New York! Oh listen to your male voice of brass vibrating with
oboes, the anguish choked with tears falling in great clots of blood
Listen to the distant beating of your nocturnal heart, rhythm and blood
of the tom-tom, tom-tom blood and tom-tom.

3

New York! I say to you: New York let black blood flow into your blood
That it may rub the rust from your steel joints, like an oil of life,

193

That it may give to your bridges the bend of buttocks and the suppleness
   of creepers.
Now return the most ancient times, the unity recovered, the
   reconciliation of the Lion the Bull and the Tree
Thought linked to act, ear to heart, sign to sense.
There are your rivers murmuring with scented crocodiles and
   mirage-eyed manatees. And no need to invent the Sirens.
But it is enough to open the eyes to the rainbow of April
And the ears, above all the ears, to God who out of the laugh of a
   saxophone created the heaven and the earth in six days.
And the seventh day he slept the great sleep of the Negro.

KAZUKO SHIRAISHI

Dedicated to the Late John Coltrane

Suddenly
He went to heaven
John Coltrane

In several ways
You were drastic about living
Out of your beauty
Beyond any meaning
A blue rain began to fall
People
Sit cross-legged on the richness of meaning
And like beggars grab the rice of sound
Eating, they weep goldly
Uncontrollably in misery

Coltrane
You have entered through
A hole in heaven

Because you died
On earth, again, one huge
Soundless hole has opened
People
Crawl to the edge of that pit

Missing him and his sounds
They clutch his thrown away shirts
Or album covers
Yearning sadly, loving him
They groan, get angry, and cry

Kulu Sé Mama
Kulu Sé Mama

Coltrane
With your extremely heavy
And short pilgrimage
Full of fleeting eternity
Spirit traveling
You were mainly blowing thoughts
Thoughts are eyes, wind
Cascades of spicy sweat
Streaming down your forehead
Thought is an otter's scream
The sexual legs of chickens
Killed by your old lady
Boiling in a pot
Women's pubic hair
Alice or Aisha
Thoughts are the faceless songs
Of pink stars
Squirming in the sky
Of every woman's womb

Hot, dark summer afternoon
Coltrane
Your 'Olé'
So full of romanticism and power
Now we don't have your 'Olé' of love
For a little while, about as long as forever,
We won't receive your
"Olé"

On this earth
In this human hot arena
In the bullring
Cicadas are crying now
Hot, dark summer
Sits by itself

No bulls, no glory
Only shadows and memory
You in my memory
Coltrane, your music

People see the colors of your sounds
So passionately
They listen with ears of dread
To the ordeal of your sounds

For forty-one years
In your very busy history
The sun often rose and sank
Orange sun, African sun, American sun
The taste of human sun
Rose and set hundreds and thousands of times
In a black, soul room
You are sunbathing
That dude the sun shines brightly
On your silent back
That dude the sun often cried
And became the sweat of blinding music
Diving into a saxophone blown by you
He cried out loud and free

Brilliant blue
Even the orange sun
Against those black, desperate cheeks
Has begun to cry incoherently
Coltrane almost became a sky
He became a cascade of will
Carrying the sounds
He made them fall
Pouring them out
We know the monsoon
In John's long lasting solo
The blazing rain continues

We are often beaten with the rainfall of sound
We are numbed
To the deepest room of our hearts
We are soaked through
The door breaks, the mast snaps
The chairs float away
Then we regain that certain consciousness

Which is volition
Which is desire
It is the cosmos announcing
The trivial existence of humans
Alone, carrying his saxophone
He takes giant steps
Walking through the cosmos
Though his stride helps us see the blue
Unstable vertebrae of earth
His expression was mostly invisible
Sometimes he mysteriously, shyly
Buried his face in a cloud

John, wandering Coltrane
Even though you are no longer on earth
I, we remember you when you were
All of a sudden
We recall you wandering for awhile
In the season without answers
With your face hidden
In that opaque cloud

While flowing slowly down the river of agony
You met the fish of pleasure
You met love
You met woman, son, friend, God
You met music and its Holy Spirit
Then you became the Holy Spirit
You became the music itself

On earth, from now on
A long, hot, dark summer continues
Even though you died
Even though your transient life ended

On earth
In whatever cold struggle
Hot passions and determinations
Are smoldering
Humans are walking on the day

John Coltrane
Your day, that day which was once alive
That day which met 'someday'
That day which dissolved the next moment

197

Coltrane
In the way I love you
I love the days you lived through
I love the season of those days
Which you survived for forty-one years
Your music, your voice
Your glory and rage
Your love and conviction
Your God, your Holy Spirit
Your cosmos with East and West
Its desperation and grief

All those I love and warm
And meditate upon
May your spirit rest in peace
Our beloved John Coltrane
A tremendous saxophone player

For the strong, black soul
Of Saint Coltrane
In heaven

ALEDA SHIRLEY

Ellington Indigos

It's the day of the penumbral eclipse and I'm driving
home, through Brown County, Indiana, and thinking
about how later we'll go outside and watch

the earth's transparent shadow cross the face
of the harvest moon. I wonder if you'll be there
when I get home: how is it I sometimes feel as if

I'm waiting for you, even when I'm the one who's late?
A kind of uneasy indolent longing, it's similar
to the one evoked in me by Ellington's pastels, or fall.

Though the autumn colors haven't yet peaked,
here and there I see a sweetgum edged in violet,
a maple dying back to pale-yellow. The soft azure

198

of an alto sax, the jagged red of a growling trumpet,
the raw gold of a clarinet—discussing Ellington's
tone palette, a jazz critic perfectly described

this landscape. Though the wind's picking up, I stop
to put down the top of the car. *It's the story,*
Ellington explained, *of a little girl who loves*

a little boy. Everyday she sits at a window
and waits for him to come by. One day he doesn't.
"Mood Indigo" *just tells how she feels.* With its trio

of clarinet and muted trumpet and trombone,
"Mood Indigo" starts, each chord shaped by small
movements in the line of a single instrument.

A slow tempo, a minimal melody. With the stealth
of sunset it moves and, suddenly, is gone. No coda,
just Duke picking out two notes on the piano.

What is it about the light of departure that reveals
the essence of things? Your physical presence—
the mere fact of your body—sometimes overwhelms me

as I hug you goodbye in the morning: I'm an hour
from both dusk and home, but I've recovered
that sense of wonder; possibilities, like a guitar's

shimmering fills, move through my mind. We could walk
along the reservoir and sip cognac from your flask.
Arrange branches of sumac in every vase we own.

Or we could brew a pot of tea, bundle up in quilts,
and sit on the terrace, awaiting the eclipse.

The Last Dusk of August

A cold front's blowing in; the fragrant air
rustles as if with the approach of rain
but the sky's clear and when I go out to call
the cat I see in the pool's deep end the lights

of a jet. They look sharp enough to slice
a diver's legs. Michael joins me for a moment, offers
a sip of his Lillet, while the cat writhes indolently
on stone still warm with afternoon. How clearly

I see her, my mother, twenty years ago,
as she sorted through my summer clothes, deciding
which of my bastiste slips should be mended,
which used for dust clothes. I sat on the bed

and watched her toss them into two soft piles,
the air so dense with light I'd have moved,
had I moved, as slowly as a bell rung in heavy oil.
Last night Michael placed a bowl of apricots

on the windowsill and kissed the insides of my elbows.
Love swelled like vertigo inside me; shown the word
in print I'd have thought it foreign, nonsense,
an odd name. But, tonight, it's longing

that fills me: I sense the season's end as I would
the bass line of a pavanne played from great distance.
Michael calls my name, suggests a drive. And so
we head east down River Road in my old convertible.

He pops Miles Davis in the tape player—"Sid's Retreat,"
"Green Dolphin Street," "Round Midnight." Music
and speed fuse and for a moment I'm no longer
in the car but behind it, the only skier on the water.

21 August 1984

She thinks at first it is rain,
or memory. Perhaps his hand,
heavy with warmth,
at the nape of her neck.
But it is neither lunar nor clairvoyant.
The shimmering is the lawn
across which three raccoons are walking.
Their spines arch softly as they disappear

into the grating under the curb.
She thinks about timing,

that rare angle that transforms incident
to magic. What does it mean
to have perfect pitch,
a green thumb,
to be in the right place at the right time?
Not everything can be explained by numbers.

The breeze smells of mown grass,
the streetlights hum and brighten
while, in the cafe, a guitarist plays harmonics.
Consider the chemistry that, out of the blue,
snaps between a man and a woman
who've passed each other at parties
for years. *Hello, how are you,*
they've said, perhaps a dozen times;

they say it again, for the thirteenth.
That these things have nothing to do
with love is not yet clear
to her, who only now understands
why the dates of jazz sessions
are listed on liner notes:
it matters that we know
when the improvisation occurred.

JOHN SINCLAIR

humphf

for big Red

they say monk
couldn't play the music. they say,
monk, he limited
by his own vision

& just can't play right. monk,
he too weird. his music
don't sound right, and he gets up
& dances

while he's playing,
like a jackleg preacher
at a revival meeting
in an old tent in north carolina.

they say monk sound too much
like a whorehouse piano player
from some pre-harlem ghetto
stuffed with back-woods renegades

& sporting women & gamblers,
street-level intellectuals. they say
monk, what is that shit
you trying to play, you just can't

do it that way,
you too way out baby,
that stuff ain't you. & monk,
in his infinite knowledge

& wisdom, shoots a grin
from behind the piano,
wiggles his ass on the stool,
lays down another few bars

of utter genius,
turns it over to the tenor player
& rises to dance beside the piano,
some more of that old north carolina boogaloo

GILBERT SORRENTINO

Broadway! Broadway!

Halloween is black and orange.
A song, as in "le clarinet du marmalade."
Some are happiest drowned
in a saxophone solo.

"Le jazz hot" rhymes à la Mallarmé
with tabasco: *vide* Bunk Johnson
astomp in New Iberia.

I saw Dexter Gordon play to six people
in a frayed suit. His golden horn had lost
its sheen. The notes gleamed.

Dexter in his brilliance.
Exquisite phrasing and perfect comedy.
A black velvet an
orange corona corona.

JACK SPICER

Song for Bird and Myself

I am dissatisfied with my poetry.
I am dissatisfied with my sex life.
I am dissatisfied with the angels I believe in.
        Neo-classical like Bird,
        Distrusting the reality
        of every note.
        Half-real
        We blow the sentence pure and real
        Like chewing angels.

"Listen, Bird, why do we have to sit here dying
In a half-furnished room?
The rest of the combo
Is safe in houses
Blowing bird-brained Dixieland,
How warm and free they are. What right
Music."
        "Man,
        We
        Can't stay away from the sounds.
        We're *crazy,* Jack
        We gotta stay here 'til
        They come and get us."

Neo-classical like Bird.
Once two birds got into the Rare Book Room.
Miss Swift said,
"Don't
Call a custodian
Put crumbs on the outside of the window
Let them
Come outside."
                    Neo-classical
The soft line strains
Not to be neo-classical.
But Miss Swift went to lunch. They
Called a custodian.
Four came.
Armed like Myrmidons, they
Killed the birds.
Miss Munsterberg
Who was the first
American translator of Rilke
Said
"Suppose one of them
Had been the Holy Ghost."
Miss Swift,
Who was back from lunch,
Said
"Which."
But the poem isn't over.
It keeps going
Long after everybody
Has settled down comfortably into laughter.
The bastards
On the other side of the paper
Keep laughing.
LISTEN.
STOP LAUGHING.
THE POEM ISN'T OVER. Butterflies.
I knew there would be butterflies
For Butterflies represent the lost soul
Represent the way the wind wanders
Represent the bodies
We only clasp in the middle of a poem.
See, the stars have faded.
There are only butterflies.
Listen to

The terrible sound of their wings moving.
Listen,
The poem isn't over.

Have you ever wrestled with a bird,
You idiotic reader?
Jacob wrestled with an angel.
(I remind you of the image)
Or a butterfly
Have you ever wrestled with a single butterfly?
Sex is no longer important.
Colors take the form of wings. Words
Have got to be said.
A butterfly,
A bird,
Planted at the heart of being afraid of dying.
Blow,
Bird,
Blow,
Be,
Neo-classical.
Let the wings say
What the wings mean
Terrible and pure.
   The horse
   In Cocteau
   Is as neo-classical an idea as one can manage.
   Writes all our poetry for us
   Is Gertrude Stein
   Is God
   Is the needle for which
   God help us
   There is no substitute
   Or the Ace of Swords
   When you are telling a fortune
   Who tells death.
   Or the Jack of Hearts
   Whose gypsy fortune we clasp
   In the middle of a poem.

"And are we angels, Bird?"
   "That's what we're trying to tell 'em, Jack
   There aren't any angels except when
   You and me blow 'em."

So Bird and I sing
Outside your window
So Bird and I die
Outside your window.
This is the wonderful world of Dixieland
Deny
The bloody motherfucking Holy Ghost.
This is the end of the poem.
You can start laughing, you bastards. This is
The end of the poem.

WALLACE STEVENS

The Sick Man

Bands of black men seem to be drifting in the air,
In the South, bands of thousands of black men,
Playing mouth-organs in the night or, now, guitars.

Here in the North, late, late, there are voices of men,
Voices in chorus, singing without words, remote and deep,
Drifting choirs, long movements and turnings of sounds.

And in a bed in one room, alone, a listener
Waits for the unison of the music of the drifting bands
And the dissolving chorals, waits for it and imagines

The words of winter in which these two will come together,
In the ceiling of the distant room, in which he lies,
The listener, listening to the shadows, seeing them,

Choosing out of himself, out of everything within him,
Speech for the quiet, good hail of himself, good hail, good hail,
The peaceful, blissful words, well-tuned, well-sung, well-spoken.

MICHAEL STILLMAN

In Memoriam John Coltrane

Listen to the coal
rolling, rolling through the cold
steady rain, wheel on

wheel, listen to the
turning of the wheels this night
black as coal dust, steel

on steel, listen to
these cars carry coal, listen
to the coal train roll.

JOHN TAGGART

Coming Forth by Day

after a composition by Ornette Coleman

Cold and, cymbals fizz with no old animals among railroad tracks,
tarrel   grass in   still   winter,
austral herons beating, beating grey ellipses over closed cities.

Ponderous women move as slowed film, the
chrome tendons in night, furious lengthening bar, broken within them,
them, intense anatomies' dark edges as eruptions along suns,
clouds, as interiors, heavier than oil, sediment on glass,
                              grass tarred, gravel afire.

Women contain things as lighted signs apart
from the darkness, motionless, split, vibrating and without hope,
      air lives in   death of   fire.

The trees fronting the sea   are as fans, reversed, the
eastern harbor, ridges, backs of buildings in smoke,
water   lives in death of   air.

Machines burn in zones of
pure aluminum. Alluvial plains with abandoned factories, upheaval,
fire lives   in death   of lands.

Ponderous women move out of frames, the
metal in palm trees, muscles, the hum of refineries no longer

them, and twisted grass the breasts with knees, ankles of black gravel,
Now, as mirrors, revolved, oiled with carbon, not holding
                              old animals,   railroad tracks.

Women are as lighted signs in dancing, when
coming upon cities from regions of winter by day,

                    birds fade out, rising.

MELVIN B. TOLSON

Lambda

[From *Harlem Gallery*]

From the mouth of the Harlem Gallery
came a voice like a
ferry horn in a river of fog:

"Hey, man, when you gonna close this dump?
Fetch highbrow stuff for the middlebrows who
don't give a damn and the lowbrows who ain't hip!
Think you're a little high-yellow Jesus?"

No longer was I a boxer with a brain bruised
against its walls by Tyche's fists,
as I welcomed Hideho Heights,
the vagabond bard of Lenox Avenue,
whose satyric legends adhered like beggar's-lice.

"Sorry, Curator, I got here late:
my black ma birthed me in the Whites' bottom drawer,
and the Reds forgot to fish me out!"

His belly laughed and quaked
the Blakean tigers and lambs on the walls.
Haw-Haw's whale of a forefinger mocked
Max Donachie's revolutionary hero, Crispus Attucks,
in the Harlem Gallery and on Boston Commons.
"In the beginning was the Word,"
he challenged, "not the Brush!"
The scorn in the eyes that raked the gallery
was the scorn of an Ozymandias.

The metal smelted from the ore of ideas,
his grin revealed all the gold he had stored away.
"Just came from a jam session
at the Daddy-O Club," he said.
"I'm just one step from heaven
with the blues a-percolating in my head.
You should've heard old Satchmo blow his horn!
The Lord God A'mighty made no mistake
the day that cat was born!"

Like a bridegroom unloosing a virgin knot,
from an inner pocket he coaxed a manuscript.
"Just given Satchmo a one-way ticket
to Immortality," he said. "Pure inspiration!"
His lips folded about the neck of a whiskey bottle
whose label belied its white-heat hooch.
I heard a gurgle, a gurgle—a death rattle.
His eyes as bright as a parachute light,
he began to rhetorize in the grand style
of a Doctor Faustus in the dilapidated Harlem Opera House:

King Oliver of New Orleans
has kicked the bucket, but he left behind
old Satchmo with his red-hot horn
to syncopate the heart and mind.
The honky-tonks in Storyville
have turned to ashes, have turned to dust,
but old Satchmo is still around
like Uncle Sam's IN GOD WE TRUST.

Where, oh, where is Bessie Smith
with her heart as big as the blues of truth?
Where, oh, where is Mister Jelly Roll
with his Cadillac and diamond tooth?

209

Where, oh, where is Papa Handy
with his blue notes a-dragging from bar to bar?
Where, oh, where is bulletproof Leadbelly
with his tall tales and 12-string guitar?

Old Hip Cats,
when you sang and played the blues
the night Satchmo was born,
did you know hypodermic needles in Rome
couldn't hoodoo him away from his horn?
Wyatt Earp's legend, John Henry's, too,
is a dare and a bet to old Satchmo
when his groovy blues put headlines in the news
from the Gold Coast to cold Moscow.

Old Satchmo's
gravelly voice and tapping foot and crazy notes
set my soul on fire.
If I climbed
the seventy-seven steps of the Seventh
Heaven, Satchmo's high C would carry me higher!
Are you hip to this, Harlem? Are you hip?
On Judgment Day, Gabriel will say
after he blows his horn:
"I'd be the greatest trumpeter in the Universe,
if old Satchmo had never been born!"

Mu

[From *Harlem Gallery*]

Hideho Heights
and I, like the brims of old hats,
slouched at a sepulchered table in the Zulu Club.
Frog Legs Lux and his Indigo Combo
spoke with tongues that sent their devotees
out of this world!

Black and brown and yellow fingers flashed,
like mirrored sunrays of a heliograph,
on clarinet and piano keys, on cornet valves.

Effervescing like acid on limestone,
Hideho said:
"O White Folks, O Black Folks,
the dinosaur imagined its extinction meant
the death of the piss ants."

Cigarette smoke
—opaque veins in Carrara marble—
magicked the habitués into
humoresques and grotesques.
Lurid lights
spraying African figures on the walls
ecstasied maids and waiters,
pickups and stevedores—
with delusions
of Park Avenue grandeur.

Once, twice,
Hideho sneaked a swig.
"On the house," he said, proffering the bottle
as he lorded it under the table.
Glimpsing the harpy eagle at the bar,
I grimaced,
"I'm not the house snake of the Zulu Club."

A willow of a woman,
bronze as knife money,
executed, near our table, the Lenox Avenue Quake.
Hideho winked at me and poked
that which
her tight Park Avenue skirt vociferously advertized.
Peacocking herself, she turned like a ballerina,
her eyes blazing drops of rum on a crêpe suzette.
"Why, you—"
A sanitary decree, I thought. "Don't *you* me!" he fumed.
The lips of a vixen exhibited a picadill flare.
"What you smell isn't cooking," she said.
Hideho sniffed.
"Chanel No. 5," he scoffed,
"from Sugar Hill."
I laughed and clapped him on the shoulder.
"A bad metaphor, *poet.*"
His jaws closed
like an alligator squeezer.

"She's a willow," I emphasized,
"a willow by a cesspool."
Hideho mused aloud,
"Do I hear The Curator rattle Eliotic bones?"

Out of the Indigo Combo
flowed rich and complex polyrhythms.
Like surfacing bass,
exotic swells and softenings
of the veld vibrato
emerged.
. . .
Was that Snakehips Briskie
gliding out of the aurora australis of the Zulu Club
into the kaleidoscopic circle?
. . .
Etnean gasps!
Vesuvian acclamations!
. . .
Snakehips poised himself—
Giovanni Gabrieli's
single violin against his massed horns.
. . .
The silence of the revelers was the arrested
hemorrhage of an artery
grasped by bull forceps.
I felt Hideho's breath against my ear.
"The penis act in the Garden of Eden," he confided.
. . .
Convulsively, unexampledly,
Snakehips' body and soul
began to twist and untwist like a gyrating rawhide—
began to coil, to writhe
like a prismatic-hued python
in the throes of copulation.

Eyes bright as the light
at Eddystone Rock,
an ebony Penthesilea
grabbed her tiger's-eye yellow-brown
beanpole Sir Testiculus of the evening
and gave him an Amazonian hug.
He wilted in her arms
like a limp morning-glory.

212

"The Zulu Club is in the groove," chanted Hideho,
"and the cats, the black cats, are *gone!*"

In the *ostinato*
of stamping feet and clapping hands,
the Promethean bard of Lenox Avenue became a
lost loose-leaf
as memory vignetted
Rabelaisian I's of the Boogie-Woogie dynasty
in barrel houses, at rent parties,
on riverboats, at wakes:
The Toothpick, Funky Five, and Tippling Tom!
Ma Rainey, Countess Willie V., and Aunt Harriet!
Speckled Red, Skinny Head Pete, and Stormy Weather!
Listen, Black Boy.
Did the High Priestess at 27 rue de Fleurus
assert, "The Negro suffers from nothingness"?
Hideho confided like a neophyte on The Walk,
"Jazz is the marijuana of the Blacks."
In the *tribulum* of dialectics, I juggled the idea;
then I observed,
"Jazz is the philosophers' egg of the Whites."

Hideho laughed from below the Daniel Boone rawhide belt
he'd redeemed, in a Dallas pawn shop,
with part of the black-market
loot set loose
in a crap game
by a Yangtze ex-coolie who,
in a Latin Quarter dive below Telegraph Hill,
out-Harvarded his Alma Mater.
• • •
Frog Legs Lux and his Indigo Combo
let go
with a wailing pedal point
that slid into
Basin Street Blues
like Ty Cobb stealing second base:
Zulu,
King of the Africans,
arrives on Mardi Gras morning;
the veld drum of Baby Dodds'
great-grandfather
in Congo Square

pancakes the first blue note
in a callithump of the USA.
And now comes the eve of Ash Wednesday.
Comus on parade!
All God's children revel
like a post-Valley Forge
charivari in Boston celebrating the nuptials of
a gay-old-dog minuteman with a lusty maid.
. . .
Just as
the bourgeois adopted
the lyric-winged piano of Liszt in the court at Weimar
for the solitude of his
aeried apartment,
Harlem chose
for its cold-water flat
the hot-blues cornet of King Oliver
in his cart
under the
El pillars of the Loop.
. . .
The yanking fishing rod
of Hideho's voice
jerked me out of my bird's-foot violet romanticism.
He mixed Shakespeare's image with his own
and caricatured me:
"Yonder Curator has a lean and hungry look;
he thinks too much.
Such blackamoors are dangerous to
the Great White World!"
. . .
With a dissonance
from the Weird Sisters,
the jazz diablerie
boiled down and away
in the vacuum pan
of the Indigo Combo.

214

WILLIAM TREMBLAY

Song for Jeannie

(written to "'Round Midnight," by T. Monk)

This is a song for you about you
& around you like a minuet cocoon of tenderness
& regret.

Jeannie, everything on this planet
is going to die, the computers are humming
the limit a hundred years.

I told my son Ben
that scientists say
our sun will super-nova,
swallowing us with its blessing
of hydrogen corollas & love
five billion years from now
& he cried like any limit makes tomorrow.

I think his tears now
& suddenly everything is important, even the wards
for the prematurely wise.

I remember the night when I met you
& you were dancing about the flower in your womb
& it was a delight that strengthened me against
the streets of New York with their bombs & dollars
& wine bottles of murder.

I remember the night we sat near the fire
the first summer of the lake
& you spoke of the rising & rising again of the flashlights
to meet the restless dead parts of ourselves.

I remember the rainbow headband you took off your waist
for me, the sweat & the grapes & the devoured
men in your tent.
I remember your hair demanding a hill facing sunset
with the will of your deceased bank-account

215

& I remember how you hugged me & said you loved me
when you knew I thought you insane,

& that's the shiv in my spine,
that we all thought you there
where you walked out the door

>   remember how we talked
>   about walking out on the prisons we make
>   that we bang our heads bloody on,
>   coming back & coming back
>   until one day we see the door
>   & take it

out of the white corridors & the shock treatment

& I can see you walking back into that fireside
talk astonishing us with all your time-travel & prophecies
in children's rhymes

& I have this vision of you running in a hospital smock
over the Hudson River in a narcosis of headlights
toward the century we have left

>   where all the broken marriages
& destroyed Californias, the desperation to find
father, mother, child & the Holy Ghost in one man
who will not kill you with his dying
his black whiskers of photographs
& his boyish smiles
>   all count, very much.

No dream of whips & multiplication tables
will black out the sun, which will be with us
til we end.

It doesn't matter whether we do it in forests
or on tugboats in the oil harbors,
that exquisite hunger in our centers
to live, to eat life,
that lovely & grieving appetite, is it—

what we are, in brilliance, hymns of comets,
is it, what we *are* kills us.

It matters & it doesn't matter
if all is cloudless skies of penance.
Nothing is there between touching
& needing to be touched.

What you suffered before us, the cold
floors of your fight with the economy of love,
that there is never enough, like there is never enough
Moses or bread.
     Your nursery school rooms are
     festooned with alphabets & zebras.

So this is the endsong of the one who knows
living is dreaming the fire of your cells
quavering over the dead lakes;
every nightmare & betrayal, every half-Catholic
half-Jewish prayer, every coveted fur coat
& cheap rhinestone matters now
as a stick in the house of beginning-to-be
is subtracted by the wind.

The song & the fire will sleep like a fern
in the rock, the silence before the next movement
stirs on the bows of Heaven:

dance, little flower of the womb, dance now!

JON C. TRIBBLE

Anaximander Lewis

Mr. Jones kicked him out
of the Horace Mann High School Band
when he went solo during the flag line's
routine, blowing notes that left the purple
and gold material hanging limp
from the still poles. It didn't

slow him down. He hitched weekends
to Memphis, catching sets on Beale Street

at any club he could sneak in.
I was still playing contrabass
clarinet when I met him and I wanted
music so bad I'd practice 'til my lips bled.

It got me sore lips.
Anaximander tried to help, told me
to love the reed, not fight it,
feel the bass line like it was growing
out of my back, through my arms and fingers,
out the bell of the horn.

I couldn't do it and quit the band
when he was kicked out. There just wasn't anything
worth hearing anymore. I sold the contrabass
and bought an old car, started driving him
to Memphis on the weekends. He talked
about how his grandfather was the first

Lewis to learn to read,
how he named all his children and grandchildren
after philosophers, hoping they'd all
be men and women of knowledge. Anaximander
laughed at that, said the only thing he read
was music, only once

for each song, after the first time
he felt the notes, knew what should go next
and how long to hold it. He let me paint *aperion*
on his clarinet case (as close as I could get
to the Greek of his namesake). He played that horn
like it was something elemental, like he could transmute

his breath as it passed over the reed
into notes that burned out the bell.

QUINCY TROUPE

The Day Duke Raised; may 24th, 1974

for Duke Ellington

1.

that day began with a shower
of darkness calling lightning rains
home to stone language
of thunderclaps shattering the high
blue elegance of space & time
a broken-down riderless horse
with frayed wings
rode a sheer bone sunbeam
road down into the clouds

2.

spoke wheels of lightning
spun around the hours high up
above those clouds duke wheeled
his chariot of piano keys
his spirit now levitated from flesh
& hovering over the music of most high
spoke to the silence
of a griot shaman/ man
who knew the wisdom of God

3.

at high noon the sun cracked
through the darkness like a rifle shot
grew a beard of clouds on its livid bald
face hung down noon sky high
pivotal time of the flood-deep hours as duke
was pivotal being a five in the nine
numbers of numerology
as his music was the crossroads
the cosmic mirror of rhythmic gri-gri

4.

so get on up & fly away duke bebop
slant & fade on in strut dance swing riff

float & stroke those tickling gri-gri keys
those satin ladies taking the A train up
to harlem those gri-gri keys of birmingham
breakdown sophisticated
ladies mood indigo
so get on up & strut across gri-gri
raise on up your band's waiting

5.

thunderclapping music somersaulting
clouds racing across the blue deep wisdom
of God listen it is time for your intro
duke into that other place where the all-time
great band is waiting for your intro duke
it is time for the Sacred Concert duke
it is time to make the music of God
duke we are listening for your intro
duke let the sacred music begin

Four, and More; for Miles Davis

1.

a carrier of incandescent dreams this
blade-thin shadowman stabbed by lightning
crystal silhouette
crawling over blues-stained pavements his life
lean he drapes himself his music across edges
his blood held tight within
staccato flights

clean as darkness & bright as lightning
reversed moments where the sound is two cat eyes
penetrating the midnight hours of moon pearls lacing
the broken mirrored waters
mississippi mean as a sun-drenched trumpet/ man
holding dreams held high on any wind/ light

voice walking on eggshells

2.

& time comes as the wrinkles
of your mother's skin shrinking inward

fly towards that compelling voice
light calling since time began
on the flip-side of spirit
you shed placentas at each stage of your music
then go down river exploring new blues

the drum skin of young years wearing down

the enigmatic search of your music
now your autumn years of shadows creeping twilight
dancers wrapped tight in cobwebs hold on
to one another
beneath fractured lights cracking the floor
their lives now prismatic poems at the point where the sun
disappears with every turning of the clock hands
spinning towards the death of light
there in the diamond point
of the river beyond the edges

the light glows smaller
grows inward becomes a seed to grow
another light illuminating the shadows
crystalline as this trumpetman

voice walking on eggshells

phosphorous as truth or blue
as luminescent water beneath the sun's eye

3.

O Silent Keeper of Shadows
of these gutted roads filled with gloomy ticking
of time-clocks/ razor-bladed turnings of hairpin corners
of these irreducible moments of love found
when love was sought
irridescent keeper of rainbow laughter
arching out of broken-off gold-capped teeth

blues man holding the sun between his teeth

soothsayer of chewed-up moments
shekereman at the crossroads of cardinal points
talisman hanging from dewdrops singing deep
sea diver of transparent rhythmic poems

221

trumpet voice walking on eggshells

your shadow is as the river snake-thin
man at flood time blood lengthening in the veins
coursing through the earth's flesh

shaman man gone beyond the skies limit

music sleeps there in the riverbed
mississippi where those calcified shining bones sleep
deep reminding us of the journey from then to now
& from now to wherever it is we have to go

so pack your bags boy
the future is right around the corner
only a stone's throw from yesterday's/ light

as is this carrier of afternoon dream music
trumpet voice walking on eggshells

this eggshell-walking trumpetman
voice hauntingly beautiful lyrical music man
gold as two cat eyes penetrating the midnight hours
as blood blackening the pavement mean music man
shadowman holding the night in the bell
of his trumpet singing

mississippi river pouring from roots of his eyes

4.

shadowman holding the night in his music
shekereman at the crossroads of cardinal points
elliptical talisman hanging from dewdrops singing
deep sea diver of haunting magical tones

trumpetman walking on eggshells

your shadow as the river at flood-time
snake-thin shaman man blade-sharp gone beyond
the skies limit music sleeps there in your coursing
river veins curl around the bones
clear as diamond points on waters of sunsets

222

there where light grows inward
your genius moving out from that source
trumpetman walking on eggshells

afternoon dreamcarrier of blues in flight
steep night climber of haunting magical poems

juju hoodooman conjuring illuminating darkness

Snake-Back Solo

(for Louis Armstrong, Steve Cannon, Miles Davis & Eugene Redmond)

with the music up high
boogalooin bass down way way low
up & under eye come slidin on in mojoin
on in spacin on in on a riff
full of rain
riffin on in full of rain & pain
spacin on in on a sound like coltrane

my metaphor is a blues
hot pain dealin blues is a blues axin
guitar voices whiskey broken niggah deep
in the heart is a blues in a glass filled with rain
is a blues in the dark
slurred voices of straight bourbon
is a blues dagger stuck off in the heart
of night moanin like bessie smith
is a blues filling up the wings
of darkness is a blues

& looking through the heart
a dream can become a raindrop window to see through
can become a window to see through this moment
to see yourself hanging around the dark
to see through
can become a river catching rain
feeding time can become a window
to see through

Coltrane, Syeeda's Song Flute

When I came across it on the
piano it reminded me of her,
because it sounded like a
happy, child's song.
                              —Coltrane

For M & P.R

To Marilyn, to Peter,
playing, making things: the walls, the stairs,
the attics, bright nests in nests;
the slow, light, grave unstitching of lies,
opening, stinking, letting in air

you bear yourselves in, become your own mother and father,
your own child.
You lying closer.

You going along. Days.
The strobe-lit wheel stops dead
once, twice in a life: old-fashioned rays:

and then all the rest of the time pulls blur,
only you remember it more, playing.

Listening here in the late quiet you can think
great things of us all, I think we will all, Coltrane,
meet speechless and easy in Heaven, our names
known and forgotten, all dearest, all come giant-stepping
out into some wide, light, merciful mind.

John
Coltrane, 40, gone
right through the floorboards,
up to the shins, up to the eyes,
closed over,

Syeeda's happy, child's song
left up here, playing.

ANNE WALDMAN

Bluehawk

Monk's gone

      blown

those keys
    his
        alone
to unlock

            your
            heart

sway

    swipe those tears away

        Monk's gone
        Monk's gone

    (pause)

            a minor chord

      asymmetry

      (accent on the "try")

    pushing the limits

        all his own
    &
        the music of the spheres
            (song the gong)
gone
Monk's gone

        Buddha fingers gone

        bluehawk

                in the sky

    soar high

Eric Dolphy

"Out To Lunch"
        :
        funny how he
takes a break

        cooking

        the real stuff
                goes on

                        in the back

                                (kitchen?)
All you bill collectors,
            official cats
                    back off

we're in the sunshine
        in the presence
            in the thick of it now

JOY WALSH

Ferguson's Conquistadores 77

Maynard cooked Vesti la Giubba
While drums played three rhythms at once
Cut Man Johnson had a love affair with his bass
Right there under red lights
The Prince was hot
And the Lebanon Love Beast was better than before
His hair exploded and his brains
Came out through the horn

Militello conversed through his flute
As the Conquistadores wove their way
Through Mexico and up the California coast

226

They made maidens and monasteries
Looted all the notes in the air
Played sounds that weren't even there

Smoke rose and the drummer Gadd
Jumped out of his skin
The music screamed beyond passion
Tripletimed ragas rolled
The night the Conquistadores
Played
        Pillaged
                And prayed.

MARILYN NELSON WANIEK

It's All in Your Head

for Deborah M.

How easily my heart falls back into habits:
a little stress, and I'm checking my pulse again
for irregular beats.
Just last year I went once a week
to the emergency room,
afraid my breath would expand
the radiant pain in my chest.
I lay among the hurt, the dying,
checking my symptoms off on a mental list.

I didn't die; I napped
on the spotless stainless steel beds.
I went home chastened, humble, thankful
to the steeplechase of my life.
Now, like a bass drum dropped down the stairs,
my heart wakes me up again at night.
I pretend I'm not afraid
as the funeral procession
comes to order under my ribs.

I wanted to twirl a baton
in the 2082 parade.

The day Mrs. Gray predicted fame for me
the sixth grade class dissolved
to an image of high-stepping white boots.
But now I stumble after, out of step,
as the band strikes up a hymn
and the colored congregation
slowly begins to move on.

The trombone fades into the distance
with the flattened-out trumpets and drums;
the women carry black parasols:
Diverne, Annie, Ray, Mary, Charlie.
Geneva, Oneida, Zilphia, Blanche,
in shabby shoes and black straw hats
rescued from the backs of their closets.
Dark dresses reserved for such occasions
flicker around their brown calves.

Their felt fedoras in their hands,
their collars too white,
their heads small
with new haircuts, my grandfathers,
my uncles, walk in the bright morning.
Pete has taken off his apron,
John, his overalls. Melvin, Rufus, Pomp,
in shiny shoes and suits, march
with Mister Tyler and the women.

I limp behind in my black hole shoes,
my hair crocheted with tangles
as it was when I was ten.
My old heart groans
when the brass light from the tuba
takes the road that winds up the hill.
I hear the sisters ahead of me
join in a church-house moan
as the band ascends into the blues.

The moan changes
to a melody vaguely familiar,
though they're too far away now
for me to hear more than snatches.
I hum along with them,
halting and out of synch,

like a jay
in a tree full of finches.

It's jazz I hear now from the height,
hands clap a rhythm like approaching rain.
I want to be a part of that music,
but I fall back again and again,
damned impossible stone.
By the time I pant up the narrow ridge
only the thin voice of a clarinet
rises from small blacks and lights.

It's too early yet for me to follow them over
from the top of my birthdate
to the other side of the dash,
where I'll be welcomed with fanfare.
This syncopation's only a habit
my heart has picked up.
So I march back home
to my husband, my son,
and my life.

WILLIAM WANTLING

A Plea for Workmen's Compensation

for T. Monk

to make up for t. monk
to take the place of t. monk
to hold sway on t. monk
to make way for t. monk
to ask grace for t. monk
make peace with t. monk
make a place for t. monk
trade places with ol' monk
trade faces with ol' monk
lake day labor—tabor bore maybe
born for thelonious monk
                    a scotch physic on former busy
                    thelonious monk

229

                         take a cue from
                         blow the blue drum
                         say the gay song
                         play the gay dog
                         do not deny for i love you monk
cador drey tune
              slow flow day soon
                                neighbor day for nay day
                                     labor again the flavor
table blessing never lessing congo blessing
                   blessings on you Great & Glorious Monk
              creative day for coming way out
              all you little monks
                   BLAH
          ? where's your soul monk ?
              plink plank plunk
                monk cant funk
                   where's
                      your
                      soul

              thelonious
                   m
                   o
                   n
                   k
                   ?
                   maybe
          charlie mingus has it
and children are born
with deep eyes
and grow up
and die
knowing nothing
feeling little
              but pain
and it continues
all go their ways
all ways the same
without change
birth
death
and in between
little but

deep wondering eyes
and pain

Oh, the bitter grows sweet
and the sweet bitter
and paths run through the grass
and towns are here and there
and trees, and often
lakes, birds
and always the wind blows
the sun rises
always too
the deepeyed children
forget, age into eyes
of glass, of stone

tumble the void
blind, dumb, alone
and always
nothing
always
pain

JERRY W. WARD, JR.

Jazz to Jackson to John

(for John Reese)

movement one: genesis

it must have been something like
sheets of sound wrinkled
with riffs and scats,
the aftermath of a fierce night
breezing through the grits and gravy;
or something like a blind leviathan
squeezing through solid rock,
marking chaos in the water
when his lady of graveyard love went

turning tricks on the ocean's bottom;
or something like a vision
so blazing basic, so gutbucket, so blessed
the lowdown blues flew out: jazz

jazz to jackson and
dust to dawn and
words for John

it must have been something like
Farish Street in the bebop forties,
a ragtag holy ghost baptizing Mississippi
on an unexpected Sunday, a brilliant revelation
for Billie telling you about these foolish things
back in your own backyard, angel eyes in the rose room,
Monk's changing piano into horn because it was zero in the
sun,
and around midnight there was nobody but you
to walk Parker and his jazz to Jackson;
yeah, brother, it must have been something
striking you like an eargasm,
a baritone ax laid into soprano wood,
like loving madly, in hurting silence,
waiting to fingerpop this heathen air
with innovations of classical black
at decibels to wake the deaf, the dumb, and the dead;
because around midnight there was nobody but you
who dug whether race records were
lamentations or lynchings: jazz

jazz to jackson and
sunset to dawn and
words for John

movement two: blues people in the corn

steal away, steal away, steal away
the heart blow/horn blow/drum drop
to bass/fives-four time beat
making a one o'clock comeback creep
behind all that jazz
beat—beepbeep—beat

steal way back to beginning
beginning
is the water

232

is the soul
is the source
is the foundation with my brothers
is Pharoah jamming in the pyramid,
sketches of Spain for a night in Tunisia;
is MJQ, Tatum, Turrentine, Tyner,
the Jazz Messengers, messiahs, crusading
headhunters tracking down the mind

cause, Lord yes, all God's people got sold
and who'da thought
owning rhythm was a crime like stealing a nickle
and snitching a dime, when we had coffers packed
with golden music and time, golden music and time
sliding from the flesh, the bone, honeysweet music;
them lollipopcicle people
with they sardine ships
(and no music to speak of)
they stole it all and sold it all
for wooden nickles, for frozen dimes: jazz

behind all that jazz
blues people in the corn, in the vale of cotton tears,
blues people in the corn,
waiting, waiting, waiting,
wrapped in esoteric patience,
waiting to steal away,
steal away, steal away
soon as Miles runs down the voodoo avenue
with some jazz to Jackson
and pipes a private number
to call a tune for John

movement three: and this, John, is our new day

and this, John, is our new day.
never say goodbye to the blues that saw you through,
nor put down the spirituals and the salty sermonettes
the drugs, the junkies, the jukebox juice, the sweat
and the pain of shelling hot peanuts, hot peanuts: jazz

and the jazz you gave to us
we give to you as jazz to Jackson and
because we really want to thank you
words for John

233

PAULETTE C. WHITE

Nina Simone

Witch Doctor Lady,
create a liberating mood—
sing
and we will move
into you,
one soul, one thought.
Go
deeper than reason,
deeper than reality.
Make your voice
a magic dream
where your vision
becomes us
and we are beautiful.

Witch Doctor Lady,
mystify the air.
Shoot it
with your firesong,
burn us
in the softest places
so that we feel,
thrill after you
when you have gone.

Witch Doctor Lady,
Nina Simone,
teach us,
bewitch us,
sing us your song.

SHERLEY ANNE WILLIAMS

Any Woman's Blues

every woman is a victim of the feel blues, too.

Soft lamp shinin
   and me alone in the night.
Soft lamp is shinin
   and me alone in the night.
Can't take no one beside me
   need mo'n jest some man to set me right.

I left many peoples and places
   tryin not to be alone.
Left many a person and places
   I lived my life alone.
I need to get myself together.
   Yes, I need to make myself to home.

What's gone can be a window
   a circle in the eye of the sun.
What's gone can be a window
   a circle, well, in the eye of the sun.
Take the circle from the world, girl,
   you find the light have gone.

These is old blues
   and I sing em like any woman do.
These the old blues
   and I sing em, sing em, sing em. Just like any woman do.
My life ain't done yet.
   Naw. My song ain't through.

1 Poem 2 Voices A Song

for Sherman McKinney

his body be arched when he play—like Miles—
only leaner legs stiff
hips forward and the top
of him seem like it drift
his shoulders be hunched protectin his gift

235

He put horn to lip and blew
that he had been through the world
blew against rock beats in clear
soprano tones.

he said it be like a battle—
him and that horn—be pain.
I know it like an hour with the blues
blowin help him call his name

                    Now,
          fragmented by the
          tripping lights, the band
          is a fusilade
          a kaleidoscope
          of sound. And then. Then
          he moves, arrogant,
          slouching across the
          stage and his raucous
          voice reverberates
          in the hand-held mike
          rapping, calling out
          a litany of
          heroes: Lummumba.
          Mao.   Martin.   Malcolm.
          Jackson. . . . yeahyeah. Yeah!

he speak when he see a brother
wave   say   what is it, dude?
they nod   say   you got it   man.
he smile cause he know it be true.

this sherman song   the one he blew:

     I been through the world

(hear it.   hear it.   hear it   feeeeel
it.   Blow!)

          but only
the best has touched me.

WILLIAM CARLOS WILLIAMS

Ol' Bunk's Band

These are men! the gaunt
unforesold, the vocal,
blatant, Stand up, stand up! the
    slap of a bass-string.
Pick, ping! The horn, the
    hollow horn
long drawn out, a hound-deep
    tone—
Choking, choking! while the
    treble reed
races—alone, ripples, screams
    slow to fast—
to second to first! These are men!

Drum, drum, drum, drum, drum
    drum, drum! the
ancient cry, escaping crapulence
    eats through
transcendent—torn, tears, term
    town, tense,
turns and backs off whole, leaps
    up, stomps down,
rips through! These are men
    beneath
whose force the melody limps—
    to
proclaim, proclaims—Run and
    lie down,
in slow measures, to rest and
    not never
need no more! These are men!
    Men!

DAVID WOJAHN

Satin Doll

It's probably the year her marriage
fails, though the photo, blackened now
on the edges of its sepia, doesn't say:
my aunt on the hood of the blue Chevy coupe,

straw hat and summer dress. It's the year
she carries the novels and notebooks
into the backyard to burn them, and when she finishes
her dress and apron are covered with ashes, rising

in what she wants to call a pillar of fire
but it is only smoke on a damp day.
She walks back to the house and her first
sickly daughter, feeling the one

inside her kick. She thinks of going
back to her maiden name, and the daughter
cries in her crib like the passionless
wind up the St. Croix River bluffs.

And when she was a child there, the day
of the grade school picnic, they found
a woman drowned on the banks. Everyone stared
and no one closed the eyes staring back.

But now it's raining on the first spring night
of 1947, six years to my birth,
and I don't want to leave her here. I want
the kitchen radio to murmur

some slithering big band and "Satin Doll"
from the Casablanca ballroom, high in Chicago's clouds.
I want her to see the women floating
in their taffeta, chilly red corsages from

their pencil-mustached men, ivory tuxedos, lotion,
and bay rum. She can almost touch them now. Duke Ellington
rises from the sprawling Steinway as the three
trombones begin their solo, horns glittering

under the spinning globe of mirrors. And now
she's dancing, isn't she? Until the cupboards shake,
until the window, already trembling with rain,
hums its vibrato, and she's holding herself in her arms

so tightly she can feel the veins
in her shoulders throb to their separate music,
until this is a song she can dance with too,
and I can let her go.

JOEL "YEHUDA" WOLK

Elegy for Kenny Dorham

> The news of Dorham's
> death spun out like
> thirty-second notes.
>
> The Old West Church,
> Boston, his
> last: to raise
> dialysis money.
>
> His message
> floated in the
> church. Trumpets
> dressed in suits
>
> and ties. The
> little mouthpiece
> for a head
> hung itself up.

C. D. WRIGHT

Jazz Impressions in the Garden

Dark as a cow. It's a downpour.
Mud on every sole in the vestibule.
A boy can lean on his oar, drift
Out of this world.
The time has come now
For the cold eyes of the rain and the writer
To bear down. This could be Harlem,
The old theater where they used to lay up
Smoking Kools in the balcony,
Tying off a vein
With something found on the floor,
Or Arkansas, a pair of antlers
Glued to a cedar board.
Which do you want, this or more of the same.
All the great dead lie on their backs
Under grass and granite
Listening to women sing, dragging their chains.
Requiem of the thunder. Roll on.

The Substitute Bassist

During the very rich times of the Duke
The trains, long and slower than funerals
In the Quarter;

Musicians went to their berths like the grave.
They were going home. Rocking.

The bass man stayed up alone
To pay his respects to the moon. He sat
In the draft of her.

Their instruments grew silent and cold
In the lining of their cases.

The hand with the glove on let up the shade.
A ground fog moved alongside the coach.

He drew in the pane
As though carving a scar in the bark,
Willow Weep for Me.

Treatment

for the children of Atlanta

this is a 16mm film of 7 minutes in which no words are spoken.
but for a few hand-tinted elements: the girl's dress, the sax,
sky at church the color is b/w.
the camera reports in the all-knowing third except in handheld
shots it reveals the driver's field of vision.

The bus rocks out of ruts and over creek rocks at pre-dawn. The driver
hasn't picked up any children. He has the radio on and a cigarette lit.
Isn't paying attention to either. His headlights are on the road, and
webs in the trees as if they were searchlights. His mind is bent. As his
posture and his face reveals. A girl dresses in purple in the dark. She
feels along the wallpaper to the kitchen, fixes oatmeal, warms coffee to
which she adds globs of honey. She makes a s/w for lunch. She starts to
eat out of the pot on the stove. Stops and gets a bowl from a high cabi-
net and sits at the table. She keeps tap with her foot to a tune she hums
only inside herself. When she goes back upstairs to comb her hair and
make an irregular part; to tinkle, she hears her parents. Their bed-
springs. A shot of them under many covers. Apparently her mother has
told her she is a love child. She understands so her listening isn't upset-
ting. She steals in her younger brother's room and leaves a bird she
folded from one sheet of paper on his nightstand. When she hears the bus
shifting at the foot of the hill she grabs sweater and tablet and flies past
the lunchsack on the bannister. The driver greets her with Hey Prin-
cess. That look. She sits close to the rear. The driver climbs the hill and
puts it in neutral under an elm stand. He jerks the handbrake. The
camera is in the back and shooting forward as he comes down the aisle,
it is behind her. He looms larger than he is and walks as if the bus was
in motion. The rape is explicit. The camera shoots out the back and side
windows every few seconds to see if anyone, another vehicle, approaches.
There are no more shots of the girl. The parents' house is shown from
the yard and from the foot of her window. Light breaks in the trees, a
cool sun. You hear the bus grind, the children, as the bus fills and pro-
ceeds. Then a field of high grass, a white church. No roads leading
there. No cars parked nearby. Slight quality of a different world. A sax-
ophone is played. A full choir accompanies. A silent congregation, all

stand, motionless. All adults. Pharoah Sanders stands in front of the choir stall in white robes. He plays with his eyes shut. He plays a curved soprano. His foot taps to an interior beat. Clearly he's an Angel. With the horn he lures. Accuses. His solo has a timeless aura. The doors of the church blow open. The driver falls onto the aisle. He begins to squirm on his belly toward the Pharoah. It's a long journey. The Pharoah wails controllably. The choir sways, claps, the congregation keeps quiet, light breaks in the trees and indistinct voices of many children fill the nave as if they were boarding a bus.

ROBERT WRIGLEY

Torch Songs

I would speak of that grief
perfected by the saxophone, the slow
muted trombone, the low unforgettable cornet.
Theirs were the paths we followed
into the sexual forest, the witch's spellbound cabin,
the national anthems of longing.

Rhythm is the plod of the human heart,
that aimless walker down deserted streets
at midnight, where a tavern's neon keeps the pulse.
A horn man licks the blood
in tow, heavy and smooth,
and a song is in the veins like whiskey.

Does it matter then that men have written
the heartbreaks women make hurt?
That Holiday and Smith sang for one
but to the other? Or is everything equal
in the testimonies of power and loss?

Now your eyes are closed,
your head leaned back, and off to one side.
Living is a slow dance you know
you're dreaming, but the chill at your neck
is real, the soft, slow breathing
of someone you might always love.

AL YOUNG

A Dance for Ma Rainey

I'm going to be just like you, Ma
Rainey this monday morning
clouds puffing up out of my head
like those balloons
that float above the faces of white people
in the funnypapers

I'm going to hover in the corners
of the world, Ma
& sing from the bottom of hell
up to the tops of high heaven
& send out scratchless waves of yellow
& brown & that basic black honey
misery

I'm going to cry so sweet
& so low
& so dangerous,
Ma,
that the message is going to reach you
back in 1922
where you shimmer
snaggle-toothed
perfumed &
powdered
in your bauble beads
hair pressed & tied back
throbbing with that sick pain
I know
& hide so well
that pain that blues
jives the world with
aching to be heard
that downness
that bottomlessness
first felt by some stolen delta nigger
swamped under with redblooded american agony;
reduced to the sheer shit

243

of existence
that bred
& battered us all,
Ma,
the beautiful people
our beautiful people
our beautiful brave black people
who no longer need to jazz
or sing to themselves in murderous vibrations
or play the veins of their strong tender arms
with needles
to prove how proud we are

Jungle Strut

Gene Ammons, 1969

Of all the nights, yours were greenest, Gene,
blue-breathing son of your boogie-bled dad
who, like you after him, left this dry world
a treasure tray of cocktails for the ear.

You loved making people high with your song
just as you must've loved soaring some yourself.
How high? Moon high, scaling neon heights like
an eagle humming along on silence and a bellyful.

Dumb hunters stalked you, staking you out shame-
lessly, especially when you were straddling air
pockets that, however turbulent, never blew away
your sound and rollicking command of aerial flight.

The wine poured from your jug (when you weren't
locked up in one) was aging and tasty. Bottoms up!

BILL ZAVATSKY

Elegy

(For Bill Evans, 1929–1980)

Music your hands are no longer here to make
Still breaks against my ear, still shakes my heart.
Then I feel that I am still before you.
You bend above your shadow on the keys
That tremble at your touch or crystallize,
Water forced to concentrate. In meditation
You close your eyes to see yourself more clearly.

Now you know the source of sound,
The element bone and muscle penetrate
Hoping to bring back beauty.
Hoping to catch what lies beyond our reach,
You hunted with your fingertips.

My life you found, and many other lives
Which traveled through your hands upon their journey.
Note by note we followed in your tracks, like
Hearing the rain, eyes closed to feel more deeply.
We stood before the mountains of your touch.
The sunlight and the shade you carried us
We drank, tasting our bitter lives more sweetly
From the spring of song that never stops its kiss.

To the Pianist Bill Evans

When I hear you
play "My Foolish Heart"
I am clouded

remembering more than
Scott LaFaro's charred bass
as it rested

against a Yonkers wall
in its transit
from accidental fire

245

like a shadowy
grace note
exploding into

rhythms of Lou
insanely driving
"Man, we're *late!*"

his long curved bass
straining the car
interior, a canvas swan

my hand clutched,
fingered, refingered:
steel strings as

of the human neck
the vulnerable neck
the neck of music

squeezed by hands
the fragile box
of song, the breath

I crushed out of music
before I killed
by accident

whatever in me
could sing
not touching the keyboard

of terrible parties
and snow
                    snow

falling as canvas and
wood and hair flamed
behind a windshield

I imagined being
trapped inside, still
see it in my heart

our terror magnified
note by note
purified each year

the gentle rise
and circle of
cinders in

February air
in their transit
from fire

into music,
into memory, a space
where heroin

does not slowly wave
its blazing arm,
like smoking ivory

teeth and fingers
scorched by the
proximity

of cigarettes laid
on anonymous piano
lips that crush

our function, in-
transigent wire,
inanimate wood

of another century
we must save by song!
for which we are paid!

continuing to be
used, insisting
our hands present

themselves
and keep
on taking our hands

PAUL ZIMMER

The Duke Ellington Dream

Of course Zimmer was late for the gig.
Duke was pissed and growling at the piano,
But Jeep, Brute, Rex, Cat and Cootie
All moved down on the chairs
As Zimmer walked in with his tenor.
Everyone knew that the boss had arrived.

Duke slammed out the downbeat for Caravan
And Zimmer stood up to take his solo.
The whole joint suddenly started jiving,
Chicks came up to the bandstand
To hang their lovelies over the rail.
Duke was sweating but wouldn't smile
Through chorus after chorus after chorus.

It was the same with Satin Doll,
Do Nothing Till You Hear From Me,
Warm Valley, In A Sentimental Mood;
Zimmer blew them so they would stay played.

After the final set he packed
His horn and was heading out
When Duke came up and collared him.
"Zimmer," he said, "You most astonishing ofay!
You have shat upon my charts,
But I love you madly."

Zimmer's Last Gig

Listening to hard bop,
I stayed up all night
Just like good times.
I broke the old waxes
After I'd played them:
Out of Nowhere, Mohawk,
Star Eyes, Salt Peanuts,
Confirmation, one-by-one;

248

Bird, Monk, Bud, Fats, Pres,
All dead, all dead anyway,
As clay around my feet.

Years ago I wanted to
Take Wanda to Birdland,
Certain that the music
Would make her desire me,
That after a few sets
She would give in to
Rhythm and sophistication.
Then we could slip off
Into the wee hours with
Gin, chase, and maryjane,
Check into a downtown pad,
Do some fancy jitterbugging
Between the lilywhites.

But Wanda was no quail.
Bud could have passed
Out over the keys,
Bird could have shot
Up right on stage,

Wanda would have missed
The legends. The band
Could have riffed
All night right by
Her ear, she never
Would have bounced.

Biographical Notes and Statements of Poetics

SAM ABRAMS, Associate Professor of Language and Literature at Rochester Institute of Technology and a Fulbright lecturer in twentieth-century American literature at the University of Athens, is the author of three books of poems. He was turned on to jazz/blues at a high school party by the Library of Congress record of Jelly Roll Morton doing "Winin' Boy Blues."

"I have no doubts that a couple of thousand years from now the names Jelly Roll Morton, Ma Rainey, Charlie Parker will be famous. Thus it is that we know of Sappho, while great Pittacus of Mytilene, her contemporary, is known only to specialists.

"But Amiri sez it better."

JAMES BALDWIN wrote twenty books, including *If Beale Street Could Talk, The Fire Next Time, Giovanni's Room, Another Country, Go Tell It on the Mountain,* and *Going to Meet the Man.* His book of poems is titled *Jimmy's Blues.* He died in 1987.

AMIRI BARAKA is the author of over twenty plays, two jazz operas, seven books of nonfiction, and thirteen volumes of poetry. He has received grants from the Rockefeller Foundation and the National Endowment for the Arts, has taught at Columbia and Yale universities, and for years has had a jazz program on public radio. He and his wife, Amina, co-authored *Confirmation: An Anthology of African-American Women* and *The Music: Reflections on Jazz and Blues.*

GEORGE BARLOW has taught at De Anza College since 1975. His work has appeared in numerous periodicals and anthologies. He has published two books, *Gabriel* and *Gumbo,* the latter of which was selected by the National Poetry Series.

GERALD BARRAX, born in 1933, is the author of *Another Kind of Rain* and *An Audience of One.* He has also contributed to several anthologies and teaches at North Carolina State University in Raleigh.

"It is difficult, almost impossible, for me to isolate the influence of jazz on my work from the influence that *all* music has had on me, my work, my whole life. I love jazz no more and no less than I love Blues, popular music, classical music, and opera. All have been equally important—*necessary* to me—and I can't rank them in value or priority. For example, the first versions of "The Singer" were called "Diva" before I revised it—rewrote it for the last time. In fact, after I'd finished it I realized that the singers to whom it is dedicated could just as well have included (and probably should have) Marian Anderson, Mahalia Jackson, Shirley Verret, Grace Bumbry, Florence Quivar, Leona Mitchell, Jessye Norman, Kathleen Battle, Leontyne Price, etc. But that's another poem."

MARVIN BELL grew up on eastern Long Island, playing cornet in bands, orchestras, combos, churches and bars. His two most recent books of poems are *New and Selected Poems* and *Iris of Creation*. He lives in Iowa City, Iowa, and Port Townsend, Washington.

"Going to Birdland to hear trombonists J. J. Johnson and Kai Winding, we were likely to see Miles Davis or Don Eliot too. The stadium dates and big record-distribution routes had yet to weaken the club system for jazz, and the artists came to hear one another and sometimes to sit in. Even then, the beer came only in paper cups, to cut down on violence, and the drinks were hustled to tables little bigger than the napkins. Still, to teenagers it *seemed* spacious and cheerful. We didn't know shit, but we knew something."

CAROL BERGÉ has written many books of poetry, including *Rituals and Gargoyles, A Song, a Chant, Alba Genesis,* and *Alba Nemesis.* Among her honors and awards are a New York State Council on the Arts Creative Artists Public Service grant for fiction and a National Endowment for the Arts fellowship in creative writing.

"In the early 60s, there were two synchronous movements in poetic technique: one was the intellectual reaching, symbolized for me by Jackson Mac Low (who, even so, was a composer and always conscious of the sonics in his poetry); the other was the sensual reaching, symbolized by the Beats, in both San Francisco and NY coffeehouses. I read poetry aloud with the jazz of California musicians and Charlie Mingus in New York back then. I was then and still am interested in syncopation, dissonance and assonance, and the correspondence of words to the body which produces them. To me, there's no separation of mind and body—both equal self, and self is made of music derived from pulse and motion. John Cage opened me to realizing the "music" inherent in all sound—I'm now aware that everything in physics/nature has tonality and specific response and rhythm in its auditory quality. A walk on the desert or in a city is the same in its production of music. Jazz is as exquisite to me as a sonata or a fugue, and often as well-made. I have a particular delight in jazz. I remember loving Lenny Tristano, Gerry Mulligan, Eddie Condon, while I was attending college; later, Dave Brubeck—these were more the cool-jazz players, and they followed Louis Armstrong, Duke Ellington, George Shearing—my first loves. Where I live now are mariachi music and ceremonial drums, and both form kinds of culturally contemporary jazz. I love the poetry of Charles Olson and that of Paul Blackburn—both based in extemporaneous variations on themes of sound/language. It seems to me that jazz music has pervaded most good poetry and prose in this country since the first world war. To me, jazz and poetry are alike in that they're both intended to be heard and felt at the same time, with a vivid appeal to the senses."

PAUL BLACKBURN, born in 1926, was a poet, a translator, and an educator. He died in September 1971.

HORACE JULIAN BOND is active in the movement of human rights and is a former Georgia state senator.

GEORGE BOWERING has published forty books, including poetry, fiction, and essays. His most recent book published in the United States is the novel *Caprice.*

EDWARD KAMAU BRATHWAITE, born in Bridgetown, Barbados, taught in Ghana from 1955 to 1962. Since that time he has been lecturing in history at the Uni-

251

versity of the West Indies. He has written many books, including *Rights of Passage, Masks, Folk Culture of the Slaves in Jamaica,* and *Black & Blues.*

RAY BREMSER'S books include *Poems of Madness* and *Blowing Mouth/The Jazz Poems, 1958–70.* A blurb for a reading in New York described him as "Jazz-ear Sound Poetry Genius, old Elvin Jones roommate, syncopating wow-sound word walloper; long ago jailbird, original NY late-1950s coffee shop Beat bard with Kerouac & Leroi Jones."

STERLING A. BROWN, born in 1901 in Washington, D.C., developed an early passion for literature. Like many of his contemporaries—including Langston Hughes, Zora Neale Hurston, Jean Toomer, Arna Bontemps, and Countee Cullen—he was profoundly influenced by the change in the political and social climate in America following World War I and the upsurge of militancy. He remains one of the great innovators of jazz-related poetry. His books include *Southern Road, The Negro in Washington, The Negro in American Fiction, Negro Poetry and Drama,* and *The Negro Caravan.* He taught for more than fifty years at Howard University, where he was Professor Emeritus until his death in 1989.

RICHARD BURNS was born in London in 1943; his mother's family were Lithuanian and Latvian Jews, and his father, a musician, was born in Warsaw. In 1964 he traveled to Italy and Greece, where he spent three years, and later moved to London and Cambridge, where he founded and organized the first international Cambridge Poetry Festival. Author of several books of poetry (including *Roots/Routes,* his first book to be published in the United States), he is also an editor of three anthologies and a translator from Italian and modern Greek.

"I was at a boarding school through my teens, one of those awful British Public Schools which aren't public and are intended to mold the Upper Classes into the nauseating zombies they are. That was in the late fifties, and we had a lot of good American jazz coming through then: Bird, Miles, Coltrane. I first heard 'Sketches of Spain' at the house of a friend who was the best drummer in the school. We'd broken out one afternoon, and his mother lived over an undertaker's shop. Somehow he got hold of a key to one of the little chapels down below his mother's flat (i.e., apartment), which had a corpse in it. He brought down his records and record player and plugged it in and we sat there playing Miles, and smoking, with the corpse of this old man lying there. I'd never heard Miles Davis before and I'd never seen a corpse before.

"The poem 'The Song of the Yellow Star' came out of my reading of a fine book called *Beyond the Blues,* Selected and Introduced by Rosey E. Pool, published by that fine poetry press, The Hand and Flower Press, Lympne, Kent, in 1962. It stuns me to think that's 28 years ago. This was a pioneering book in England, and to me, aged nineteen, it opened up new dimensions. The passage which affected me most in her fine introduction was this:

> One could even say that many of the sufferings of Afro-Americans have parallels in human history in many places on this earth. I may even add that the socio-artistic interest I have had in American Negro writing even since 1925, when I discovered Countee Cullen, intensified and became extremely close and personal (to the point of identification) after my own experiences during five years of Nazi reign, underground work and imprisonment in occupied Holland. Yellow Jew-stars sewn on garments have only to be substituted for darker skins and African features.

"That's how 'The Song of the Yellow Star' got written. I've written other poems since then which show a jazz influence in structure, freewheeling rhythms, improvisations in poetic space, and so on, but this poem to me still captures the intensity of my first love of jazz, and my own identification (as a Jew) with the sources of jazz."

HAYDEN CARRUTH is the author of twenty-six books published over the past thirty-five years, most of them poetry, some of them criticism and fiction. His most recent books are *The Selected Poetry of Hayden Carruth* and *Sitting In: Selected Writings on Jazz, the Blues, and Related Topics.* He teaches in the graduate creative writing program at Syracuse University.

CYRUS CASSELLS is the author of a highly acclaimed first book, *The Mud Actor,* one of the 1982 National Poetry Series and a nominee for the 1982 Bay Area Book Reviewers Award in Poetry. He is also the recipient of the 1983 Callaloo Creative Poets Prize at Stanford University and of several creative writing fellowships. He has recently completed a manuscript, *Sinera,* translations of the poet Salvador Espriu, Catalan Spain's leading contender for the Nobel Prize.

"As a poet, I'm particularly inspired by the complex beauties and improvisational glories of black classical music. I love the daredevil freedom of scat singing, the way great jazz artists tuck their talent and discipline fearlessly under their wings—and take off: they're joyous spiritual acrobats seeking the splendor of the moment; like them, I don't want to miss a beat."

MAXINE CASSIN was born in New Orleans and has lived there all her life. She was co-founder and co-editor in 1955 with Richard Ashman of *The New Orleans Poetry Journal.* Her books include *Nine by Three* (shared with Robert Beum and Felix Stefanile), *A Touch of Recognition,* and *Turnip's Blood.*

"For me, jazz is not so diametrically opposed to poetry—though I cannot speak from the first-hand experience of a musician. It is that breathtakingly unexpected but never accidental improvisation which begins to soar from a simple melodic line—the imaginative leap which characterizes both art forms at their best.
"In thinking of a way to describe this phenomenon, I cannot help calling to mind William Matthews' brilliant tour de force, 'Bmp Bmp.' Here Bechet is '. . . playing against the regular disasters / of the melody his love for flight and flight's / need for gravity. . . .'
"Obviously, the poet cannot do what the musician does, but how strong that longing is to get those licks in! In my own case, the poems seem to spring from some kind of thwarted urge and intense identification with those feverish, yet cool spirits who pipe to us from so many New Orleans haunts.
"Years ago at Preservation Hall I stood with Kathleen Raine listening to 'Down by the Riverside,' transported as she was—wordless, too; but eventually the words stir in us to become poems when we are finally back at work—'isolated in the circle of our lamplight.' "

GRACE CAVALIERI is the author of five books of poetry, the most recent of which is *Bliss.* She has had eighteen plays produced throughout the country for stage and radio. She is the producer and host of "The Poet and The Poem," a program on public radio stations which now celebrates its twelfth year.

FRED CHAPPELL, Professor of English at the University of North Carolina at Greensboro, is author of several volumes of poetry, five novels, and a collection of short stories. His most recent book is *First and Last Words.*

"I enclose my only jazz piece I care for, a poem, 'The Highest Wind That Ever Blew.' One of the reasons that I do care for it is that, by way of the trombonist

253

Bill Pape, I got a fan letter about it from Mr. Clark Terry. He called it an M.F. and carried a copy to Mrs. Lucille Armstrong."

WANDA COLEMAN, a former welfare mother, now works as a medical secretary/ transcriber. Her books include *Mad Dog Black Lady, Imagoes,* and *Heavy Daughter Blues.* She has received fellowships in poetry from the National Endowment for the Arts and the Guggenheim Foundation. Best known for her dramatic performances, she has given more than three hundred readings/events and toured Australia in 1986. Her most recent recording, in tandem with poet Michelle Clinton, is *Black Angeles.*

"The power of the word to evoke time the power of the word to make change the power of the word to uproot to make whole to sever the power to be heard long long long after silence."

CLAIRE COLLETT was born in Bradford, England, but brought up in South Wales.

LEO CONNELLAN is the author of *The Clear Blue Lobster-Water Country.* He is the 1982 recipient of the Shelley-Memorial Award. He has written several books of poems, including *New and First Collected Poems.*

"I am now 55 years old. When I was 24 I wanted to catch the horror and reality of male-oriented chauvinism that always disgusted me and also a period that actually existed in New York City that I wanted to catch somewhat before it was gone. I was *very* conscious, in those days, that our 'little new country, America' was often looked on with contempt, even by great poets. . . . Since I was even then trying to be original, I talked well into the night about this often with poets like the Bombay Indian poet Tambimuttu who had been T. S. Eliot's editor at Faber & Faber right before WW II and I often spoke to Kenneth Fearing and to Maxwell Bodenheim and even once to e. e. cummings about the things that disturbed me and so I *presumed* and took a risk as all poets who wish to be read later must take and I actually wrote a book titled *Another Poet In New York* which has the obligatory New York City subway poem (to go against Robert Lowell's, Hart Crane's, Kenneth Fearing's, etc.) and my Staten Island Ferry Poem and a poem to stand up to Garcia Lorca's Ignatio poem, which no poet will ever be able to do—and in the book I got a jazz poem . . . it was all true too. There *was* a real Johnny Romero who had a place with a Village back yard garden on Minetta street, or Minetta Lane between famous Village streets."

GILLIAN CONOLEY'S first collection of poems is *Some Gangster Pain,* and her manuscript *Tall Stranger* was awarded a 1988 Artist's Fellowship from the Washington State Arts Commission. Her poems have appeared in *Poetry, Poetry East, Crazyhorse,* and *Denver Quarterly's* special poetics issue.

CLARK COOLIDGE was born in 1939. A musician since his high school days, he was drummer with the Serpent Power, a San Francisco rock group. His books of poetry include *Space* and *Suite V.*

"The feel is that time has a precise center. Like tightroping on a moving pulley clothesline, you're always trying to keep up midway between the poles. It really gets that sharply physical. As a drummer you're holding time's cutting edge in your righthand (ride cymbal), a simultaneity of holding and shaping. You occupy the center of the sonic sphere, the world, and ride it and bear it, inviolable (why heroin is Bop's perfect chemical). And everything that happens there happens once and at once. Once and Ounce, Groove and Chord, Wave and Particle: the Complementarity of Bop.

"Touch is essential. Can you touch time? Consider Kenny Clarke's 'magic cymbal,' which he 'kept level' and 'when somebody would sit in on drums and use his set, it would sound like the top of a garbage can, but when he played it, it was like fine crystal.'

"Time is a substance if you hear   you can get on and ride. I have always found metric feet awkward as a base for my lines. Rather the unceasing teem of that top cymbal at the back of my room.

"Max Roach is imprinted on my nervous reflex. I sit at my desk helplessly tapping out his snare and bass exchanges between thoughts. Sometimes I feel the space between people (voices) in terms of tempos. The rush of an idea, a Blakey press-roll. That characteristic Roy Haynes snare and sock-cymbal figure a definitely constructed image, perhaps over to one side but more important than the main action, a sort of very bright cam. Klook's brushes a landscape in my sleep.

"Then there is the famous door of Elvin Jones: 'The length of my solos doesn't mean anything. When I go on for so long, I am looking for the right way to get out. Sometimes the door goes right by and I don't see it, so I have to wait until it comes around again. Sometimes it doesn't come around at all for a long time.'

"These days I ask myself again and more acutely the relation (if there is one?) between language forms and the wordless shapes of time. Perhaps there is no direct exchange. All I can be sure of is that I am able to possess them both within one body and one mind."

GREGORY CORSO, born in 1930 in New York, was a prison inmate from 1947 to 1950. In the fifties he attracted widespread attention in a series of poetry readings in the East and the Midwest. He is the author of many books, including *Gasoline, The Mutation of the Spirit,* and *Elegiac Feelings American.*

JAYNE CORTEZ was born in Arizona, grew up in California, and is currently living in New York City. She is the author of six books of poetry, most recently *Coagulations: New and Selected Poems.* She has made four recordings; her most recent is *Maintain Control.* Her work has been published in many journals, magazines, and anthologies, including *A Book of Women Poets, Powers of Design, Confirmation, New Black Voices, Free Spirits, Black Scholar,* and *UNESCO Courier.* She has lectured and read her poetry alone and with music throughout the United States, West Africa, Europe, Latin America, and the Caribbean. She received the New York Foundation for the Arts poetry award in 1987, and two National Endowment for the Arts fellowships, in 1980 and 1986.

ROBERT CREELEY, born in 1926, taught at Black Mountain College from 1955 to 1956 and has taught at various universities and colleges all over the world since then. He has written a number of poetry books and in 1982 published *The Collected Poems of Robert Creeley, 1945–1975.*

TOM DENT, after living in New York, where he was part of the "Umbra" group, returned to his native New Orleans in 1965 and worked with the Free Southern Theater, a civil rights theater group which toured "movement" towns of the south. He is the author of *The Free Southern Theater by the Free Southern Theater* (with Gilbert Moses and Richard Schechner), *Magnolia Street,* and *Blue Lights and River Songs.* He currently serves as executive director of the New Orleans Jazz and Heritage Foundation, which presents the annual New Orleans Jazz Festival each spring.

255

OWEN DODSON, born in 1914, is the author of several books, including *Powerful Long Ladder* and *Come Home Early, Child.* His work has received a number of fellowships and awards, including a Guggenheim fellowship, the *Paris Review* prize, and a Rockefeller Foundation fellowship. He died in 1983.

GEORGE ECONOMOU, born in 1934, taught at Long Island University from 1961 to 1983, when he became department chair of English at the University of Oklahoma. His poems, translations, and criticism have appeared in many journals, magazines, and anthologies. He has written several books of poetry, including *Harmonies and Fits,* as well as numerous books on medieval literature.

"I hope this poem ["33⅓ RPM"] demonstrates as well as states the influence of jazz on my work. To grow up American is to grow with the sounds of jazz nurturing our souls along with our speech and our oceans, winds, waters and birds. Jazz is our land's musical nature. The life of our words shaped into songs depends on it."

RICHARD ELMAN: Born, Brooklyn. Ran to Manhattan at an early age to Three Deuces, Birdland, Onx, Club Savannah. Heard Kid Ory's Farewell concert with Chippy Hill, attended Syracuse; MA Stanford. Novelist and poet. Early loves: Fats Navarro, Bird, Tad Damaron, Prez, Moody's Mood In Love. First important book read: *Really The Blues* by Mezz Mezzrow. Used to scat on the corner with Louis Donchebag and Milty Mayface—Jewish blues. Twenty-one books published, wives, children. Currently lives in Stony Brook, NY, not far from the great blues singer Mose Allison.

JOHN ENGELS's *Cardinals in the Ice Age,* his sixth collection of poetry, was selected by Philip Levine as one of five winners in the 1986 National Poetry Series competition. He is the recipient of a Fulbright award for Yugoslavia, as well as Guggenheim and National Endowment for the Arts fellowships. He teaches at St. Michael's College in Vermont.

"The poem ['In the Palais Royale Ballroom in 1948'] was in the beginning an attempt to deal in an affectionately ironic way with what was in my youth my most passionate fantasy. But it took me a couple of years to write it; during that time I turned fifty, upon which the irony intensified at the same time that nostalgia established its claims. The embouchure is gone forever, but I remember how it felt."

CLAYTON ESHLEMAN, born in 1935, is the author of many books, including *Indiana, The Gull Wall,* and *Core Meander.* He has translated Neruda, Vallejo, and Artaud—to name a few—and has received numerous awards and fellowships. He currently edits the magazine *Sulphur.*

FATISHA, born in 1940, is a poet and playwright of New York. During her career she has developed a strong reputation in public readings, in anthologies, and in jazz & poetry performances.

" 'From Star to Sun We Are Going' was written simply because I believe that the beauty in Miles Davis' sound corresponds to an inner beauty—regardless of how crazy, mean and evil people say Miles is . . . this is not the total human. The poem also implores Miles to set aside crazy and inane activity and be about the beauty of self-actualization—better than a Star—be another SUN!"

256

SASCHA FEINSTEIN is a tenor player from New York City who recently completed an MFA (poetry) and is currently working on a Ph.D. in twentieth-century literature. He has published jazz-related poems, essays, and interviews in several journals, including *The Missouri Review, The Green Mountains Review,* and *The North American Review,* and has published a chapbook of jazz-related poems titled *Summerhouse Piano.* He believes in many of Monk's philosophies, particularly that "the tenor sax is here to stay."

LAWRENCE FERLINGHETTI, one of the most influential of the Beat poets, is the author of a great many books of poetry, including *A Coney Island of the Mind, Who Are We Now?* and *A Trip to Italy and France.* He has written several plays, recorded his work, and contributed to several anthologies.

CALVIN FORBES was born in Newark, New Jersey, and received an MA degree from Brown University in 1978. He was writer in residence at Howard University from 1982 until 1987 and has taught at Emerson College, Tufts University, the University of Copenhagen, and the University of the West Indies. He published *Blue Monday* and received a Fulbright fellowship in 1981. He is currently working on a novel and a new volume of poetry and living in Washington D.C.

"Jazz is one music out of the music of the cosmos. There are many musics. Poetry is one. Dancing, a real people's artform, another. None is greater or less than any other. Afro-Am Jazz grows out of the collective soul consciousness of African-Americans and the source is there to be tapped by all—tap dancers—rap dancers—all who care (can care) about beauty can be beautiful. All the arts are one big happy (?) family sharing the same mother and father. Though different, what they learn from one another means none is disowned unless one wants to be bought and sold. Slave to the dollar. In my opinion, Black Literary artists (especially) have suffered under the illusion of an inferiority complex—as if music— JAZZ—was superior and had therefore sole claim to legitimate Black expression. True or false? Some of us who worshiped forgot that we all are children of the same God. None greater. We are all Gods, Priests, Magicians, if any of us are. I don't want to be a musician (or in the latest guise, a film maker) because I am already one and all."

ALICE FULTON, born in 1952, is the author of *Dance Script with Electric Ballerina* and *Palladium.* In 1984 she received the Consuelo Ford Award from the Poetry Society of America, and she was granted a fellowship from the Michigan Society of Fellows for 1983–1986.

"I began listening to popular music when I was 12, and through it I discovered jazz and blues. My interest in music led me to work as a radio announcer, and during 1976–77 I was the all-night jazz d.j. on WMHT-FM, Schenectady, New York.

"Analogies are often made between poetry and painting, but for me, poetry's concerns and ambitions have more in common with music. Even when the subject of my poems is not specifically musical, the poems' sound and its enjambments are influenced by some of the technical questions and resolutions of jazz. I try to write a line with a pushy, impulsive edge, an energetic phrasing that propels the reader along. Just as a jazz singer will stretch one note over several bars, bending the melody and meaning, I sometimes like to withhold sense until the end of a sentence, using line breaks to indicate underlying meanings and false stops along the way. Rather than following rules that say one must write in one tone throughout one poem, or stick to one level of diction, I am interested in intentionally changing tones in ways that surprise or move the poem to another level, and in playing density of language off lyricism. Too many poems are being written as if from a guidebook. The experiments of jazz music, including time changes, exchanges of dissonance with melody, and unconventional dynamics, have encouraged me to risk parallel inventions in my work."

CHRISTOPHER GILBERT'S first book, *Across the Mutual Landscape*, was chosen by Michael Harper as winner of the 1983 Walt Whitman Award of the Academy of American Poets. Trained in clinical and cognitive psychology, he has worked as a psychotherapist and is a psychologist associated with the Worcester Youth Guidance Center, the Cambridge Family, and the Children's Service in the Boston area.

DANA GIOIA'S poems have appeared in many magazines, including *The Paris Review, Poetry, The New Yorker,* and *The Hudson Review.* In 1984 he was chosen by *Esquire* in their first register of "Men and Women under 40 Who Are Changing the Nation." An executive with a major American corporation, he has a published a collection of poems called *Daily Horoscope.*

ELTON GLASER was born in New Orleans and raised there and in Slidell, Louisiana. Since 1972 he has taught at the University of Akron in Akron, Ohio, where he lives with his wife and two children. His first full-length book of poems is *Relics.* His second book, *Tropical Depressions,* won the Iowa Poetry Prize. He has also won the Theodore Roethke prize from *Poetry Northwest,* the Hart Crane Memorial Poetry Award from *Icon,* and fellowships from the Ohio Arts Council and the National Endowment for the Arts.

"When Wallace Stevens says that 'music is feeling, then, not sound,' I know what he means. When I listen to Robert Johnson testifying on 'Tipitina,' my whole body understands that music. And I want my poetry to work the same way, to enter the reader so that he is at one with the language, moved as the poem moves.

"I grew up in and around New Orleans, and the music of my childhood goes deeper than anything I have listened to since then. I am not talking about Dixieland jazz, the music most outlanders associate with New Orleans, tired toetappers in the tourist traps on Bourbon Street. My downhome music is rhythm 'n' blues. My ears were educated on the great piano players of New Orleans, blues-based tunes with a hot Caribbean spin, the parade strut of the drums, and a saxophone break that would tear the hide off any alligator cruising in Bayou St. John.

"The greatest of them all was Professor Longhair, who summed up the soul of New Orleans for me. His exuberance and funky sophistication, his goofy lyrics and relentless right hand, did not travel well—but then most New Orleansians prefer not to stray too far from home. You can't get crawfish in Ohio, and the red beans don't have the same flavor when cooked in a cold climate. But all I have to do is put 'Big Chief' on the stereo and I am back on Decatur Street with an oyster po-boy in one hand and a longneck Dixie beer in the other, in serious training for the daylong rigors of Mardi Gras.

"All those performers—Jesse Hill, Huey Smith, Ernie K-Doe, Irma Thomas, Art and Aaron Neville, and others too numerous to bring up here—remain an inspiration for me. Their rhythms, their phrasings, their innovative variations within a tradition are never very far from me when I sit down to write a poem. The poem does not have to be about New Orleans, either: their influence is general, not particular; sustaining, not temporary; ingrained, not superficially applied.

"When the blues gets up and walks like a man, it becomes the embodiment of human experience. It goes where the poem has to go too: 'free-lancing out along the razor's edge,' in Robert Lowell's phrase. My poems seek to transmute the pain of life into something not only bearable, but also beautiful; and this transformation must take place through language, through sound and rhythm and strikingly apt images. The R & B music of New Orleans, glamorous and sleazy and bold, is my lifeline to home, my wild honey in the wilderness, the syncopated back beat of my poems."

VINCE GOTERA is currently writing a collection of poems largely on Filipino-American life and culture entitled *Madarika*—a Tagalog word meaning "homeless wanderer." He won the 1988 Mary Roberts Rinehart Award in poetry. He currently teaches at Humboldt State University in California.

"Just as jazz counterpoints the classical and the improvisational, poetry should live on a tightrope. Balance real and irreal, lyric and narrative, the figure and the letter. Poetry should eat nails *and* eclairs."

LEE MEITZEN GRUE is a poet and fiction writer who lives in New Orleans and whose books include *Trains and Other Intrusions: Poems* and *French Quarter Poems.* In 1984 she received a National Endowment for the Arts grant for short fiction and has just been awarded a grant by the Jazz and Heritage Foundation for a book of poetry, *In the Sweet Balance of the Flesh.* She has won a PEN Syndication Prize for short fiction and is now working on a novel.

"My writing has long been influenced by the New Orleans musicians I listen to, and by the cadence of New Orleans everyday talk. The musicians are usually people I've known and admired for years. Hearing their work develop as their lives changed, I began to write poems in which jazz was used as literary allusion. Particular artists known for a certain sound—singers for certain songs—evoke the metaphor of their lives; their names, the titles of the songs, invest the poems with myth not available without these references.

"I love blues metaphors—strong colloquial speech—the ambience created by live jazz in a neighborhood club. I feel grateful that happy chance had me born in Louisiana. The primary source for the sound of my work is the African spoken tradition, but there's a strong flavor of the Irish in one section of New Orleans, the Italian another, and, of course, French. The French language came here in several different ways: the Frenchmen who came directly to New Orleans from France, the Acadians of Nova Scotia, and the creoles of the West Indies; all these voices are unique, but blend and take on piquant qualities by their associations with each other, just as seasonings exchange flavors in a good pot of gumbo. We've recently added Asians. By using cadence and breath pauses to express these voices in a poem or story, and by using allusions to certain songs or musicians I add strong flavors to my work—make it taste right—sound right—smell like my time and place."

MARILYN HACKER'S "Elegy for Janis Joplin" is from her book *Presentation Piece,* which received the National Book Award in poetry for 1975. Her other books include *Separations, Assumptions,* and *Love, Death, and the Changing of the Seasons.* She is editor of the *Kenyon Review.*

"The foreground music of my late adolescence was, on the one hand, that of Miles Davis, Ornette Coleman, John Coltrane and Max Roach; and, on the other, the very different vocal traditions of Odetta, Miriam Makeba, and Nina Simone. As a writer, my relation to music has always been more that of say, Ma Rainey, than that of the poetry-and-jazz buffs of the 1950s: I'd love to write things that could be sung, but am not enamored of the contemporary spoken-poem-as-perfor-mance-by-poet. I can't recall the early '60s without a Motown & country sound-track. Later in the decade, I rubbed elbows & pool cues with Janis Joplin more than once in Gino & Carlo's bar in North Beach. Unaccompanied Ladies were outlaw/exiles almost anywhere still, and, when I joined the crowds that filled the Fillmore Auditorium, she spoke and sang to my condition."

MICHAEL S. HARPER's books of poetry are *Dear John, Dear Coltrane; Debridement; History Is Your Own Heartbeat; Song: I Want Witness; Nightmare Begins Responsi-bility; Images of Kin; Healing Song for the Inner Ear.* He has won two National Book Award nominations, as well as awards given by the National Institute of Arts and Letters and the Black Academy of Arts and Letters. He has been the director of the graduate writing program and first holder of the Israel J. Kapstein Professorship of English at Brown University, where he has taught since 1970.

"Blues and jazz and the American language [are] part of America. And I'm sorry that everybody feels more comfortable when they go to England. And I mean that very seriously. I mean, I think we can learn a great deal from Words-worth and Coleridge but they're all Englishmen, you know, coming out of this tradition that's a thousand years old. They can look back to Chaucer. But the American language and the American idiom is entirely different, and it has com-ponents in it that don't exist . . . in England. And we have to get to the point where we feel a little more comfortable. . . . Jazz music is so indigenous to Amer-ican culture that even if you have a predilection not to like it you have to really be informed about it if you want to be informed about American culture."

HOWARD HART, born in 1927, is the author of four books of poetry, three plays, and two translations of French drama. As a New York–based musician during the fifties and early sixties, he worked as a contributing editor to the *Village Voice.* His poetry books include *Selected Poems: Six Sets, 1951–1983.*

ROBERT HAYDEN was born in Detroit, Michigan, in 1913. He won a number of international awards for his poetry. His books include *A Ballad of Remembrance, Words in the Mourning Time, The Night-Blooming Cereus,* and *Angle of Ascent: New and Selected Poems.* He died in 1980.

DAVID HILTON, born in 1938 in Oakland, California, went to graduate school at the University of Wisconsin, Madison, and since 1971 has taught English at Anne Arundel Community College near Baltimore. His books include *Huladance, The Candleflame,* and *No Relation to the Hotel.*

"I go for the strong, sonorous, 'hard' line; I like music, loud or lush; and *craft*— Yeats, Roethke, Williams, Hopkins, and contemporaries like Levertov, Heaney, Merwin form my notion of what should be done. A real line of poetry is in some way *accentual;* you can hear the beat."

EVERETT HOAGLAND's poetry and short fiction have appeared in numerous recent periodicals and anthologies, as well as in *Black Velvet,* his collection of love poems. He is professor of English at Southeastern Massachusetts University. His awards include the 1974 Gwendolyn Brooks Award for Fiction, awarded by *Black World Magazine,* and a 1975 Creative Artists Fellowship funded by the Massachusetts Arts and Humanities Foundation for his poetry.

ANDRE HODEIR is a French composer, arranger, and prolific writer of jazz. His books include *Jazz: Its Evolution and Essence, Toward Jazz,* and *The Worlds of Jazz.* Especially as a jazz critic, he is one of the most distinguished in the field.

GARRETT HONGO, co-author of *The Buddha Bandits Down Highway 99,* has published two books of poems, *Yellow Light* and *The River of Heaven.* Among his awards are the "Discovery"/*The Nation* award and a National Endowment for the Arts fellowship. He teaches at the University of Oregon, where he is director of the creative writing program.

LANGSTON HUGHES, 1902–1967, left behind a wealth of poems, novels, short stories, plays, song lyrics, translations, children's books, and recordings. His book *The Weary Blues* might be considered the first serious attempt at confronting the range and mixture of poetry and jazz. With Sterling A. Brown, he remains one of the greatest blues poets in history.

LYNDA HULL'S poetry has been published in the *New Yorker, Poetry, Antioch Review,* and *The Missouri Review.* Her first book of poems, *Ghost Money,* received the 1986 Juniper Prize, the annual poetry award sponsored by the University of Massachusetts Press. She has received a Pushcart Prize, a fellowship from Yaddo, and in 1989 an award from the National Endowment for the Arts.

LAWSON FUSAO INADA received two creative writing fellowships from the National Endowment for the Arts, has served on the Literature Panel for the Endowment, and is the former chair of the Coordinating Council of Literary Magazines. His poetry has appeared in numerous collections and is part of the Encyclopedia Britannica filmstrip series on American literature. His is the author of *Before the War,* the first volume of poetry by an Asian-American to be published by a major firm. He is an editor of two major Asian-American anthologies, *AIIIEEEE!* and *THE BIG AIIIEEEE!*

"Regarding poetry/jazz, I'm about the same age as friends/colleagues such as Baraka, Al Young, Ish Reed, Jayne Cortez. . . . Michael Harper and I go way back; we caught The Trane from coast to coast. . . . Further back, when I was an aspiring bassist instead of an aspiring poet, I knew another aspiring bassist named Jay; well, years later, he turns out to be *poet* Jay Wright!

"I just turned out to be me. By dint of history, necessity, I've whittled my own reeds and got my own chops together. Sort of, I suppose, blowing shakuhachi versaphone. Then, too, by dint of geography, I've had to do a Rahsaan and become my own group by developing various techniques of poetry."

KEN IRBY, born in 1936, has written several books of poetry, including *The Roadrunner, Relation: Poems, 1965–66,* and *The Snow Queen.* He has contributed to several anthologies and currently teaches at the University of Kansas.

ROD JELLEMA was born and raised in Michigan, educated there and in Scotland, and is Professor of English at the University of Maryland. Winner of two poetry fellowships from the National Endowment for the Arts, his latest book of poems is *The Eighth Day: New and Selected Poems.*

"I listened deeply to old 78's of King Oliver, Jelly Roll Morton, the Hot Five, Teagarden, and Bix while flunking out of high school. Without meaning to, I learned something which years later crossed over to the making of poems: the joy and exhilaration of taking chances, leaping into phrases without knowing how they were going to end. I learned to trust the movements of sounds and spaces far beneath and beyond the charts.

"On the way to discovering this trust in creative process, I spent freely the fringe benefit I had picked up. Listening hard to those old records, I learned to discriminate between good and mediocre, between brilliance and flashiness, between the authentic and the commercially successful. It gave me, I think, a kind of grid on which to measure ideas, books, poems, lines.

"If there is any body of creative work which the poet in me has used as a model, it is probably the recorded output of clarinetist Johnny Dodds."

TED JOANS, painter, trumpet player, jazz poet, has recited his poems in Greenwich Village coffeehouses and in the middle of the Sahara Desert. He is as much at home in Harlem, USA, as he is in Haarlem, Holland—and Paris and Stockholm and Timbuktu. His collection of jazz-related poetry is titled *Black Pow-Wow.*

JOE JOHNSON was born in Harlem in 1940. He is a poet, short-story writer, and critic for *Crisis* magazine.

"I believe in both life and spirit; spirit moves life and poetry moves spirit. Most of my adult life, I've denied that I'm a poet, but now I acknowledge spirit and claim my poetry. I live."

STEVE JONAS was born on December 1, 1921, in Atlanta, Georgia. His real name was Rufus Jones. He died in Boston on February 10, 1970. His mother died when he was fourteen, and he was raised for a while by an uncle in New York City; however, there are no records to confirm this fact. As he often spoke of an uncle, he also spoke of having a sister who lived in New York City. Raffael DeGruttola, a poet and close friend of Jonas's, reflects:

"Steve loved jazz and was always interested in searching out its roots and following its evolution in the new young musicians. He had a fantastic jazz record collection and you would always hear jazz upon entering his apartment. In his late twenties and early thirties, he would have many parties at his apartment in the old South End of Boston, and one would always find many jazz musicians who would stop by to listen to Steve's 'sides.' Often during these parties, he would read his poetry over the sounds of jazz and casual talk, as friends would socialize."

BOB KAUFMAN, born in 1925, was known in the United States as "The Original Be-Bop Man" and in France as "The Black American Rimbaud." His three volumes of poetry are *Solitudes Crowded with Loneliness, The Golden Sardine,* and *Ancient Rain: 1956–1978.* He died in 1986.

SYBIL KEIN is a New Orleans poet, playwright, and musician. Her work has been published in numerous texts and journals. Ten of her twenty-eight plays have been produced in the US and abroad. A one-hour taped recording of her poetry is housed in the National Archives. She is a professor of English at the University of Michigan at Flint. *Gumbo People,* poetry in Creole, represents the first contribution of literature in the New Orleans Creole language to American letters.

"Writing poetry is another way of making music."

JACK KEROUAC, born in 1922, has had an extraordinary influence on West Coast writers. In his lifetime he published a number of books, including a collection of poetry, *Mexico City Blues.* He is, arguably, the most significant figure in the Beat movement. He died in 1969.

"I want to be considered a jazz poet blowing a long blues in an afternoon jam session on Sunday. I take 242 choruses; my ideas vary and sometimes roll from chorus to chorus or from halfway through a chorus to halfway into the next."

ETHERIDGE KNIGHT, born in 1931, he has received numerous honors and awards for his various literary contributions—a National Endowment for the Arts grant, a National Book Award, a Pulitzer Prize nomination, and a Guggenheim fellowship. His books of poetry include *Poems from Prison, Belly Song and Other Poems,* and *The Essential Etheridge Knight.*

"The influence of jazz in my poetry is natural. Like most Black people—especially those of us who were born in the south—I grew up in an atmosphere that was permeated with music: blues, gospel, and jazz. I was conceived in the Great Song of the Universe. And before I was born, I boogied in my mother's belly while she sang her songs in the country churches and clubs in northern Miss. So jazz is not an abstraction to me, it is a physicality (so is all music really). We speak rhythms, ask anyone who stutters. Our speech patterns—the intonations, inflections, nuances—are to a larger degree determined by the music of our lives. We talk jazz and we walk jazz. I came of age with jazz. Got my first 'piece' listening to Cootie Williams in the background. And when I die I hope Coltrane is played at my funeral, 'cause jazz has been very important to my life, and therefore to my poetry."

KENNETH KOCH is a prolific writer of plays, novels, books on education, and poetry, including *Selected Poems.* He lives in New York City and is Professor of English at Columbia University.

YUSEF KOMUNYAKAA is Associate Professor of English at Indiana University. He has published three books of poetry: *Copacetic, I Apologize for the Eyes in My Head* (which won the San Francisco Book Center Award in 1986), and *Dien Cai Dau.* His home is in Bloomington, Indiana, and, for part of the year, in Australia.

RICHARD KOSTELANETZ, an experimental poet and fiction writer living in New York, has published numerous collections of his poems, in addition to critical essays collected in *The Old Poetries and the New.* He has recently been working with language in audio, video, film, and holography.

ART LANGE is the author of *Needles at Midnight, Evidence, The Monk Poems,* and *Glee: Song.* His poems have appeared in journals as widespread as *Partisan Review, New American Writing, B City* and *Oink!* His music criticism has appeared in countless periodicals, and he is a former editor of *down beat* magazine.

"As you can see, *The Monk Poems* consists entirely of poems using the titles of compositions by Thelonious Monk as their titles. There is *not* meant to be any other specific reference to the music in the poetry, neither in terms of content, subject, or form—outside of some musical references which pop up here and there, and the influence that Monk's rhythmic sense has had on me, but these are both rather arbitrary and vague. The poems are in *no* sense an attempt to explain, elucidate, illustrate, or translate Monk's music in words."

PHILIP LARKIN'S books of poetry include *The North Ship, The Less Deceived, The Whitsun Weddings, High Windows,* and *The Complete Poems of Philip Larkin.* From

1961 to 1971 he wrote jazz reviews for the *Daily Telegraph;* a collection of these reviews can be read in *All What Jazz.* He died in 1985.

PHILIP LEVINE has written ten books of poems during the past twenty years— among them *Selected Poems.* He has received many awards: the American Book Award, the National Book Critics Circle Award, and the Lenore Marshall Award. He lives in Fresno, California, where he teaches for part of the year.

"The first true artists I met were jazz musicians, many of whom were my class- mates at Wayne University during the late Forties & the great Detroit jazz era. I'm talking about Tommy Flanagan, Barry Harris, Bess Bonnier, Kenny Burrell, Pepper Adams. They were a living example to me that you could live your life on your own terms, you could do your art, & you could tell the great American nonsense to go its own way. They were a model of truth & grit when I needed it most."

LARRY LEVIS'S books of poetry include *Wrecking Crew,* winner of the US Award of the International Poetry Forum; *The Afterlife,* the Lamont Selection of the Academy of American Poets; *The Dollmaker's Ghost,* selected by Stanley Kunitz as winner of the National Poetry Series Open Competition; and *Winter Stars.* His other awards include fellowships from the National Endowment for the Arts and the Guggenheim Foundation.

LYN LIFSHIN has published more than seventy books and chapbooks, including *Raw Opals, Red Hair and the Jesuit, Rubbed Silk, Dance Poems, The Daughter May Be Let Go,* and *Many More Madonnas.* A speaker at more than five hundred readings across the country, she also has taught poetry and prose writing for years at universities, colleges, and high schools throughout the Northeast. She has won more than a dozen writing awards and grants, including the Jack Kerouac award in 1984 for *Kiss the Skin Off;* poetry prize, *Centennial Review,* 1985; *New York Quarterly Sadin Award,* 1986; poet in residence at the University of Rochester, 1986; poet in residence at the Antioch Writer's Conference, summer 1987; and Footwork Award, 1987.

N. J. LOFTIS was born in Chicago in 1943. He has degrees from Fisk University and Columbia University. His books include *Exiles and Voyages* and *Black Anima.*

JOHN LOGAN, born in 1923, has taught at numerous colleges and universities. His awards include grants from the Rockefeller Foundation, the Guggenheim Foundation, and the National Endowment for the Arts, as well as the Morton Dauwen Zabel Award of the National Institute. He has published numerous books, including *Only the Dreamer Can Change the Dream: Selected Poems.* He died in 1987.

MINA LOY, poet, painter, and designer and manufacturer of lampshades, lived from 1882 to 1966. Her books of poetry include *The Last Lunar Baedeker and Time Tables: Selected Poems,* and she contributed to several anthologies.

NATHANIEL MACKEY is the author of *Eroding Witness* and *Bedouin Hornbook.* He edits the literary magazine *Hambone* and teaches at the University of California, Santa Cruz.

CLARENCE MAJOR is the author of seven novels (among them, *My Amputations* and *Such Was the Season*); eight poetry collections (the most recent two, *Surfaces*

264

and *Masks* and *Some Observations of a Stranger at Zuni during the Latter Part of the Century)*; and two books of nonfiction. He has contributed short works to forty anthologies and over one hundred and fifty periodicals in a dozen countries. He has read his work and lectured in cities across America, throughout Europe, and in North and West Africa. He is the recipient of numerous honors, among them a National Council on the Arts award, a Pushcart Prize, a Fulbright, and a Western States Book Award for fiction. He teaches American literature and creative writing at the University of Colorado in Boulder.

Dionisio D. Martinez, born in Cuba, now lives in Tampa, Florida. His poetry and short prose has appeared in many magazines and journals, including *American Poetry Review, Iowa Review, Caliban, Anthology of Magazine Verse & Yearbook of American Poetry* (1986–87 edition). *Dancing at the Chelsea* is his first book of poems. Lately he has developed a weakness for any woman who whistles by heart the entire first movement of *Eine Kleine Nachtmusik* as she walks into the kitchen in the morning, somewhere between the first light and the coffee.

"And there's really nothing I can say about the poems, how I write them, why, etc. You see, I just write them. I think too many poets are wasting so much time talking so much bull about writing instead of just writing the damn stuff. I hate to explain things."

William Matthews is the author of several books of poems, including *Rising and Falling, Flood, A Happy Childhood, Foreseeable Futures,* and *Blues If You Want.* He has twice been awarded fellowships from the National Endowment for the Arts and has received fellowships from the Guggenheim Foundation and the Ingram Merrill Foundation. He currently teaches at the City College of New York and is president emeritus of the Poetry Society of America.

Victoria McCabe's books include *John Keats' Porridge* and *Until Death.* Her work has appeared in a number of magazines, including *The American Poetry Review, The Hollins Critic, Kansas Quarterly, New Letters, Shenandoah,* and she has two manuscripts in circulation, *The Failed Suicide* and *Night Company.* She teaches at Regis College in Denver.

"For me, it is much more comfortable—natural—to go at this backwards—to speak of the music as poetry, to align the shared crises and curatives, to say, stumblingly, how that connection works for me. As a poet with an ignorant ear, I nevertheless respond to the whole man beneath the intensely personal staccato lines of someone like Albert Ayler—whose music catches, holds, and names the condition of the human soul, especially the creative human soul as it is located in our time. The music is the rhythmic paradigm for the struggle of the artist—it *says* the enormous energy and rigorous concentration that are demanded, it *says* the attitudinal independence, the essential strangeness, and the brave emotional improvisation that are necessary; it *says* too, insistently, how difficult and complex the instrument itself is. And it says, somehow, a sweetness, the innocence that lingers. Finally: fearlessness—you know, even if you know nothing of music, that he was taking chances every breath, every minute—which the artist must always do to attain the coherence of voice, the timbre 'charged with meaning to the utmost possible degree.' For me, the ideas that emerge from the music provide a clarity for the work I am doing. This poem is by way of homage to the spirit that informs."

Kenneth McClane's books of poetry include *Out Beyond the Bay, To Hear the River, A Tree Beyond Telling: Poems, Selected and New,* and *Take Five: Collected*

Poems, 1971–1986. He teaches English at Cornell University and has given lectures and readings around the country. A collection of personal essays, *Walls,* is forthcoming.

COLLEEN J. MCELROY is an inveterate traveler, traveling being a passion honed in her youth as an Army brat. In 1988 she was in Yugoslavia on a Fulbright fellowship. She writes poetry, fiction, screenplays, stageplays, and reviews. Her books include seven collections of poetry: *The Mules Done Long Since Gone, Music From Home, Lie and Say You Love Me, Winters without Snow, Queen of the Ebony Isle,* and *Bone Flames.* She has published a collection of short fiction, *Jesus and Fat Tuesday,* and has just completed her first novel, *Study War No More.*

"My love is language—writing is a vehicle I can use to shape, to enjoy, to grow into language. Language was always a way to reach out of myself. As a child, I was fascinated with how words sound, feel, taste—and how people said what they needed to say between words, with gesture, body language, and inflection. As a student, I studied language (and languages) and began to understand the importance of words and the spaces between them. As a writer, I am concerned with the beauty and music of language, with the joy of forming and controlling sounds that expressed the self as fluidly as a dancer's body movements, the way in which language, like an artist's clay, can be sculpted into many nuances of voice."

HEATHER MCHUGH lives near salt water and always has; she is a passionate jazz and R & B fan. Her books include *Dangers, A World of Difference, To the Quick,* and *Shades.* Among her awards are fellowships from the National Endowment for the Arts and the Rockefeller Foundation. She teaches at the University of Washington and in the nonresidential writing program at Warren Wilson College, but lives on an island in Maine.

JACK MICHELINE has published many books, including *River of Red Wine, I Kiss Angels, In the Bronx and Other Stories, Poems of Dr. Innisfree, Yellow Horn, Street of Lost Fools, Last House in America, Letter to Jack Kerouac in Heaven,* and *A Man Obsessed Who Does Not Sleep Who Wanders About the Night Mumbling to Himself Counting Empty Beer Cans.* His work has been included in six anthologies, and he has recorded his readings on cassettes. He regularly performs accompanied by tenor saxophone.

"In 1956 I read with the Charlie Mingus Jazz workshop at the Half Note on Hudson Street in Manhattan. The group included Booker Irwin, Shafi Hadi on sax, Danny Richmond on drums. Some one-armed cornet player I don't remember and some guy on flugel-horn. That night I received twenty dollars' worth of jazz records (Debut Records) for winning "The Revolt in Literature Award." Nat Hentoff, Jean Sheppard, and Charlie Mingus were the judges. Charlie was an inspiration cause I never won anything in my life before. New York at that time was jumping with jazz. When I wrote and walked the Manhattan streets I'd always bump into Cecil Taylor late at night. He was a walking Jazz Poem.

"Jazz Poetry comes from the streets, comes out from the streets. Mario Jorrin the photographer walked in a daze above the city. Freddy Mogubgub was a walking piece of jazz. Jazz Poetry is the rhythms of life in continual movement. It is not a technical gift; it is intuitive and flows from the heart and out from the windows and into the sky and above the stars.

"Later in San Francisco, I met sweet Bobby Feldman, a tenorman. He is the best for my poetry. He knows my rhythms and my notes. Sometimes I stop and he blows on. We weave in and out like a river of time. He's a gas to work with.

Bob Kaufman and Marty Matz were also fine Jazz Poets. The last time I saw Charlie Mingus was at the Great American music hall where he spotted me in the audience and had me come up and read a few poems. Danny Richmond sang some songs that night. It was a great reunion."

VASSAR MILLER, nominated for the Pulitzer Prize in 1961, has published seven volumes of poetry, including *Selected and New Poems: 1950–1980.* Her work has appeared in fifty anthologies and hundreds of periodicals. Three of her books have won the annual poetry prize of the Texas Institute of Letters. Recently she edited an anthology of poetry and fiction by and about those handicapped with motor and sensory dysfunctions.

ROGER MITCHELL'S books of poetry include *Letters from Siberia, Moving, A Clear Space on a Cold Day,* and *Adirondack.* His essays and reviews have appeared in various journals, most recently in *American Poetry Review, The Ohio Review, American Book Review,* and *Triquarterly,* among others. His awards include the Midland Award and a creative writing fellowship from the National Endowment for the Arts.

"Like most middle-class white boys who grew up in the fifties, I found jazz. It was the rock music of its time and told us all there was a completer truth, a wholer mind than the one we had been spoon-fed in the suburbs. Oddly, though, I found jazz at home. My parents bought the 1938 Benny Goodman Carnegie Hall jazz concert album when it came out in the late 40's. My father tapped his fingers to music. He had a set of "bones" which he got out now and then and shook for us. I picked up a stick one time climbing a mountain. Long, tapering and dry, it had an impressive bounce off table tops, jar lids, window sills, anything hard and flat. To protect the furniture, my parents bought me a snare drum, and later a bass drum and a cymbal. I would go down in the basement and put 'Sing, Sing, Sing' on the record player, turn up the volume as loudly as I dared, and pretend to be Gene Krupa. How my parents stood it I do not know and still do not ask.

"When I went off to college, though, I took a blitz course in jazz. It was not offered for credit. It meant going to record stores—in the days when they had listening booths—and pretending you wanted to buy all twenty records you took into the booth with you. It meant going to the clubs in the city—this was Boston—and on an average night hearing Vic Dickenson, Charlie Mariano, the Basie band. Ellington, MJQ, Lennie Tristano, and many more. Three hours nursing one beer. It meant learning a new vocabulary and dressing differently. When I came home at Christmas my freshman year, I was wearing a pink shirt (a *pink* shirt), pegged pants, and a knitted tie (the last time on record, I believe, that the adolescent revolt kit included a tie). I had a new copy of Josh White's album, *Josh at Midnight,* and I played by favorite blues number for my mother. I had never paid any attention to the words. I probably didn't even understand them. But it was 'Jelly, Jelly,' and my mother gave a little squeal of horror and ran out of the room.
"Later, and I don't think this was unrelated, I decided I wanted to be a poet, not a doctor."

JOHN MONTGOMERY, author and compiler of books on Jack Kerouac and friend of Jack, Ginsberg et al., is also a character in Kerouac books. *Hip, Beat, Cool and Antic,* his first book of poetry, appeared recently.

"Jim Christy, author of Montgomery article in *Encyclopedia of Beat Generation Authors,* says that he composes in jazz rhythms. I am not aware of this. My taste in jazz is for the Chicago period.

"I do not believe that poetry is music but rhythms are essential to the extent that chanting is a message. I consider Rexroth, Ferlinghetti and MacLeish the important contemporaries."

JACK MUELLER was born in Philadelphia. He lived and studied in Europe and Asia for four years and has been active in San Francisco poetry circles for more than ten years. His poems and art work have appeared in many little magazines and national anthologies. He is the author of five books of poetry. including *Prussian Blue* and *The Paramorphs: Prose Poems*. He has read his poetry at many clubs and colleges, lectured in universities around the US, and is at present teaching literary history at the University of California Extension. Director of the National Poetry Association, which hosts the annual National Poetry Week Festival, he lives with his wife, his daughter, and his flute in Berkeley, California.

"Poetry, like jazz, obeys emerging form. The sound and shape is followed, joined, and carried forward. The music teaches the musician, the poem teaches the poet. In both cases, it is an active process of doing two things at once: thinking and singing, playing and solving, taking in and making up.

"Each time you start, by reed of tongue or sax, you join the moving equilibrium of life, and while inside you work to make another measure we can all admire."

LISEL MUELLER, born in 1924 in Hamburg, Germany, came to the United States in 1939 and worked initially as a social caseworker, receptionist, library assistant, and free-lance writer and reviewer. Among her many books are *Dependencies, The Private Life,* and *The Need to Hold Still.* Her work has been widely anthologized.

HARRYETTE MULLEN grew up in Texas, has spent time in New Mexico and California, and currently lives in Ithaca, New York. She is the author of *Tree Tall Woman,* and her poetry has been included in the anthologies *Washing the Cow's Skull* and *In Celebration of the Muse.* Her short stories have appeared in *Her Work, South by Southwest, Lighthouse Point,* and *Common Bonds.*

JAMES NOLAN, born in New Orleans in 1947, has traveled extensively, particularly in India and Spain. He has written several books of poetry, including *Why I Live in the Forest* and *What Moves Is Not the Wind,* as well as having translated Pablo Neruda's *Stones of the Sky.*

"Is a jazz poem one that uses some of the structural elements of jazz, that is, call-response, repetition & variation of theme, improvisation within form, etc., or is it one that sounds good when read right with jazz accompaniment, like Barry Wallenstein's stuff? I decided to send you what I have, in the past, felt inspired to perform *with* jazz because the poem answers *to* jazz the way a child answers to its mother. So these are the poems that jazz begat. Words got to fooling around with jazz, folding it into the soft curves that made them feel right—or sometimes jazz seduced words to carry them higher and deeper than they could ever go on their own—and these poems were born. But I don't know what they are or which world they properly belong to, which is why I like to read with musicians: to keep the family together. But you can't dance to them, and most of them look awfully tedious or flat on the page, so I'm afraid most of them will have to go on being the little bastard misfits they are."

FRANK O'HARA was born in 1926, grew up in Worcester, Massachusetts, and studied at Harvard, where he helped to found the Poets' Theatre, and at the Uni-

268

versity of Michigan's graduate school. During the sixties he became a leading figure in a group of writers who came to be known as the New York Poets. He wrote six books of poems and, after his death in 1966, a selection of his work was published with the title *Collected Poems*.

KENNETH PATCHEN, born in 1911, is the author of a great many books of fiction, plays, and poetry, including *Before the Brave, Selected Love Poems,* and *The Argument of Innocence.* In the 1950s he began reading his poetry to the accompaniment of jazz. In later years he would become famous in poetry circles as one of the pioneers of this technique. He died in 1972.

ROBERT PINSKY'S books of poetry include *Sadness and Happiness, An Explanation of America, History of My Heart.* He has received awards from the National Institute of Arts and Letters and the Guggenheim Foundation. He teaches in the graduate creative writing program at Boston University.

"I had a happy, funky small-town childhood, with some ethnic twist. A poor student, I was assigned in the eighth grade to what was known as the Dumb Class. This had at least two consequences: I was tracked into Spanish, rather than French, and through a strange bit of scheduling, the Dumb Class had free time to register for band and learn instruments. (For some years after this bureaucratic quirk, the Long Branch High School Orchestra and Marching Band was a distinctly rough group.)

"By high school, I was ambitious to make a career as a jazz player. My heroes include Lester Young and Stan Getz. I played tenor with a combo we called the DownBeats (sixteenth notes for the 'D' and 'B'), mostly such gigs as weddings, Elk's Club parties (one New Year's Eve I played while my mom and dad won the Mambo contest), proms, etc. At the Catholic high school, we played show tunes in a Lawrence Welk tempo set by a nun. At poolside of the Colony Surf Club we played cha-chas wearing pink ruffled shirts. At the Paddock Lounge we played while a mafia *colonello* sat at a table with aides and a white telephone. The daydreams of jazz glory that threaded through these low engagements gradually changed—because I just wasn't a very good musician—into daydreams of being a writer. I think that my work and ambitions as a poet are based, like a jazz chorus, on improvisation and surprise, variations on a theme, the building and breaking of expectation, and above all on the kind of sexy, sensuous rhythm that teases and despises boredom."

STERLING D. PLUMPP is Associate Professor in the Black Studies Program, University of Illinois at Chicago. He is the author of *Portable Soul, Half Black, Half Blacker, Black Rituals, Steps to Break the Circle, Clinton, The Mojo Hands Call, I Must Go, Somehow We Survive* (ed.), and *Blues: The Story Always Untold.* He is a poetry editor with *Black American Literature Forum* and an advisory editor with *Literati Chicago* and *Another Chicago Magazine.*

"Two things come to my mind whenever I am confronted with the word jazz: black experience and a method for articulating the parameters of that everchanging experience musically when on instruments, with the voice, or god forbid, on the page. Thus jazz for me implies improvisation, the ability to negotiate a chaotic mode into some coherent and manageable pattern through articulation. Yet jazz, spirituals, and blues as well as their stepchildren—gospel, du-wop R & B, Soul—all are connected, on the same African Continuum. I accept James Baldwin's observation that it is only through his music that the Black man has been able to tell his story and I further accept the function black art, poetry in partic-

269

ular, had in the African cultures which my ancestors were snatched from. My premise is that those African cultures from which my ancestors were ruptured, underwent centuries of cultural genocide, yet held their secrets in the fragments which were not crushed. Thus I see the attempt of slaves to forge a world view, vision, out of the fragments of their memory and the alien experience in America as being one of communal improvisation. They articulated, changed and articulated until they came up with the 'Negro Spirituals.' 'I Hear the Shuffle of the People's Feet' is my way of charting that journey from African cultures to field hollers and whips in a strange hostile land. However, the ability of the African to articulate, via improvisation, a vision became a principal way for him to maintain his humanity and self of ancestry. While I recognize the distinction of the music developed in Congo Square in New Orleans and played on various European instruments—cornets, trumpets, saxophones, drums, pianos, trombones, and bass— as jazz, I view it as an extension and fuller development of the spirituals and blues but on instruments. My poem sought to merge the 'I' of the individual artist into the experience of the 'we' in the African's experience in America. I used a variety of ideas from the music some people call jazz; polyphony, quick shift of emphasis, the articulation of a personal vision within the context of a collective constant. In the poem Africans survived and made gains through their collective ability to improvise: make jazz with their feet in their liberating African dances."

ISHMAEL REED is the author of numerous books of poetry and fiction, including *Conjure, Chattanooga, Secretary to the Spirits,* and *New and Collected Poems.* His honors include a nomination for a Pulitzer Prize in poetry, a National Endowment for the Arts fellowship for creative writing, and a Guggenheim Foundation award for fiction.

KENNETH REXROTH, poet, translator, playwright, essayist, and painter, published a wealth of material in many areas. Among his prestigious awards are a Guggenheim fellowship, a Rockefeller grant, and an Academy of American Poets Copernicus Award. He taught at various universities and gave poetry readings throughout the world. When he died in 1982, he left behind brilliant collections of poetry that still influence and inspire.

KATE RUSHIN, born in 1951, grew up in both Camden and Lawnside, N.J. She has given numerous readings and has run writing workshops for children and adults. In 1978 she was awarded fellowships from the Massachusetts Artists' Foundation and the Fine Arts Work Center in Provincetown. She is a recipient of the 1988 Grolier Poetry Prize, and currently earns her living as a member of the New Words Bookstore Collective.

"I love music of all kinds. I am especially in awe of the beauty that African-American musicians create. I want my poetry to sing.

"One night, I was listening to the radio while I was washing dishes. When I heard the words to Lou Reed's 'Walk on the Wild Side' and listened closely to the voices of the Black women singing background vocals, a flood of memories, emotions, images, questions and observations crashed together in my consciousness. That moment inspired and informed 'The Black Back-Ups.' "

IRA SADOFF has published several books of poetry, most recently *Emotional Traffic.* He has also published a novel, twenty-five short stories, translations, and essays— including an essay on Ben Webster in *The Missouri Review.* He has edited two magazines, *The Seneca Review* and *The Antioch Review,* and taught at the Iowa

270

Writer's Workshop. He currently directs the creative writing program at Colby College.

Sonia Sanchez, born in 1934, has written several books of poetry, including *We a BaddDDD People* and *A Blues Book for Blue Magical Women*. She has also published several plays, and her work has been frequently anthologized. Among her awards are a PEN Writing Award and a National Institute of Arts and Letters grant.

Carl Sandburg, one of the pioneers of jazz-related poetry, lived from 1878 until 1967 and published extensively. His books of poetry include *Early Moon, Harvest Poems, 1910–1960,* and *Honey and Salt.* He remains one of the important poets of the twentieth century.

Robert Sargent was born and educated in the Deep South but came to Washington, D.C., as a Naval officer in World War II and remained after the war as a civil servant. He began writing poetry in the 1950s and has been widely published in literary reviews and a number of anthologies. His books of poetry include *Now Is Always the Miraculous Time* and *Aspects of a Southern Story.*

"I was born in New Orleans, and although my family moved away from there when I was young, my older brother went to college there, and in the late 1920s used to bring home phonograph records of King Oliver, Louis Armstrong's Hot Five, NORK, and others, which I would play by the hour. By the time I went to college I was a committed jazz lover.

"Later, when grown, I moved back to New Orleans. My poem 'Touching the Past' describes a happening of that period.

"It was natural, then, that when I began to write poetry, my interest in jazz would be reflected in some of the poems."

Mandy Sayer, born in Sydney, Australia, in 1963, is the only writer in a family of musicians. She has studied and performed dance in Australia and the United States. Her novel, *Mood Indigo,* won the 1989 Australian/Vogel Literary Award.

Asger Schnack, a Danish writer, has published numerous books in his native language, as well as several that have been translated into English. Among those translations are books on David Bowie and Bob Dylan, as well as his long poem, *Aqua.*

Jan Selving received a BA in English literature from Indiana University and is pursuing an MFA in creative writing.

Léopold Sédar Senghor was born in Joal, Senegal, in 1906. He began his secondary studies in Dakar and continued his education in Paris. In 1959 he became president of the legislative assembly of the Mali Federation, and when he withdrew from the Federation, he was elected president of the Republic of Senegal. He has written several books of poetry, and his work has been widely translated.

Kazuko Shiraishi is a Japanese poet born in 1931 in Vancouver, British Columbia. She was a member of the VOU avant-garde literary group from 1948 to 1953 and, with Kazuo Ono, has mounted a series of poetry/dance performances. Her poetry in translation includes *Seasons of Sacred Lust.* Kenneth Rexroth, one of the translators of *Seasons of Sacred Lust,* wrote in the book's introduction:

"If you hear her read aloud, with or without jazz accompaniment, you know that, even if you don't speak a word of Japanese, Shiraishi is the last and the youngest and one of the best of the generation of Beats in America, the Angry Young Men in England, Vosnesensky in the U.S.S.R."

ALEDA SHIRLEY'S poems have appeared in several journals, including *American Poetry Review, Georgia Review, Poetry, Shenandoah, Prairie Schooner,* and *Virginia Quarterly Review.* One of her poems was included in the 1985 edition of the *Anthology of Magazine Verse and Yearbook of American Poetry.* In 1986 her first book of poetry, *Chinese Architecture,* received the Poetry Society of America's Norma Farber First Book Award. She has also received a National Endowment for the Arts grant.

JOHN SINCLAIR, born in 1941, has written a number of books of poetry, including *We Just Change the Beat: Selected Poems, Song of Praise: Homage to John Coltrane,* and *thelonious: a book of monk.* He has also written books on writing and music, written liner notes, been included in several anthologies, given a number of performances with his own musical group, and edited several magazines.

GILBERT SORRENTINO is the author of some twenty books of fiction, poetry, and criticism, the most recent of which is *Rose Theatre.* He is a professor of English at Stanford University.

JACK SPICER, born in 1925, published several books of poetry, including *The Collected Books of Jack Spicer.* He died in 1965.

WALLACE STEVENS was born in 1879. He received many awards for poetry in his lifetime, including the Bollingen Prize, the National Book Award (twice), and the Pulitzer Prize. His books include *The Collected Poems of Wallace Stevens* and *Opus Posthumous.* He died in 1955.

MICHAEL STILLMAN lives in Woodside, California, and maintains close friendships with the Djerassi Foundation Resident Artists Program. "In Memoriam John Coltrane" comes from an unpublished sequence called *Memories of Grace Street,* which describes his years teaching literature and playing jazz (saxophone and flute) in Richmond, Virginia. His twenty-nine sequences of original haiku were published as *An Eye of Minnows.* He is completing a book of original lyrics to jazz classics called *Mermaid Songbook* and a book of poems called *Making Nothing Happen.*

"Jazz is a universal language. In the final decade of our century, as totalitarian and authoritarian systems melt away, jazz can be understood as an expression of the energy, the impulse, the drive that brings down injustice. It belongs to everyone. It begins in slavery—'Who aint a slave? Tell me that' says Ishmael—but soon makes a break for freedom."

JOHN TAGGART was born in Guthrie Center, Iowa, and educated at Earlham College, the University of Chicago, and Syracuse University. He has edited his own poetry magazine, *Maps,* which included a special John Coltrane issue. He has published several volumes of his own poetry, among which are *Dodeka, Peace On Earth,* and *Loop.* A collection of his jazz-related poems, *Prompted,* is to be published with drawings by Bradford Graves. He lives in Shippensburg, Pennsylvania.

"The first jazz that made itself available to me was 'The Drum Thing' on John Coltrane's *Crescent* album. It was a story, a narrative; it had something to do with a journey across a wide expanse. And it was with a journey or simply a straggling procession of musicians in mind that I began the poem. It's tempting to say the music gave me the poem. The contribution of the music, however, was more an instigation, a prompting to begin, than a complete template.

"It was the first poem which truly pleased me. It seemed to exist apart from me, to have an object existence of its own. And I knew that, without the music of John Coltrane and Elvin Jones, it would have had no existence at all.

"Helped in the on-going work of composition and protected from becoming a parasite of personality, the poet is pleased and happy. What more could be desired? This was my feeling in writing the later poems prompted by jazz. Ornette Coleman's 'Lonely Woman' on his *The Shape of Jazz to Come* album involved yet another journey across a wide expanse; and Lester Young's playing, whether with the smaller Kansas City groups or with the Basie big band, had a behind-the-beat poignancy that involved him in a pursuit by green meteors and other personages of the night.

"I made a grid from the sheet music from 'Lonely Woman.' The idea was that my lines, shaped in compliance, might take on some of the rhythmic character of the music. Even as I did this I suspected it would not be enough to transpose already transposed music into poetry. There would have to be transformation. Not 'jazz poems,' they would have to start from and go away from jazz. They would have to end up somewhere else.

"The music could be blues—what Ornette always plays and what tends to come through whatever the context Lester was playing in—and the poems themselves could be elegiac occasions. In 'Coming Forth by Day,' the poem that takes off from Ornette, ponderous women move among the deaths of fire, air, and lands.

"Odysseus encounters the sirens once. The growing, undeniable intensity of admiration and love and the existence of recordings mean a constant encounter and re-encounter. In this circle of repetition there is always a call, there is always a being spoken to. *The vision seeks the man.* In the area of decision of jazz the members cannot help but to hear the call and what is being spoken.

"Once having come to jazz, like language, there is no leaving. There is only the trying to decide against being turned into the called and bespoken, there is only the constant trying to decide to stay alive."

MELVIN B. TOLSON was born in 1900. He was an educator, poet, and dramatist. In addition to teaching at several universities, Tolson was mayor of Langston, Oklahoma, and a columnist for the *Washington Tribune.* He was chosen Poet Laureate of Liberia in 1947, and his work has been widely anthologized. His books include *Harlem Gallery, Rendezvous with America,* and *Libretto for the Republic of Liberia.*

WILLIAM TREMBLAY was born in Massachusetts and raised in a French-Canadian household. Since 1973 he has taught at Colorado State University, where he is Professor of English, Chair of the Creative Writing Program, and Editor of *Colorado Review.* His books of poems include *Crying in the Cheap Seats, Second Sun: New and Selected Poems,* and *Duhamel: Ideas of Order in Little Canada.*

"In the summer of '53, my brother Gerry came home on furlough from the Air Force & turned me on to jazz. He put on a Pacific Jazz LP of Don Byrd & Gigi Gryce doing 'Over the Rainbow,' a tune I recognized from *The Wizard of Oz,* only it was so bent, the horns were twined so caduceus-like it changed me. I liked other kinds of music still, but jazz always had more finesse, more sex, *more to say* in it than rhythm 'n blues or country. Some poets hear Beethoven or Debussy as they're writing: I hear King Pleasure singing lyrics to a Charlie Parker blues—not all the time, but the drive, accenting, gets into the lines, 'the musical phrase.' My poem 'Song for Jeannie' was written to ' 'Round Midnight,' by Thelonious Monk; I was fortunate enough to perform the poem concert-style with a jazz combo in the Boulder Theatre, March 9, 1982. Some of the best moments of my life have been with jazz: Charles Lloyd's 'A Cry in the Night' turned me into a city where dark men prowl for love; I heard Miles Davis play 'Kind of Blue' in the Village Vanguard when I was a seventeen-year-old alien at Columbia University; I heard John Coltrane play 'My Favorite Things' at the Newport Jazz Festival (1963) as a Naragansett Bay fog turned pink in the bandshell & his soprano sax cut me open. Poets & jazz musicians have much in common; they're visionaries, mostly, turning the world inside-out through their instruments to show the feeling side. In this love of jazz my guardian angel is Jack Kerouac."

JON C. TRIBBLE was born in Little Rock, Arkansas. Having graduated from the University of Arkansas–Little Rock, he is working on an MFA in poetry.

QUINCY TROUPE, born and raised in St. Louis, Missouri, is Professor of American and Third World Literature at the College of Staten Island (CUNY) and also teaches in Columbia University's graduate writing program. He has edited two anthologies and published three volumes of poetry: *Embryo, Snake-Back Solos,* and *Skulls along the River.* With the full cooperation of Miles Davis, he has published *Miles: The Autobiography.* His poetry and fiction have been published in more than one hundred magazines and journals; his poetry, essays, and articles have been translated into several languages. He lives with his family in New York City.

JEAN VALENTINE was born in Chicago and raised mostly in New York and Boston. She has published six collections of poetry, most recently *Home. Deep. Blue. New & Selected Poems.* She has earned fellowships from the Guggenheim Foundation, the Bunting Institute, and the Rockefeller Foundation and has received awards from the National Endowment for the Arts and the New York State Council for the Arts. She teaches at Sarah Lawrence College, New York University, and the West Side Y. She lives in New York City.

ANNE WALDMAN is the author of eleven books of poetry, including *Makeup on Empty Space, Skin Meat Bones,* and *Helping the Dreamer: New and Selected Poems.*

"My older brother was a jazz fiend. Sidney Bechet. Charlie Parker. I liked Anita O'Day and Sarah Vaughan and John Coltrane and Miles Davis and Brubeck and Gerry Mulligan and Mingus. I used to be able to play some bars from a Horace Silver composition on the piano. My former sister-in-law was married to Steve Lacy and at that time I used to observe Thelonious Monk at their loft occasionally. He was the greatest. Like a Buddha."

JOY WALSH is the author of *Locating Positions* and *Rough Trade.* She is editor of "Textile Bridge Press," and she also edits "Moody Street Irregulars: A Jack Kerouac Newsletter." She studied music on a college scholarship and later earned degrees in English and the humanities. Her poetry, essays, and reviews have been published in the United States, Japan, Australia, and Europe. She has recently completed a novella and is working on two novels. In 1983 she received a writer in residence grant from the Just Buffalo Literary Center.

"I continue to examine the difference between plastic hipness and those who swivel the globe on their own natural bones. My poetry reflects this examination."

274

MARILYN NELSON WANIEK'S books of poetry include *For the Body* and *The Mama Poems.* She is co-author with Pamela Espeland of *The Cat Walked through the Casserole,* a book of poems for children. Among her awards is a fellowship from the National Endowment for the Arts. Married and the mother of two young children, she is a professor of English at the University of Connecticut.

"The inspiration of 'It's All in Your Head' is primarily visual: the jazz funerals of New Orleans. The imagery of a Black jazz band, followed by mourners, dominates the poem. Yet in the process of composition I was aware, as I always am, of a strong melodic line—the voice of a reader—which sounds to me like a saxophone. This melody, as I hear it, is superimposed upon what I hear as a fairly regular system of stresses: 'I didn't die, I napped / on the spotless stainless steel beds,' for example. Here I hear the voice rising on 'didn't' and 'napped,' and to a lesser degree 'spotless' and 'stainless,' while emphasis falls on those words (or their first syllables). The words improvise a melody. I think the lines in the first few stanzas are longer and more rhythmically regular to indicate the slow march tempo of the funeral march. In the seventh stanza the lines grow shorter, the tempo less regular. The voice here is higher: perhaps a solo: the rest of the band has stopped for the saxophone. I'm not sure this makes any sense, and I'm almost embarrassed to write it, but I stop when I'm writing, to clap out the tempo against the sound of my reading a line. Sometimes I have to go against the rhythm I want to get the sense I intend, but for me, both melody and rhythm are essential."

WILLIAM WANTLING was born in 1933 in what is now East Peoria, Illinois. He fought in Korea, where he was wounded in action and spent ten days in a coma. When he returned to the States, he became addicted to heroin and eventually served five years in San Quentin after pleading guilty to possession. While in prison, he discovered poetry. His several books of poetry include *San Quentin's Stranger,* his selected poems. He died in 1974.

JERRY W. WARD, JR., has lived in Mississippi since 1949 and is Professor of English at Tougaloo College. His poetry, essays, and reviews have appeared in many journals, magazines, and newspapers. His work-in-progress includes *A Gathering of Roots,* a study of five black southern writers.

"Although most of my work is not lyric, much of it since the mid-1960s has been influenced by efforts to imitate certain sound structures and through innovations present in that great body of music called jazz. At another level, allusion to specific jazz artists and compositions is my method of connecting verbal and nonverbal artistry. For the poems most influenced by jazz, there is an implied audience, and a limited one at that. The poems that can be performed with musicians or 'played' through the voice are the most successful, because audiences can sense the jazz esthetic more immediately.

"I have listened to jazz since I was around thirteen or fourteen, but I only began to perceive connections between jazz and poetry when I read Langston Hughes and the anthology *Beyond the Blues* during my college years. I am most influenced, I think now, by the jazz artist's imagination and respect for craft."

PAULETTE C. WHITE, a native of Detroit, is a painter and a poet. Her poems have appeared in magazines such as *Deep Rivers* and *Broadside Annual,* as well as in a collection of her poetry titled *Love Poem to a Black Junkie.*

SHERLEY ANNE WILLIAMS was born in 1944. She is a poet, a novelist, a dramatist, and a writer for television. Her books of poetry include *Give Birth to Brightness* and *The Peacock Poems,* which was nominated for a National Book Award.

WILLIAM CARLOS WILLIAMS is the author of many books of criticism, fiction, and poetry, including, of course, *The Collected Earlier Poems* and *The Collected Later Poems.* He remains one of the most important figures in twentieth-century poetry. His first real introduction to jazz was in 1945, when he visited New York City and heard Dixieland trumpeter Bunk Johnson. The literary results were twofold: an unfinished novel called *Man Orchid* and the poem "Ol' Bunk's Band." He died in 1963.

"We poets have to talk in a language which is not English. It is the American idiom. Rhythmically, it's organized as a sample of the American idiom. It has as much originality as jazz."

DAVID WOJAHN'S books of poetry include *Icehouse Lights,* the 1981 winner of the Yale Series of Younger Poets Award and the 1983 winner of the William Carlos Williams Book Award of the Poetry Society of America, *Glassworks,* and *Mystery Train.* Among his other awards is a fellowship from the National Endowment for the Arts. He teaches at Indiana University.

"Like so many members of my generation, I grew up listening not to jazz, but to the insistent assertions of rock and roll, a music that—like jazz—carries with it a distinct cultural milieu, a sensibility. For a good many members of my generation, jazz *culture* is accessible only through recreation in the imagination, through a retrieval that tries to look back a bit nostalgically to the time in which jazz played a paramount role in American life. That jazz does not play the role in our lives that it once did is not the fault of jazz, and not something I want to concern myself with here. But a particular jazz song, Ellington's 'Satin Doll,' became a crucial element in a poem I wrote which takes its title from the Ellington tune. The poem is not *about* Ellington, nor is it about the song; the poem is instead meant to seem to travel back in time, to offer a kind of consolation to a figure very much like my aunt, who suffered more than her fair share of human tragedy at one point in her life. Somehow, the Ellington song became the device by which the poem could seem to communicate with her over the years, to help me evoke a particular moment in her life, a moment which occurred several years before I was born. Without the reference to the song, this communication would not have been possible in the poem. A romantic notion? Yes, but sometimes we need such notions, both in poetry and in music. Thanks to Duke Ellington for helping me to remember this."

JOEL "YEHUDA" WOLK, proud new father who drives a taxi in San Francisco, takes night journalism courses at San Francisco State University, is writing a screenplay for Pilot Productions, and is sustained by his North African–Italian wife's soul food. He was admitted into the 1989 edition of the *Directory of American Poets and Writers* under "Performance Poet."

C. D. WRIGHT is a native of the Arkansas Ozarks. Her most recent collections of poetry are *Translations of the Gospel Back into Tongues* and *Further Adventures with You.* She has been the recipient of fellowships from the National Endowment for the Arts, the Bunting Institute, and the Guggenheim Foundation as well as the 1986 Witter Bynner Award in Poetry from the American Academy and Institute of Arts and Letters. With poet Forrest Gander she edits *Lost Roads Publishers.*

ROBERT WRIGLEY was born in East St. Louis but has lived for the last fifteen years in the West. He is Professor of English at Lewis-Clark State College in

Lewiston, Idaho. His books include *The Sinking of Clay City* and *Moon in a Mason Jar*. He often wishes he were Oscar Peterson.

"I honestly haven't any grand theories of 'poetics,' though I would say that poetry—like any art—ought to be made with passion. As I tell my writing students—*mean it.*"

AL YOUNG is the author of many books of fiction, prose, and poetry, including *The Blues Don't Change: New and Selected Poems* and *Bodies & Soul: Musical Memoirs*. He is editor, with Ishmael Reed, of the anthology *Yardbird Lives!* and the editor and publisher, with Ishmael Reed, of *Quilt Magazine*. He has taught writing at Stanford University, the University of California, and the University of Washington and has been appointed Distinguished Andrew Mellon Professor of Humanities at Rice University.

BILL ZAVATSKY, born in 1943 in Bridgeport, Connecticut, worked as a pianist in the southern Connecticut area from the age of fifteen to twenty-five. He studied harmony at the New School and privately with Hall Overton. His two books of poetry are *Theories of Rain and Other Poems* and *For Steve Royal and Other Poems*. His poems have also appeared in *Diamonds Are Forever: Artists and Writers on Baseball* and *Up Late: American Poetry Since 1970*. "Elegy" was set to music for jazz group and string quartet by Norwegian pianist-composer Egil Kapstad and was recorded by vocalist Sheila Jordan in Norway in 1985. He teaches at the Trinity School in New York City.

"To write the text of 'Elegy,' which was commissioned for the sleeve of the album *You Must Believe in Spring* by Bill Evans's manager, Helen Keane, I listened for days to a pre-release cassette of the music. I was thinking hard about Bill, who had died not long before, and whom I knew well during the last few years of his life, and I was thinking of the great and austere French poet Paul Eluard, whose nobility and clarity helped me find the tone that Bill's music seemed to demand.

" 'To the Pianist Bill Evans,' written over a decade earlier, came out of years of familiarity with the recordings of the Evans trio that featured the late Scott LaFaro, with special reference to its version of 'My Foolish Heart.' Someone had told me that the car in which LaFaro had died had burned, and that he had seen the musician's charred bass in a repair shop. (I don't know how much of this is true.) Anyhow, that image got me started, and the music carried me forward."

PAUL ZIMMER, Director of the University of Iowa Press, has read poems at more than one hundred colleges, has recorded his poems for the Library of Congress, and has been awarded writing fellowships from the National Endowment for the Arts in 1974 and 1981. In 1985 he was given an American Academy and Institute of Arts and Letters Literary Award. His poems have been widely anthologized, and his books include *The Ribs of Death, The Republic of Many Voices, The Zimmer Poems, With Wanda: Town and Country Poems, The Ancient Wars, Earthbound Zimmer, Family Reunion: Selected and New Poems,* and *The American Zimmer.*

"I discovered jazz when I was a teenager living in Ohio in the late 1940s. My first joys were Duke Ellington, the beboppers and the Jazz at the Philharmonic recordings. I have been a fan ever since. I have always felt 'poetic' when listening to jazz, but I resisted making poems about this experience for many years, mostly because I generally do not like poems about other art. But then I was able to find several ways to make interesting (I hope!) poems without trying to marry the other art of jazz. I am very happy that these have worked out. But aside from these more direct poems, jazz and the blues are—or at least the rhythms and feeling—always present in my work."

Music Appendix

INDIVIDUAL MUSICIANS

Cannonball Adderly
  Michael S. Harper, "Cannon Arrested"
Gene Ammons
  Ira Sadoff, "At the Half-Note Cafe"
  Al Young, "Jungle Strut"
Louis Armstrong
  Fred Chappell, "The Highest Wind That Ever Blew: Homage to Louis"
  Tom Dent, "For Lil Louis"
Albert Ayler
  Victoria McCabe, "For Albert Ayler"
Chet Baker
  Richard Elman, "Chet's Jazz"
Count Basie
  Jayne Cortez, "Solo Finger Solo"
Sidney Bechet
  Philip Larkin, "For Sidney Bechet"
  William Matthews, "Bmp Bmp"
Bix Beiderbecke
  Dana Gioia, "Bix Beiderbecke (1903–1931)"
Buddy Bolden
  Robert Sargent, "Touching the Past"
Anthony Braxton
  Grace Cavalieri, "The Liberation of Music"
Ray Charles
  Horace Julian Bond, "The Bishop of Atlanta: Ray Charles"
  Heather McHugh, "Sleep, after Ray Charles Show and Hurricane Report"
Ornette Coleman
  Sam Abrams, "In the Capability"
  Steve Jonas, "One of Three Musicians"
  Kenneth Rexroth, "Written to Music"
  John Taggart, "Coming Forth by Day"
John Coltrane
  Amiri Baraka, "AM/TRAK"
  Edward Kamau Brathwaite, "Trane"
  George Economou, "33⅓ RPM"
  Michael S. Harper, "Dear John, Dear Coltrane"
  Michael S. Harper, "Here Where Coltrane Is"
  Garrett Hongo, "Roots"
  Nathaniel Mackey, "Ohnedaruth's Day Begun"
  William Matthews, "Blues for John Coltrane, Dead at 41"
  Sonia Sanchez, "a/coltrane/poem"
  Kazuko Shiraishi, "Dedicated to the Late John Coltrane"

279

Michael Stillman, "In Memoriam John Coltrane"
Jean Valentine, "Coltrane, Syeeda's Song Flute"
Miles Davis
  Gregory Corso, "For Miles"
  Fatisha, "From Star to Sun We Are Going"
  Quincy Troupe, "Four, and More; for Miles Davis"
Eric Dolphy
  Etheridge Knight, "For Eric Dolphy"
  Anne Waldman, "Eric Dolphy"
Kenny Dorham
  Joel "Yehuda" Wolk, "Elegy for Kenny Dorham"
Duke Ellington
  Jayne Cortez, "Rose Solitude"
  Léopold Sédar Senghor, "Blues"
  Aleda Shirley, "Ellington Indigos"
  Quincy Troupe, "The Day Duke Raised; may 24, 1974"
  David Wojahn, "Satin Doll"
  Paul Zimmer, "The Duke Ellington Dream"
Bill Evans
  Bill Zavatsky, "Elegy"
  Bill Zavatsky, "To the Pianist Bill Evans"
Maynard Ferguson
  Joy Walsh, "Ferguson's Conquistadores 77"
Dexter Gordon
  Yusef Komunyakaa, "February in Sydney"
Stephane Grappelli
  Roger Mitchell, "For Stephane Grappelli"
Sonny Greer
  Howard Hart, "Sonny Greer"
Coleman Hawkins
  William Matthews, "Coleman Hawkins (d. 1969), RIP"
  Ken Irby, "Homage to Coleman Hawkins"
Billie Holiday
  Carol Bergé, "Piaf and Holiday Go Out"
  Cyrus Cassells, "Strange Fruit"
  Lisel Mueller, "January Afternoon, with Billie Holiday"
  Frank O'Hara, "The Day Lady Died"
Lena Horne
  James Baldwin, "Le sporting-club de Monte Carlo"
Alberta Hunter
  Lyn Lifshin, "Alberta Hunter"
Bunk Johnson
  William Carlos Williams, "Ol' Bunk's Band"
Elvin Jones
  Michael S. Harper, "Elvin's Blues"
Janis Joplin
  Alice Fulton, "You Can't Rhumboogie in a Ball
    and Chain"
  Marilyn Hacker, "Elegy"
Rahsaan Roland Kirk
  David Hilton, "Blind Saxophonist Dies"
Leadbelly
  Jack Kerouac, "221st Chorus" [From *Mexico
    City Blues*]

280

George Lewis
    William Matthews, "Alice Zeno Talking, and Her Son George Lewis
        the Jazz Clarinetist in Attendance"
Professor Longhair
    Elton Glaser, "Elegy for Professor Longhair"
Charles Mingus
    Jayne Cortez, "Into This Time"
    Dionisio D. Martinez, "Three or Four Shades of Blues"
    Dionisio D. Martinez, "Three or Four Shades of Blues (2)"
Thelonious Monk
    Tom Dent, "After Listening to Monk"
    Sascha Feinstein, "Monk's Mood"
    Yusef Komunyakaa, "Elegy for Thelonious"
    Art Lange, "Blues Five Spot"
    Art Lange, "Monk's Dream"
    Art Lange, "Monk's Point"
    John Sinclair, "humphf"
    William Tremblay, "Song for Jeannie"
    Anne Waldman, "Bluehawk"
    William Wantling, "A Plea for Workmen's Compensation"
Fats Navarro
    Richard Elman, "Driving Home"
Charlie Parker
    Robert Creeley, "The Bird, the Bird, the Bird"
    Owen Dodson, "Yardbird's Skull"
    Christopher Gilbert, "Horizontal Cosmology" [Sections 1, 4]
    Michael S. Harper, " 'Bird Lives': Charles Parker"
    Bob Kaufman, "Walking Parker Home"
    Jack Kerouac, "239th Chorus" [From *Mexico City Blues*]
    Larry Levis, "Whitman:"
    Ishmael Reed, "Poetry Makes Rhythm in Philosophy"
    Jack Spicer, "Song for Bird and Myself"
Billie Pierce
    Lee Meitzen Grue, "Billie Pierce's Jazz Funeral"
Bud Powell
    Clayton Eshleman, "Un Poco Loco"
    Clarence Major, "Un Poco Loco"
    William Matthews, "Bud Powell, Paris, 1959"
Ma Rainey
    Sterling A. Brown, "Ma Rainey"
    Al Young, "A Dance for Ma Rainey"
Django Reinhardt
    Vince Gotera, *"Hot Club de France* Reprise on MTV"
Max Roach
    Etheridge Knight, "Jazz Drummer"
Sonny Rollins
    Paul Blackburn, "Listening to Sonny Rollins at the Five-Spot"
Pharoah Sanders
    George Bowering, "Pharoah Sanders, in the Flesh"
    C. D. Wright, "Treatment"
Nina Simone
    Paulette C. White, "Nina Simone"
Bessie Smith
    Robert Hayden, "Homage to the Empress of the Blues"

Art Tatum
   Philip Levine, "On the Corner"
   William Matthews, "Unrelenting Flood"
Cecil Taylor
   Joe Johnson, "Cecil Taylor" [Excerpt]
Sophie Tucker
   Vassar Miller, "Dirge in Jazz Time"
Fats Waller
   Robert Pinsky, "History of My Heart" [Section I]
Ben Webster
   Howard Hart, "Ben Webster and a Lady"
Lester Young
   Ted Joans, "Lester Young"
   William Matthews, "Listening to Lester Young"

BLUES MUSICIANS (GENERAL)

Langston Hughes, "Dream Boogie"
Langston Hughes, "Jazzonia"
Langston Hughes, "Morning After"
Langston Hughes, "The Weary Blues"
Wallace Stevens, "The Sick Man"
Sherley Anne Williams, "Any Woman's Blues"

NEW ORLEANS AND EARLY JAZZ MUSICIANS (GENERAL)

Sterling A. Brown, "Cabaret"
Sterling A. Brown, "New St. Louis Blues"
Maxine Cassin, "Three Love Poems by a Native"
Sybil Kein, "Jazz"
John Logan, "Chicago Scene"
James Nolan, "Presenting Eustacia Beauchaud: Ward 3"
Carl Sandburg, "Jazz Fantasia"
Robert Sargent, "Tin Roof Blues"

VOCALISTS (GENERAL)

Gerald Barrax, "The Singer"
Colleen J. McElroy, "The Singer"
Kate Rushin, "The Black Back-Ups"
Robert Wrigley, "Torch Songs"

REFERENCES TO SEVERAL JAZZ ARTISTS

Marvin Bell, "The Fifties"
Hayden Carruth, "Paragraphs" [Sections 11, 26, 27, 28]
Jayne Cortez, "Tapping"
Rod Jellema, "Stop-time"
Ted Joans, "Jazz Is My Religion"
Ted Joans, "Jazz Must Be a Woman"
Jan Selving, "Dancing to Ellington"
Gilbert Sorrentino, "Broadway! Broadway!"
Quincy Troupe, "Snake-Back Solo"
Paul Zimmer, "Zimmer's Last Gig"

IMPROVISATIONS WRITTEN ABOUT OR TO JAZZ

Lawrence Ferlinghetti, "Sometime During Eternity . . ."
Andre Hodeir, "Outside the Capsule"
Richard Kostelanetz, "STRINGFOUR"
Richard Kostelanetz, "STRINGFIVE"
Asger Schnack, "Aqua" [Excerpt]
Melvin B. Tolson, "Lambda" [From *Harlem Gallery*]
Melvin B. Tolson, "Mu" [From *Harlem Gallery*]

MEDITATIONS ON JAZZ

Carol Bergé, "The Recounting of Gods"
Richard Burns, "The Song of the Yellow Star"
Wanda Coleman, "At the Jazz Club He Comes on a Ghost"
Claire Collett, "Midsummer"
Leo Connellan, "Mommy's Hubby"
Gillian Conoley, "The One"
Clark Coolidge, "The Great"
Robert Creeley, "Broken Back Blues"
John Engels, "In the Palais Royale Ballroom in 1948"
Christopher Gilbert, "Resonance"
Lee Meitzen Grue, "Jazzmen"
Robert Hayden, "Soledad"
Andre Hodeir, "Outside the Capsule"
Lynda Hull, "Hollywood Jazz"
Lawson Fusao Inada "Plucking Out a Rhythm"
Rod Jellema, "Four Voices Ending on Some Lines from Old Jazz Records"
Bob Kaufman, "Bagel Shop Jazz"
Bob Kaufman, "Battle Report"
Bob Kaufman, "War Memoir"
Bob Kaufman, "War Memoir: Jazz, Don't Listen to It at Your Own Risk"
Kenneth Koch, "The History of Jazz"
N. J. Loftis, "Black Anima" [Section 9]
Mina Loy, "The Widow's Jazz"
Jack Micheline, "Blues Poem"
John Montgomery, "Snowmelt from Yesteryears"
Harryette Mullen, "Playing the Invisible Saxophone *en el Combo de las Estrellas*"
James Nolan, "Jazz Poem for the Girl Who Cried Wolf"
Kenneth Patchen, "Latesummer Blues"
Sterling D. Plumpp, "I Hear the Shuffle of the People's Feet"
Carl Sandburg, "Jazz Fantasia"
Léopold Sédar Senghor, "New York"
Aleda Shirley, "The Last Dusk of August"
Aleda Shirley, "21 August 1984"
Marilyn Nelson Waniek, "It's All in Your Head"
Jerry W. Ward, Jr., "Jazz to Jackson to John"
C. D. Wright, "Jazz Impressions in the Garden"

ANONYMOUS OR RELATIVELY UNKNOWN JAZZ MUSICIANS

George Barlow, "In My Father's House"
Ray Bremser, "Blues for Harold"
Sascha Feinstein, "Buying Wine"

283

Calvin Forbes, "Drum Crazy"
Everett Hoagland, "Jamming"
Everett Hoagland, "The Music"
Kenneth McClane, "At the Bridge with Rufus"
Jack Mueller, "Death Jazz: A Review"
Mandy Sayer, "Choofa"
Jon C. Tribble, "Anaximander Lewis"
Sherley Anne Williams, "1 Poem   2 Voices   A Song"
C. D. Wright, "The Substitute Bassist"

Acknowledgments

The editors would like to thank Carolyne Wright for her encouragement and assistance during the early stage of preparing this anthology.

For quoted prose passages in the preface, we would like to thank Random House for permission to reprint from Ralph Ellison's *Invisible Man* and Robert Hass for permission to reprint from his essay "A Poetry Craft Lecture," originally published in *Poetry Flash.*

Every effort has been made to trace copyright for the poems included in this anthology. We gratefully acknowledge the following permissions:

Sam Abrams. "In the Capability" from *The Post-American Cultural Congress* by Sam Abrams. Copyright © 1974 by Sam Abrams. Reprinted by permission of the author.

James Baldwin. "Le sporting-club de Monte Carlo" from *Jimmy's Blues* by James Baldwin. Copyright © 1983 by James Baldwin. Reprinted by permission of Richard Curtis Associates, Inc. and Michael Joseph Ltd.

Amiri Baraka. "AM/TRAK" from *Black Magic Poetry* by Amiri Baraka. Copyright © 1969 by Amiri Baraka. Reprinted by permission of Sterling Lord Literistic, Inc.

George Barlow. "In My Father's House" from *Gumbo* by George Barlow. Copyright © 1981 by George Barlow. Reprinted by permission of the author.

Gerald Barrax. "The Singer" from *An Audience of One.* Copyright © 1980 by University of Georgia Press. Reprinted by permission of the author.

Marvin Bell. "The Fifties." Previous appearance in *Jazzscene* (Sept. 1989). Copyright © by Marvin Bell. Reprinted by permission of the author.

Carol Bergé. "Piaf and Holiday Go Out" and "The Recounting of Gods" from *Poems Made of Skin* by Carol Bergé. Copyright © 1968, 1969 by Carol Bergé. Reprinted by permission of the author.

Paul Blackburn. "Listening to Sonny Rollins at the Five-Spot" from *The Collected Poems of Paul Blackburn* by Paul Blackburn. Copyright © 1985 by Joan Blackburn. Reprinted by permission of Persea Books.

Horace Julian Bond. "The Bishop of Atlanta: Ray Charles." Copyright © by Horace Julian Bond. By permission of the author.

George Bowering. "Pharoah Sanders, in the Flesh." Copyright © by George Bowering. By permission of the author.

Edward Kamau Brathwaite. "Trane" from *Black & Blues* by Edward Kamau Brathwaite. Copyright © 1976 by Edward Kamau Brathwaite. Reprinted by permission of the author.

Ray Bremser. "Blues for Harold" from *Blowing Mouth / The Jazz Poems 1958–70* by Ray Bremser. Copyright © 1978 by Ray Bremser. Reprinted by permission of the author.

Sterling A. Brown. "Cabaret" and "New St. Louis Blues" from *The Collected Poems of Sterling A. Brown* selected by Michael S. Harper. Copyright © 1980 by Sterling A. Brown. "Ma Rainey" from *The Collected Poems of Sterling A. Brown* selected by Michael S. Harper. Copyright © 1932 by Harcourt Brace Jovano-

285

286

287

289

292

SASCHA FEINSTEIN, a poet and jazz saxophonist, is the author of a chapbook, *Summerhouse Piano.* His jazz-related poetry, essays, and interviews have appeared in numerous journals, including the *Missouri Review, Green Mountains Review,* and *North American Review.*

YUSEF KOMUNYAKAA, Associate Professor of English and Afro-American Literature at Indiana University, is the author of *Copacetic, I Apologize for the Eyes in My Head* (which won the San Francisco Poetry Center Award in 1986), *Dien Cai Dau,* and four chapbooks.